DESIGNING QUALITY AUTHENTIC ASSESSMENTS

This book examines the principles and practice of authentic assessment. It seeks to answer the following questions. What is authentic assessment? How is authentic assessment different from 'performance assessment' or 'alternative assessment'? How can authentic assessment support learner-centred education, especially when a performance-oriented culture favours pen-and-paper examinations?

The book is structured into two major parts. The first, 'Principles of authentic assessment design', provides readers with a conceptual explanation of authenticity; the principles for designing quality authentic assessments for valid evidence of student learning; and guidance about how to develop quality rubrics to structure assessment tasks.

The second part of the book, 'Theory into practice' provides examples developed by teachers to demonstrate an understanding of authentic assessment. The subject areas covered include humanities, languages, mathematics, sciences, character and citizenship. Two case studies are discussed to demonstrate how authentic assessment can be used to comprehensively address key learning objectives in a variety of curriculum contexts.

This book provides practitioners with concrete examples on how to develop authentic assessment to suit their own context and also enhance their students' learning. The book will also enable teachers to face assessment challenges present in our changing world.

Tay Hui Yong is Senior Lecturer with the Curriculum, Teaching and Learning Academic Group at the National Institute of Education, Nanyang Technological University, Singapore. She has previously served in secondary schools as a teacher, a head of department, the dean of curriculum and as vice principal. Currently, she teaches courses to a wide range of learners in her areas of expertise, particularly authentic assessments and self-regulated learning. She has published on other areas of assessments, e.g., use of technology. Above all, she is interested in all things that will enhance students' learning experiences in school.

ASSESSMENT IN SCHOOLS: PRINCIPLES IN PRACTICE

Assessment in Schools: Principles in Practice offers a collection of titles that provide accessible exploration of individual assessment concepts, while collectively providing a comprehensive overview and discussion of assessment practices in schools. This research-informed and practice-oriented book series aims to make assessment theory accessible by explaining its implications and applications in practice, providing guidance on designing and implementing quality assessment practices, giving authentic examples from current practices, and offering on-going support to readers through media-rich resources on accompanying websites.

Some key assessment competencies to be covered in the series are:

- Designing quality authentic assessments;
- Understanding and using rubrics;
- Developing self-assessment for reflective and self-directed learning;
- Formative assessments practice as part of an effective teaching and learning process.

Tay Hui Yong (National Institute of Education, Singapore)
Kelvin Tan Heng Kiat (National Institute of Education, Singapore)
Valentina Klenowski (Queensland University of Technology, Australia)

Designing Quality Authentic Assessments
Tay Hui Yong
with contributions from Pam Hook, Ben Jenkinson, Eric Chong King Man and others

For more information about this series, please visit: https://www.routledge.com/Assessment-in-Schools-Principles-in-Practice/book-series/ASPP

DESIGNING QUALITY AUTHENTIC ASSESSMENTS

Tay Hui Yong

WITH CONTRIBUTIONS FROM PAM HOOK, BEN JENKINSON,
ERIC CHONG KING MAN AND OTHERS

Routledge
Taylor & Francis Group

LONDON AND NEW YORK

First published 2018
by Routledge
2 Park Square, Milton Park, Abingdon, Oxon OX14 4RN

and by Routledge
711 Third Avenue, New York, NY 10017

Routledge is an imprint of the Taylor & Francis Group, an informa business

British Library Cataloguing-in-Publication Data
A catalogue record for this book is available from the British Library

Library of Congress Cataloging-in-Publication Data
A catalog record for this book has been requested

ISBN: 978-1-138-89650-5 (hbk)
ISBN: 978-1-138-89652-9 (pbk)
ISBN: 978-1-315-17913-1 (ebk)

Typeset in Bembo
by Deanta Global Publishing Services, Chennai, India

CONTENTS

ACKNOWLEDGEMENTS

This book would not be possible for the following people:

- Kelvin Tan for proposing and supporting the series of books.
- Kelvin Tan and Val Klenowski for their valuable comments that helped improve the book.
- Pam Hook, Ben Jenkinson and Eric Chong King Man for contributing chapters.
- The many teachers, especially the mathematics department of Wellington Girls' College, New Zealand, who contributed their work so that others in the fraternity can benefit from their examples.
- Mr Nik Voon for the use of the photo on the book cover.

INTRODUCTION[1]

Teachers will not take up attractive sounding ideas, albeit based on extensive research, if these are presented as general principles which leave entirely to them the task of translating them into everyday practice – their lives are too busy and too fragile for this to be possible for all but an outstanding few. What they need is a variety of living examples of implementation, by teachers with whom they can identify and from whom they can both derive conviction and confidence that they can do better, and see concrete examples of what doing better means in practice.

(Black & Wiliam, 1998, p. 10)

There has always been keen interest in classroom assessments. And though there is a wealth of research and theorising in this area, practitioners keen on improving classroom assessment practices are sometimes left to their own devices to think of how to apply these principles in their own contexts.

This series of books, *Assessment in Schools: Principles in Practice*, aims to be a situated resource, particularly for busy teachers who want accessible and practical help in their classroom assessment practices. The series offers the flexibility for readers to focus on specific areas or systematically develop the whole range of assessment competencies.

The assessment competency in focus in this particular book is designing quality authentic assessments (AA). AA is not new to the scene but what exactly is it? There is still a lack of clarity among practitioners. For example, the term is often used interchangeably with "performance assessment" and "alternative assessment". As such, the book opens with Chapter 1 that intends to clarify the concept of AA, with the help of literature in this area and made concrete with many examples designed by classroom teachers. It will also try to problematise the concept of "authenticity" (to what? and to whom? and for what?). This discussion will help readers see the need to ground practical considerations on a theoretical basis (presented in Chapter 2). In fact, Chapter 2 will be a valued resource for readers who are keen to delve more deeply into the theory and research on AA. It presents important work from the past (Dewey's theory of an educative experience) and more contemporary perspectives (social cultural and social cognitive theories) as theoretical arguments for AA. It also includes a quick overview of seminal pieces of AA research.

For readers who are concerned with the "How to", they can turn to Chapter 3. Here, they will learn about Messick's construct-based approach to guide them in designing AA. As with the other chapters, the examples will illustrate the process. In addition, these examples are accompanied by the teachers' reflection on why and how they designed the AA being featured.

Chapter 4 follows with guidance on how to design quality rubrics to measure the learning outcomes targeted by the AA. Written by Hook, this chapter presents Structure of Observed Learning Outcomes (SOLO) taxonomy as a possible framework for designing rubrics. SOLO, developed by academics Biggs and Collis (1982), has been used in many schools across the world to provide a powerful scale for summative and formative assessment rubrics. Practical examples of declarative and functioning knowledge rubrics (text based and visual) show how using SOLO as a framework can make next steps for learning visible in ways that enthuse and upskill every student to make learning progress.

This first half of the book ends with Chapter 5 addressing an important question, perhaps the elephant in the room: the relevance of AA in an increasingly performance-oriented culture where high stakes examinations are very much of the paper-and-pen mode. This chapter argues that now, more so than ever, AA is relevant, or necessary even, to nurture in our learners the critical 21st-century skills of critical and inventive thinking and collaboration.

Part II of the book features examples of AA mainly from Singapore but also from a few other countries. Each chapter begins with an overall description of the setting for the AA in the particular subject area, before presenting a range of AA designed for different levels. The rationale, curriculum standards and design principles are rich details that show that there is no one fixed model for designing AA. Rather it is from the well-considered application of theoretical principles presented in Part I. To help readers make the theory–practice link, questions are embedded in the chapter to guide reflection.

Each chapter will also offer something unique to further illustrate practical considerations. Chapter 6 presents a range of humanities subjects but all focussed on inquiry. In Chapter 7, readers can compare how language skills are assessed in English, Chinese and Malay; while in Chapter 8, readers can compare how teachers from different countries approach mathematical modelling. Chapter 9 will show how the same student outcome (e.g., scientific inquiry) is interpreted for different age groups. Chapter 10 looks at how different institutions, including that of a school for Islamic education, assess non-cognitive aspects such as character traits. I have also intentionally included two examples of AA designed for students who are deemed less academically inclined. (In Singapore, they are in the Normal

(Technical) track.) This is because research suggests that those who scored low on traditional, standardized assessment perform better with AA (Darling-Hammond, Ancess & Falk, 1995).

The last two chapters of Part II are case studies of the use of AA in two different parts of the world (Australia and Hong Kong). The contributions by Jenkinson and Chong show the full context of how the AA is part of their overall curriculum. It is hoped that by the end of the book, with the theory made clear with the many examples designed by practitioners themselves, readers will have the confidence to develop a form of AA to suit their own school context to enhance the students' learning.

Note

1 Please note that the work of the teachers included in this book is in no way representative of Ministry of Education's views and policies.

References

Biggs, J. B. & Collis, K. F. (1982). *Evaluating the Quality of Learning: The SOLO Taxonomy.* New York: Academic Press.

Black, P., & Wiliam, D. (1998). *Inside the Black Box: Raising Standards Through Classroom Assessment.* London: School of Education, King's College.

Darling-Hammond, L., Ancess, J., & Falk, B. (1995). *Authentic Assessment in Action: Studies of Schools and Students at Work.* New York: Teachers College Press.

PART I

Principles of authentic assessment design

1

WHAT IS "AUTHENTICITY" IN AUTHENTIC ASSESSMENT?

Introduction

This chapter intends to clarify the concept of "authentic assessments" (AA). It begins by examining it against other assessment terms. The examples will also serve to illustrate the concepts being discussed, particularly the concept of "authenticity" (to what? and to whom? and for what?) with reference to prominent writers in the field.

- As part of show-and-tell during an English language class, seven-year-old students are asked to bring their favourite fruit. They take turns to make an oral presentation in front of their classmates, describing the fruit and explaining why they love it.
- After lessons on physical properties of materials, students work in groups to create a boat with a given list of suggested materials. They will present their boat, justifying their choice of materials. They will also be required to test out their boat: to travel 1.5 m with the aid of a battery-operated fan, in the shortest time.
- At the end of a series of lessons on the four stages of statistical studies: Collection, organisation, display (pictogram, bar graph, pie chart, line graph) and interpretation of data, students conduct a survey to find out how often schoolmates eat fast food, and display results in a statistical diagram, justifying their choice.

Clarifying types versus purposes of assessments

These are examples of assessment tasks that teachers have designed (see previous page). Do you consider these examples to be one or some of the following?

- Alternative assessments?
- Performance assessments?
- Authentic assessments?

SOME WORKING DEFINITIONS

Alternative assessments
Meaningful assessments that are not "traditional" (which is typically paper-and-pen).

Performance assessments
Tasks that require learners to produce product or behaviours that directly reflect the range of knowledge and skills they have learnt.

It is understandable that teachers find these terms confusing because oftentimes, they are used interchangeably. "Alternative assessment" is a broad term to refer to assessments that differ from conventional ones which are often associated with paper-and-pen tests. As such, one type of alternative assessment in the language class is performance assessment (e.g., choral reading of a poem) especially if the conventional assessment involves a paper-and-pen essay. However, it is not to be taken for granted that the conventional is always of the paper-and-pen mode, e.g., in physical education classes where the conventional involves performance and the alternative may involve a paper-and-pen quiz. Hence, it is always helpful to define clearly at the start of the discussion what constitutes "conventional" and, hence, as a corollary, what constitutes "alternative".

For example: Until recently in Singapore, Primary 1 students (seven-year-olds) had to sit for written examinations. These paper-and-pen assessments have since been replaced with assessments like show-and-tell. Now, show-and-tell is a common assessment mode found in primary schools. So, is it considered *alternative* assessment?

Also, consider the example of portfolios and project work, which are considered alternative assessment in schools but are, in fact, common place in vocational institutions. In short, assessments are not, by default, either alternative or not but are defined by what is conventional in the particular context.

Another step towards greater clarity is to differentiate between mode (alternative, authentic, performance assessments) and purpose of assessment (formative or summative).

SOME WORKING DEFINITIONS

Summative purposes
Concerned with summing up or summarising the achievement status of a student, and is geared towards reporting at the end of a course of study especially for certification.

Formative purposes
Concerned with gathering assessment information from dialogue, demonstration and observation in ways that enhance on-going learning.

Different modes of assessments can serve either formative or summative purposes. However, because the conventional paper-and-pen test is often summative in nature, alternative assessments are often associated with formative purposes. Nonetheless, it is obvious that high-stakes examinations can serve formative purposes (e.g., when examiners give quality feedback to the candidate) and alternative assessments can be used to report on student achievement.

In short, the assessments shown on page 1 can be viewed as

- alternative if they are not part of the conventional assessments; or
- formative if the assessment information is used to enhance on-going learning.

Example 1.1

Example of how alternative assessments can serve both formative and summative purposes

Subject: English language and information and communications technology
Contributed by Diana Chua May Ling
Topic: Cyber wellness
Target Group: 15-year-olds (Secondary 3)
Standards: Plan and present information and ideas for a variety of purposes

Planning and organisation

- Identify purpose and audience of speaking and representing, and set goals in the context of assigned or self-selected topics.
- Generate ideas and details appropriate to the purpose, audience, context and culture.
- Gather, evaluate, select and synthesise facts and ideas from a variety of print and/or non-print sources, appropriate to the purpose, audience, context and culture.

Presentation

- Pronounce clearly and accurately consonants, vowels, consonant clusters and vowel combinations
- Speak clearly and eloquently using the appropriate voice qualities

Task

This is an EL/ICT collaborative project that all Secondary 3 students participate in annually. The project aims to first allow students to find out for themselves through research and collaborative efforts what cyber wellness is all about, why it is important and how it can be preserved in cyberspace to ensure the safety of online users; second, apply what they have learnt in visual comprehension and construct posters to succinctly capture the essence of cyber wellness; and third, do an oral presentation of their cyber wellness posters in a succinct and convincing manner to raise awareness of the topic among their peers. This is both a summative assessment task but it is also formative through the many opportunities for peer and teacher feedback to help students improve their posters and oral presentation.

But is it AA? That is the topic of the next section.

What is "authentic assessment"?

Having discussed alternative and formative assessment, let us examine more closely the other two terms, *performance-based assessment* and *AA*. Performance assessments require the student to make a product or demonstrate some behaviour that the assessor desires to measure. Examples that teachers are familiar with are the show-and-tell or portfolios mentioned earlier. AAs can be thought of as a "more realistic subset of performance assessments" (Messick, 1994, p. 5) because they require performances that parallel those in the real world. In short, every AA is performance assessment, but not vice versa (Meyer, 1992).

In Singapore language class, it is common for students to write narrative essays. However, such a performance assessment task can become an AA as well. For example, Secondary 2 students (14-year-olds) were asked to apply their narrative writing skills to write stories for pre-school children. Prior to the writing process, the students were supported with a talk by a writer who gave them tips and they borrowed children's story books from the library as reference. The project culminated with the students reading their stories to children at kindergartens.

Contributed by Rasidah Bte Mohd Rasit

Teachers sometimes ask, "How much 'real life' does one need to put into an assessment before it is considered 'authentic'?" I suggest that rather than thinking of AA as binary (either it is authentic or it is not), it may be more fruitful to ask three questions:

1. What is "authentic" about the assessment?
2. What is it "authentic" to?
3. What is the purpose of such "authenticity"?

Generally, teachers' answers to (1) are clearer than to (2) and to (3). They cite including some real-life elements in their assessments, believing that this will make learning more meaningful for their students. However, there is little elaboration on how and why these aspects make the assessments more relevant to the child. It is thus instructive to look at what the literature has to say about questions (2) and (3). Generally, writers make references to three types of contexts for "authenticity": the working world outside school, the world of the student and the world of the discipline. I will present each of them separately, supported by examples.

"Authentic" to the working world outside school

One writer often quoted in AA literature is Wiggins. In one of his earlier articles, he argued that since schools "teach to the test", we should design tests worth teaching to. He called these "authentic tests" (1989, p. 44) that will "test those capacities and habits we think are essential, and test them in context" (p. 41). In contrast, assessments that are decontextualized are, by definition, invalid and dysfunctional (Wiggins, 1993a) because the students' success tells us little of their performance in contexts outside of school.

What Wiggins considers as authentic was revised over the years. The first version involved four criteria: work that is truly representative of performance in the field involving teaching and learning of the criteria to be used in the assessment, much greater self-assessment than in conventional testing, students presenting and publicly defending their work (1989). A few years later, he elaborated on the qualities of the assessment task (1993b, p. 229):

- Engaging, worthy problems in which students must use knowledge to fashion performances effectively and creatively. The tasks are either replicas of or analogous to the kinds of problems faced by adult citizens and consumers or professionals in the field.
- Faithful representation of the contexts facing workers in a field of study or in the real-life "tests" of adult life, including that of options, constraints, and access to resources.
- Non-routine and multi-stage tasks that require a repertoire of procedural knowledge and planning skills.
- Tasks that require students to produce a quality product and/or performance.

Wiggins' rationale for exposing students to the real-life contexts faced by adults is to introduce the students to criterion performances that they will face later in life. So, if we expect working adults to communicate and collaborate, then they should be expected to exhibit these skills at school. It is also argued that since assessments closely simulate real life applications, students will be better able to transfer the learning from the classroom to beyond the school walls. At the very least, assessors can have greater confidence in inferring the students' present competency because it is revealed directly through their performance. For example, in contrast to the various AAs described in the following pages, a timed written examination with several unconnected essay questions will yield less valid inferences about how the learners harness their knowledge and skills to negotiate a complex task.

These examples show how teachers designed assessments to relate to the real-life contexts of the working world.

Example 1.2

Subject: Maths
Contributed by Jeffrey Lee Tze Wei
Target Group: 10-year-olds (Primary 4)
Topic: Area and perimeter

- Determine one dimension of a rectangle given the other dimension and its area/perimeter.
- Determine the length of one side of a square given its area/perimeter.
- Determine the area and perimeter of figures made up of rectangles and squares.

Task

Instructions to students: As a building contractor, you have been asked by your client, Fresh Meat Farm, for a plan to build fences around the farm to hold the chickens. Fresh Meat Farm has stated the following requirements:

- The length of each piece of fence is 1 m.
- The cost of each piece of fence is $29.
- The fences are to be built to cover an area of exactly 36 m^2.

Work as a group of four to propose to Fresh Meat Farm the best solution to the problem.

Example 1.3

Subject: Food and consumer education
Target Group: 13 years old (Secondary 1)
Contributed by Jocelyn Tay
Topic: Food management – methods of cooking and culinary skills

- Compare and contrast the effects of using different methods of cooking on food properties (taste, texture, appearance).
- Distinguish, compare and analyse the differences in the results of the sensory properties in food products:
  - Appearance (colour, size, crumb, shape).
  - Flavour (salty, sweet, bitter, acidic, sour).
  - Texture (grainy, smooth).

Task

Instructions to students: You have recently started your own muffin shop and one of your customers gave feedback that your muffins have little dome (i.e. the top is flat). You decide to find out the cause by investigating the effect of using different types of flour (plain and self-raising flour) on muffins in terms of its appeal (e.g., height, texture, internal appearance).

In this project work, you are required to do planning, research, problem-solving and evaluation in order to meet the requirements. It is designed to allow you to show your ability to apply your knowledge and skills in food management – methods of cooking and culinary skills.

Wiggins' accent on posing complex performance tasks in realistic settings or close simulations is the definition generally quoted or elaborated on in later writing (e.g., Darling-Hammond, Ancess and Falk, 1995; Maclellan, 2004; Tanner, 2001). However, there was debate on the referent for the real-life context. Gulikers, Bastiaens and Kirschner (2004) argue that in the case of evaluating competency, the assessment should require students to demonstrate the same competencies as experts would use in a real-life situation. Authenticity is operationalised using a five-dimensional framework (5DF) in terms of these five dimensions:

- the resemblance of the task (to the complexity and ownership levels of real-life criterion situation);
- physical context;
- social context;
- assessment form (a quality product or performance that students can be asked to produce in real life);
- and criteria to the professional practice situation.

Example 1.4

This is an example of AA designed using the 5DF approach. Figure 1.1 explains how the task adheres to the approach.

Subject: Maths
Contributed by Tan Chih Yuan
Level: 16-year-olds (Secondary 4)
Topic: Optimisation

Resemblance of task to real life situation: This task requires students to apply Mathematical Modelling (MM) to use their understanding of optimization to solve a real-world problem. However, to make the task more manageable for students, some guidelines have been provided on initial research area, and consultations with teacher are available.

Physical context: Students are given substitute materials and four weeks to construct their prototype. (It is noted that design engineers working on this full-time may not have the luxury of so many days.)

Social context: Like typical company project teams, students need to work collaboratively in groups to accomplish the task.

Assessment result: The AA requires submission of both a report and prototype which is typically expected in real life.

Criteria: The elements of the MM process, which are the actual processes that engineers go through, are used as evaluation criteria.

FIGURE 1.1   How task adheres to the 5DF approach.

Relevant standards

- Apply mathematics concepts and skills to solve problems in a variety of contexts within or outside mathematics, including:
    - identifying the appropriate mathematical representations or standard models for a problem; and
    - using appropriate mathematical concepts, skills (including tools and algorithm) to solve a problem.

- Understand the nature of the mathematical modelling process, including:
    - formulating a real-world problem into a mathematical model by making suitable assumptions and simplification and identifying suitable mathematical representations;
    - applying mathematics to solve the problem;
    - interpreting the mathematical solution in the context of the problem; and
    - refining and improving the model.

Task

Instructions to students: Students work in teams to research on milk packaging in the market with the goal of designing one that is modern looking and with good cost savings. A written report on the findings and a prototype of the proposed milk packaging is expected for submission.

"Authentic" to the student's world

However, one notes that the work of Gulikers and associates revolves round a vocational institution. As such, they rightly place more emphasis on designing assessments that resemble situations that professionals starting out are confronted with in their working life. Assessments at this stage, designed to resemble the professional real world, can be the bridge between learning in schools and working life; or, as Havnes (2008) puts it, assessments serve as *boundary objects* (p. 111) to facilitate student learning across the boundaries of education and work. In addition, the consumers of the assessment results from a tertiary institution, the prospective employers, would be concerned about the predictive validity of the assessment results. Predictive validity is the degree to which future performance can be predicted by current assessment performance (Gulikers et al., 2008). It is a reasonable argument that the closer the tertiary institution's assessment resembles professional practice, the greater the predictive validity of the assessment results. But younger students cannot, and, arguably, should not have to, deal with the authenticity of a real complex professional situation. It may be more meaningful for authenticity to be interpreted in terms of resemblance to their everyday lives. For example, these students will find comparing income tax rates across different countries harder to relate to than evaluating mobile phone plans of telcos to decide which they should personally subscribe to.

In other words, a real-life setting may be more meaningful if it offers something of personal interest or relevance to the learners (Tay, 2015). This is perhaps Dewey's message (1938, p. 77) when he argues:

> Just as the individual has to draw in memory upon his own past to understand the conditions in which he individually finds himself ... students cannot be prepared to understand either problems (of present) or the best way of dealing with them without delving into their roots in the past.

This focus on the learner's prior knowledge is echoed in more contemporary writers. They propose that if learning is "an active process of mental construction and sense making" (Shepard, 2000, p. 6), then assessment should facilitate this "sense making" by engaging the learners in purposeful tasks designed to elicit their background knowledge (Wolf, Bixby, Glenn & Gardner, 1991; James & Lewis, 2012). Chapter 2 will elaborate further on this link between learning and assessment.

Example 1.5

Subject: Physics
Contributed by Traven Loh Wei Chuen
Target Group: 14-year-olds (Secondary 2)
Topic: Household electricity

• Set up circuits containing electrical sources, switches, lamps

Task

Instructions to students: Students work in groups to design and construct a table lamp based on the concepts of electricity that they have learned over the past three weeks. They are given instructions on the criteria needed for the lamp and a table lamp kit that consists of the wiring, bulbs, battery holders and switches. They will then submit their table lamps about a week after the lesson ends and the teacher will use a checklist to grade their table lamps.

Example 1.6

In another school, Secondary 4 students (16-year-olds) are encouraged to use language in real world settings by submitting letters to the local daily newspaper, *The Straits Times*, to express their views on current affairs.

Relevant standards:

- Produce a variety of texts for creative, personal, academic and functional purposes, using an appropriate register and tone
- Provide information, explain an issue/situation, and/or express and justify a point of view/proposed action, so as to persuade the reader to accept the point of view/proposed action
- Present, explain and justify the writer's position on an issue/situation or proposed action, so as to persuade the reader to accept the position/proposed action

The letter reproduced below is one example. More examples can be found at: https://nyghcti.wordpress.com/category/muse/

Nurture a generation that learns differently, bravely

In the recent Budget debate, the words "enterprise" and "innovation" were often mentioned, with regard to improving Singapore's economy. As a highly globalised country, Singapore is well equipped with opportunities and assets for start-ups and entrepreneurship. Yet, fresh entrants to the workforce do not seem to be making full use of these resources. While the cause of this seeming lack of entrepreneurship and originality may lie in prevalent "kiasu" mindsets, which have deterred many budding entrepreneurs from taking a bold leap of faith ("'Kiasu' culture is stifling originality in business: NMP"; April 6), it is my contention that deeper roots lie in our education system.

Singapore's education system receives world acclaim for its successes in standardised and international test scores. But I wonder if enough is really being done to nurture 21st century competencies and skills, such as creativity and innovation. Even though many new initiatives, such as the Applied Learning Programme, have been launched, students are still assessed primarily with summative examinations, which, in many ways, determine their next steps in life. Much as we say that we want to depart from a streaming culture, an ethos of risk aversion and a focus on paper qualifications, the structures that exist within our education system invariably reinforce "kiasuism" and a climate of risk aversion. Very few students bother leaving their comfort zones, given that the stakes are perceivably high, and this runs antithetical to the spirit of adventure required for entrepreneurship.

If we genuinely want young Singaporeans to depart from the "safe route" of studying hard, getting good grades, graduating with a degree and then securing a stable job, structures that privilege and advantage conservative learners must be relooked to allay the anxiety that comes with departing from traditional routes to success. This might, in many ways, also change how students learn, which is a key grouse of many parents, educators and students themselves – that students are learning for the test.

We have made significant headway in assessing students holistically, for example, by assessing critical thinking and application skills, and oral presentation and communication skills. But the reality is that current assessment modes still fall short in measuring how well students deal with uncertainty and novel problems that require higher levels of critical, creative and inventive thinking.

The future is an unknown entity and the demands of tomorrow will always change. How should we prepare youth for uncertainty and flux? The key is to nurture a generation that learns differently, bravely and with a genuine sense of curiosity.

Contributed by Zhu Hongyue (Miss)
Published 23 April 2016[1]
(http://www.straitstimes.com/forum/letters-in-print/
nurture-a-generation-that-learns-differently-bravely)

"Authentic" to the discipline

Like Wiggins, Archibald and Newmann (1988) were critical of the type of learning often found in school, which they described as "trivial, meaningless, and contrived by students and adult authorities" and proposed that achievement should be measured through tasks that are "worthwhile, significant, and meaningful – in short, *authentic*" (p. 1). But unlike Wiggins, they considered it insufficient for "authenticity" to be simple participation in real world experiences. Instead, "If intellectual work is to be authentic, it must be based on rigorous thinking and grounded in substantive knowledge of the disciplines" (Newmann, 2000, p. 2). After all, each discipline has its own way of viewing and thinking about the world (McArthur, 2012). Thus, for students to experience the discipline (or subject) in an authentic way, they need to be inducted into the behaviour and discourse found in that discipline (McConachie et al., 2006).

This approach of taking reference not from the real-world dimension but from the perspective of the discipline, offers some advantages. At the very least, it guards against wasting resources on simulating a superficial "real world" setting not relevant to the construct, for example, asking students to dress up like lawyers to debate historical perspectives.

Examples of AA that simulate the behaviour of experts in the field are discussed below.

Example 1.7

Subject: Geography
Contributed by Jacqueline Lee Wui Lin

Level: 15-year-olds (Secondary 3)
Topic: Coastal environments

Relevant standards

- Explain how coastal areas can be managed in a sustainable manner.
- Assess the impact of tourism on an area and explain how tourism can be made sustainable.

Task: A geographical inquiry performance task that involves field investigation at real world sites

Instructions to students: In the first three quarters of 2014, international visitor arrivals to Singapore dipped 4% while tourism receipts rose by 0.1% to $17.8 billion (Singapore Tourism Board, 2014). To retain Singapore's economic competitiveness amidst regional competition, there is a need to enhance Singapore's tourist attractions to ensure sustained growth in the tourism sector. You are a group of researchers tasked to study the feasibility of building a tourist resort at East Coast Park. You will be required to study the influence of coastal processes and assess the suitability of the site for a coastal resort.

Example 1.8

Subject: Mathematics
Contributed by Lok Jia Ming
Level: 13-year-olds (Secondary 1)
Topic: Statistics (data collection and analysis)

Relevant standards

- Using mean, mode and median as measures of central tendency for a set of data.
- Using the mean and standard deviation to compare two sets of data.

Task

Instructions to students: You are an entrepreneur looking to open a stall in the school. But before that, you need to find out more information. Work with your team to decide what sort of data to collect on the existing stalls. You must present your informed decision based on findings from the analysis of your data.

"Authenticity" as a permutation of the three

So, which of the three – working world, student's world and discipline – should AA designers refer to for authenticity? Perhaps these three referent contexts are not mutually exclusive; they can be thought of as overlapping subsets of the real world as shown in Figure 1.2.

Each circle may be of a bigger or smaller size to reflect its dominance relative to the other two, depending on the learner (e.g., age, profile). For the younger learners, like those in primary school, the predominant focus will be that of relating the task to their real-life experience, e.g., show-and-tell about their favourite fruit.

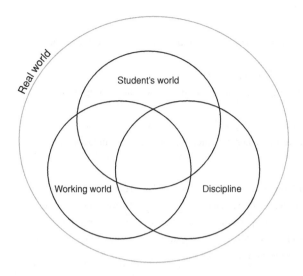

FIGURE 1.2   Different referent contexts for authenticity.

Reproduced with permission from Tan Kelvin, Koh Kim Hong and Tay Hui Yong; Authentic Assessment in Schools 2e; figure 1 (p. 328); Pearson Education South Asia Pte. Ltd.

The area of the working world will thus be less significant (thus smaller) as a reference for teachers designing AA for this cohort of students. In contrast, this referent of professional work will feature more prominently (i.e., larger) in the case of older students about to enter the working world, e.g., writing business proposals at the secondary school.

There are, conceivably, situations that will satisfy two or all three different considerations at the same time, as illustrated by the overlapping subsets of the real world. For example, an AA asking students to trace their school's history can be designed to reflect

- the students' life (i.e. the school they are currently in);
- the professional work of an historian handling primary sources material; and
- the discipline through the required tasks (e.g., defining essential questions, sorting through source material, drawing conclusions and presenting persuasively).

These two examples show how assessments on the same topic, "Man's impact on the environment", can be designed with a different emphasis to suit the learners and the level of disciplinary and professional knowledge expected of them at their age.

Example 1.9

Subject: Science
ontributed by Noorfaezah Binte Sadon
Level: 12-year-olds (Primary 6)
Topic: Terrarium-making

Relevant standards

- Show an understanding of the roles of evaporation and condensation in the water cycle.
- Recognise the importance of the water cycle.
- Observe, collect and record information regarding the interacting factors within an environment.
- Give examples of man's impact (both positive and negative) on the environment.
- Discuss the effect on organisms when the environment becomes unfavourable.

Task

Instruction to students: Students are to work in groups to construct a terrarium using guidelines provided. They observe the water cycle (evaporation, condensation, rain) occurring in the terrarium and set up a simple scientific experiment using the scientific process to find out the effect of global warming on plant growth. Students are to collate their findings and present them to the class.

Example 1.10

Subject: Science
Contributed by Chow Ban Hoe
Level: 16-year-olds (Secondary 4)
Topic: Environmental science

Man and his environment

- Demonstrate knowledge and understanding in relation to scientific and technological applications with their social, economic and environmental implications.

Task

Instruction to students: As a team of environmental science experts, your group of four has been approached by the governor of Bandar Awang to do an environmental assessment and review of the feasibility of the plans proposed by SamCorp (see further information following this instruction). Your team needs to examine major *arguments for* and *against* the proposal, identifying key factors and views from different stakeholder groups (e.g., citizens, government, farmers, nature groups, workers, SamCorp) in the following aspects:

a. *Social* (e.g., human and vehicle traffic, urban development, appreciation of nature);
b. *Economic* (e.g., infrastructure, livelihood of people, revenue for government, income for investing company); and
c. *Environmental* domains (e.g., air and water pollution, effects on human health, public hygiene, deterioration of land).

In the report, your team should make explicit reference to the information presented in the scenario, as well as other relevant knowledge in science and technology to be used as support for your recommendation. Also state clearly any assumption(s) you have made regarding the scenario.

Read the following scenario

A waste-management company, SamCorp has purchased land to the north-east of a coastal tropical city, Bandar Awang with the intention of building a major waste treatment and recycling facility. The land is currently covered by an extensive mangrove wetland. Most people from the city of 600,000 citizens have little to do with the area and some complain that it is "just a mosquito-infested swamp". Minimal environmental investigation has been conducted at the site. However, preliminary research has identified the wetland as a possible habitat for the threatened great-billed heron and estuarine crocodile.

This new waste treatment and recycling plant will replace the current landfill system, where for the last 50 years; waste has been dumped and buried in an old quarry to the west of the city. Some types of waste amounting to 60% are also incinerated at this location. The landfill site has enough space to last for another five years. Fifty workers will lose their jobs when this site is closed down. It is also believed that the run-offs after heavy rains have been polluting waters in Sungei Awang.

The construction of the proposed facility will cost approximately $56 million and the facility will require 60 to 100 employees on-site when it becomes fully operational. The sale of recycled materials, such as glass, steel, paper, aluminium, other metals and organic garden compost, is predicted to result in an overall profit of $8.5 million per year. The facility will require an upgrade of roads, water services, the sewerage system and electricity in the region. Approximately 60% of Awang wetland will be cleared on-site and the water will be drained.

The SamCorp proposal includes the planting of a screening belt of non-indigenous trees, designed to hide the facility from the view of residents in the newly built housing estate. It is also planned that many trucks will transport material to and from the site, 16 hours a day. People in the new estate have started to express concerns about the pollution that may be produced by the new facility.

Summary

This chapter seeks to clarify what AA are. It is suggested that they are:

- performance assessments that are set in a real-world context;
- possibly alternative assessments (if the conventional involves paper-and-pen); and
- either formative or summative depending on how the assessment information is used.

It is helpful to also consider what the assessment is "authentic" to:

- the working world;
- the student's world; or
- the discipline.

Each of these referents serves a purpose and has a theoretical basis that will be elaborated upon in the following two chapters.

Quick quiz

1. Are paper-and-pen assessments "inauthentic"?
   Answer: Not necessarily. They can be crafted to include elements that allude to the real world and/or the students' world.
2. What is one advantage of having assessments that reflect the problems faced in real life?
   Answer: It introduces students to the kinds of challenges they will face in the future; facilitates transfer of learning; gives us greater confidence in inferring students' competency.
3. Why is it important to include considerations of the discipline in designing AA?
   Answer: In a way it is corollary to "authenticity" residing in the working world: if learners are to engage in the discipline or subject in the way that the professionals in the field do, they need to show their capacity in the processes used by these professionals- though at a level suitable to them.

Reflection questions

Now refer back to the 5 examples given at the beginning of the chapter.

- In what way(s) would you consider them to be AA?
- What reference for authenticity did each assessment take: the working world, the students' world and the world of the discipline involved? Discuss this with your colleagues/course mates.

Note

1 http://www.straitstimes.com/forum/letters-in-print/nurture-a-generation-that-learns-differently-bravely

References

Archibald, D. A., & Newmann, F. M. (1988). *Beyond Standardized Testing: Assessing Authentic Academic Achievement in the Secondary School.* Reston, VA: National Association of School Principals.

Darling-Hammond, L., Ancess, J., & Ort, S. W. (2002). Reinventing high school: Outcomes of the Coalition Campus Schools Project. *American Educational Research Journal, 39*(3), 639–673.

Dewey, J. (1938). *Experience and Education.* New York: Touchstone.

Gulikers, J., Bastiaens, T., & Kirschner, P. (2004). A five-dimensional framework for authentic assessment. *Educational Technology, Research and Development, 52*(3), 67–87.

Havnes, A. (2008). Assessment: A boundary object linking professional education and work. In A. Havnes & L. McDowell (Eds.), *Balancing Dilemmas in Assessment and Learning in Contemporary Education* (pp. 101–114). New York: Routledge.

James, M. & Lewis, J. (2012). Assessment in harmony with our understanding of learning: Problems and possibilities. In J. Gardner (Ed.), *Assessment and Learning.* (2nd ed., pp. 187–206). London: SAGE Publications.

Klenowski, V. (2009). Assessment for learning revisited: An Asia-Pacific perspective. *Assessment in Education: Principles, Policy and Practice, 16*(3), 263–268.

Maclellan, E. (2004). Authenticity in assessment tasks: A heuristic exploration of academics' perceptions. *Higher Education Research & Development, 23*(1), 19–31.

McArthur, K. G. (2012). The Metalinguistic Protocol: Making disciplinary literacies visible in secondary teaching and learning. *Reading Horizons, 52*(1), 26–55.

McConachie, S. M., Hall, M., Resnick, L., Ravi, A. K., Bill, V. L., Bintz, J., & Taylor, J. A. (2006). Task, text, and talk: Literacy for all subjects. *Educational Leadership, 64*(2), 8–14.

Messick, S. (25–26 October 1994). Alternative modes of assessment: Uniform standards of validity. Paper presented at the Evaluating Alternatives to Traditional Testing for Selection, Bowling Green, OH.

Meyer, C. A. (1992). What's the difference between authentic and performance assessment? *Educational Leadership, 49*(8), 39–40.

Newmann, F. M. (2000). Authentic intellectual work: What and why? [Electronic Version]. *Research/Practice, 8.* Retrieved 24 September 2017, https://www.researchgate.net/publication/255607299_Authentic_Intellectual_Work_What_and_Why_1

Shepard, L. A. (2000). The role of assessment in a learning culture. *Educational Researcher, 29*(7), 4–14.

Tanner, D. E. (2001). Authentic assessment: A solution, or part of the problem? *High School Journal, 85*(1), 24–30.

Tay, H. Y. (2015). Setting formative assessments in real-world contexts to facilitate self-regulated learning. *Educational Research for Policy and Practice. 14*(2), 169–187.

Tan, K. H. K., Koh, K. H., & Tay, H.Y. (Ed.) (2015). *Authentic Assessment in Schools.* Singapore: Pearson.

Wiggins, G. (1989). Teaching to the (authentic) test. *Educational Leadership, 46*(7), 41–47.

Wiggins, G. (1993a). Assessment: Authenticity, context and validity. *Phi Delta Kappan, 75*(3), 210–214.

Wiggins, G. (1993b). *Assessing Student Performance.* San Francisco: Jossey-Bass Publishers.

Wolf, D., Bixby, J., Glenn, J., III & Gardner, H. (1991). To use their minds well: Investigating new forms of student assessment. *Review of Research in Education, 17*, 31–74.

2

WHY BOTHER WITH "AUTHENTICITY" IN ASSESSMENTS?

Introduction

This chapter will present important work from the past (Dewey's theory of an educative experience – Dewey, J. (1938). *Experience and Education*. New York: Touchstone.) and more contemporary perspectives as theoretical arguments for authentic assessment (AA).

---

1. Looking back at Chapter 1, what referents do you think each of the writers uses for "authenticity" (refer to Chapter 1)?
2. What are some of the assumptions that the writers have made (see below) in these statements about the effect of AAs? Are they valid assumptions?

The following are excerpts from Tan, K., Koh, K. H. and Tay, H.Y. (Eds.), (2015). *Authentic Assessment in Schools* (2nd ed.), Singapore: Pearson.

- AA is aligned with instruction as it allows teachers to evaluate students' abilities to solve problems in real-world contexts. AA discourages rote learning and copying, but instead lends an opportunity to develop students' creativity and ability to integrate knowledge and to complete complex tasks in real-life applications. In addition, AA can assess students' analytical skills, oral expression and written skills as well as their ability to work collaboratively with peers (p. 84).
- The desired goal of every mathematics classroom is not only to be fair and accurate when assessing students but also to make sure that each student will be able to apply the knowledge and skills gained in the classroom later in life. Hence, there is a need for an assessment tool that is authentic to the "real world" … authentic tasks provide the context for thinking and reasoning,

the setting for collaborative learning, the use of mathematical tools, and the cultivation of attitudes and dispositions in mathematics. In essence, the rich context of the authentic task promotes not only mathematical thinking but also essentially life skills that learners need for their future success.

(pp. 115–116)

What is the appeal of AA that generated claims such as the ones shown earlier? Some sceptics have argued that its appeal may lie in all the positive notions conjured up by the term "authentic" such as being genuine, realistic and accurate (Cumming & Maxwell, 1999). It is also hard to argue against "real world" experience if the alternative is a contrived one (Abernethie, 2006). Or perhaps, the appeal can be attributed to reaction against the excesses of the use of discrete items emphasizing a narrow range of skills that are often disconnected from what the students will face outside school (Resnick, 1987). In contrast, AA appeals because of "the simplicity of its central idea: students' experiences in school should more closely resemble the experiences they encounter in real life" (Cronin, 1993, p. 78). As the student applies information learnt to a particular real-world situation, to create a critical response and then to explain or defend it, the student draws higher-order thinking skills (e.g., cause and effect analysis, deductive or inductive reasoning, experimentation and problem solving).

This is what Kreber (2013) terms as a "correspondence view" of authenticity in that the assessments are "situated within, or correspond to, the 'real world' or appropriate social and disciplinary contexts" (p. 11). The assumption is that because of "their correspondence to the 'real world', the learning tasks are perceived as relevant by students and, therefore, lead students to become more engaged in their learning" (p. 11). But are there theoretical bases for these claims?

Contemporary views of learning

WHAT ASSESSMENT WOULD DEWEY RECOMMEND?

Dewey did not write about assessments, but one can perhaps infer from his belief that "all genuine education comes about through experience" (1938, p. 25). However, he cautions not all experiences are equally educative. For any experience, including that of assessment, to be educative, they need to adhere to two principles:

Principle of continuity

Because "experience does not occur in a vacuum" (p. 40), "every experience both takes up something from those which have gone before and modifies in some way the quality of those which come after" (p. 35). As such, it is the responsibility of the teacher to "utilize the surroundings, physical and social, that exist so as to extract from them all that they have to contribute to building up experiences that are worthwhile" (p. 40).

Principle of interactivity

An experience is always what it is because of a transaction taking place between an individual and what, at the time, constitutes his or her environment, whether the latter consists of persons with whom he or she is talking about some topic or event, the subject talked about being also a part of the situation; or the toys with which he or she is playing; the book he or she is reading (pp. 43–44). The immediate and direct concern of an educator is then with the situations in which interaction takes place (p. 45). Dewey is quick to point out that the two principles of continuity and interaction are not separate from each other.

Revisit the two examples at the beginning of the chapter. In what way do they satisfy Dewey's two principles?

It was once thought that knowledge reflected an external stable reality located outside the knower and could be transmitted unchanged to the minds of the learner. This empiricist (positivist) epistemological stance has given way to the interpretative or constructive paradigm that all knowledge is considered to be created/constructed, rather than discovered. Learning occurs as students engage with the world through activity and reflect on their experiences and consequence of their actions (Elwood & Murphy, 2015).

This view, that learning must be understood in terms of the relational dependency of the learner, has its roots in constructivist theory. Because constructivism has a long history, there are many strands, one of which may be traced back to John Dewey who even at the turn of the twentieth century was already advocating the importance of the child's experience in the learning process. It is not just a case of presenting the curriculum in a more motivating form; the issue is more fundamental than that. To him, "Learning is active. It involves reaching out of the mind. It involves organic assimilation starting from within", growing out of the child's "own past doings, thinkings", "within the range and scope of the child's life" (Dewey, 1902, p. 208).

His view is echoed by more contemporary writers who see learning as "an active process of mental construction and sense making" (Shepard, 2000, p. 6): the learner constructs knowledge through actively making sense of the new information and decides how to integrate it with previously held concepts and information.

This active processing of knowledge on the child's part was empirically demonstrated through the work of Piaget. Through observing and interacting with them while they worked on exercises Piaget set, he sought to map out the distinct stages of cognitive development in children and the approximate age at which the transitions took place: sensorimotor (18 months old); pre-operational (7 years old); concrete operational (12 years old); and formal operational. His theorizing of the twin processes of assimilation (fitting a new experience into the schema, an existing mental structure) and accommodation (revising an existing schema because of a new experience) has also helped us understand how children construct meaning out of their experiences.

However, the notion that knowledge acquisition is a solitary process within the mind of the learner, hidden from view, was itself challenged by Vygotsky (1978) who suggested that meanings and understandings grow out of social encounters. He concluded this after observing that when children were tested on tasks on their own, they rarely did as well as when they were working in collaboration with an adult, even if the adult was not teaching or guiding them. Just merely engaging with the adult enabled them to refine their thinking.

Hence, he proposes "an essential feature of learning is that it creates a zone of proximal development; that is, learning awakens a variety of internal developmental processes that are able to operate only when the child is interacting with people in his environment and in cooperation with his peers" (Vygotsky, 1978, p. 90). The perspective that learning occurs in interactions between the individual and the social environment has been termed the socio-cultural learning theory (James & Lewis, 2012).

This concept of zone of proximal development has received vastly different interpretations. Some, like Bruner, see it as the distance between problem-solving abilities when assisted by or collaborating with more experienced people. Hence, Bruner emphasises the pivotal role played by the instructor to "scaffold" the knowledge so that it can be most readily grasped by the learner (Bruner, 1966).

Other writers include a societal perspective in interpreting the zone of proximal development. Engeström defines it as "the distance between the everyday actions of individuals and the historically new form of societal activity that can be collectively generated as a solution to the double bind potentially embedded in … everyday actions" (Engeström, 1999, p. 66). These contemporary writers focus attention on the structure of social practice rather than privileging pedagogy as the source of learning, arguing that "learning must be understood with respect to a practice as whole, with its multiplicity of relations – both within the community and with the world at large" (Lave & Wenger, 1991, p. 114).

As a result, research on cognitive development has entered a new phase. Up to this point, contextual factors were seen as moderators of cognitive growth. But theorists are now beginning to stress "an *inextricable* link between contextual constraints and the acquisition of knowledge" with cognition considered as "*typically* situated in a social and physical context and is rarely, if ever, decontextualized" (Butterworth, 1992, p. 1). This came about when the role of perception in the foundations of thought was more thoroughly explored. As explained by Butterworth, "Perception *presupposes* context" (p. 3) as what is perceived as a figure depends entirely on what is perceived as ground, in other words, the context. Hence, what is otherwise identical behaviour is given a different meaning in a different context. In fact, the Latin root of context comes from *contexere* meaning "to weave together", "to join together" or "to compose". Hence, context is the interconnected whole that gives meaning to the parts.

Implications of learning theories on assessment

The new epistemology of knowledge requires us to re-evaluate how we assess learning. This is especially when it is almost universally acknowledged that assessments greatly affect teaching and learning in schools. Assessment communicates what is important and has a backwash effect (Biggs, 1996) on where both teachers and learners channel their energy (Boud & Falchikov, 2007).

As such, if learning is not about passively receiving the knowledge to be stored and tested later, assessment should no longer be a static, one-shot measure testing discrete bits of information (Bransford & Schwartz, 1999; Shepard, 1991). Instead, if learning results from students trying to make sense of the world, then assessment should facilitate this sense-making by engaging them, the learners, in purposeful tasks designed to elicit their background knowledge as well as connect them to the skills that they will need in their future. Such assessments would thus satisfy the two principles Dewey advocated in an educative experience: that of interactivity and continuity.

In addition, because of the new understanding that cognitive abilities are developed through socially supported interactions, "school learning should be authentic and connected to the world outside of school not only to make learning more interesting and motivating to students but also to develop the ability to use knowledge in real-world settings" (Shepard, 2000, p. 7). Another implication of such a perspective is that the "social and cultural experiences that students and teachers bring to assessment situations" cannot be ignored (Elwood & Murphy, p.187).

James and Lewis (2012) have highlighted some characteristics of assessment that would be coherent with socio-cultural perspectives, among which are:

- "situated" since the learning cannot be separated from the context in which it is embodied;
- focussed on "agency" on the part of the learner because it is the way the learner uses his resources that is of most significance; and
- holistic and qualitative evaluation, rather than atomised and quantified as in measurement approaches.

A good fit for the characteristics described so far appears to be AA. The real-life contextualization of the assessment task helps harness the learners' interests (Messick, 1994) because they see relevance to their present or future life.

But the argument goes beyond just making assessments more engaging for learners. Proponents of AA also say inferences made on the basis of AA are of sound predictive validity because the learner's performance gives us a good indication of their ability to apply that learning in the future. In addition, there is consequential validity because when learners perceive the task to be meaningful, "their responses are reasonably accurate indications of what they can do" (Wiliam, 2008, p. 273).

In addition to yielding valid inferences of the learning we value in students, AA can serve double duty by bringing about such learning (Boud, 2000). In other words, they are assessments of learning as well as assessments for learning. Black, Harrison, Lee, Marshall & Wiliam (2004) define assessment for learning as any assessment for which the first priority in its design and practice is to serve the purpose of promoting students' learning. Unlike the "inert, procedural knowledge" (Boaler, 1993, p. 56) that is often associated with closed-ended, discreet testing; the learning that is embedded in open-ended nature of AA results in an understanding that is more flexible and transferable to new situations (Boaler, 1998).

Boaler's study compared open and closed mathematical approaches in two schools over three years. In the school that was very much based on chalk-and-talk and textbook practice, students were found to develop "inert, procedural knowledge" (p. 56) that was of limited use in unfamiliar situations. In contrast, in the other school, through an open, project-based environment that also allowed students to exercise choice, students were "encultured into a system of working and thinking that appeared to advantage them in new and unusual settings" (p. 59).

What does research say?

What light have empirical studies shed on the effect of AA? The fact is that there have been few such studies, at least in school settings. Even when challenged with criticism that their rhetoric advocating AA was misleading and "largely unsup-ported by data" (Terwilliger, 1997, p. 24), both Newmann and Wiggins could not offer convincing evidence to the contrary in their reply (Newmann, Brandt, & Wiggins, 1998). The works they cited were usually journal articles (e.g., in *Educational Researcher*) or guides (e.g., Newmann, Secada, & Wehlage, 1995) on how to implement alternative assessment. In addition, there are even fewer studies reporting reliability and validity. It could be that AA advocates find that such quan-titative indicators come from an epistemological stance anathema to theirs; choos-ing instead predominantly qualitative research more consistent with contextualist perspectives, resulting in "a plethora of anecdotal, rather than empirical evidence" (McAlister, 2000, p. 25). The following section presents briefly two well-known studies and three more recent ones.

One study, cited by Newmann and Wiggins and many other researchers, is a case study of AA in action in five schools where widespread evidence of in-depth learning, intellectual habits of mind, and high-quality products were reported (Darling-Hammond, Ancess, & Falk, 1995). They found it heartening that the students involved in the research were typically those who scored low on traditional, standardized assessment. Yet, they were able to master complex content and higher order skills.

The other study often cited to support AA is the *School Restructuring Study* that involved 24 public schools across 16 states. The report included data from 504 observed lessons at various elementary, middle and high school levels (Newmann, Marks, & Gamoran, 1995). As part of their study, they looked for *authentic achievement* defined in terms of construction of knowledge, disciplined enquiry and value beyond school; and AA tasks included the following examples for 4th-grade students

- for mathematics: using measurement, fractions and fraction computation, students draw a diagram of a bookcase with given specifications (length of boards and number of compartments at certain levels); and
- for social studies: a year-long study of the community that culminated with a presentation of plans to improve the neighbourhood.

The study found that when teachers create more challenging and interesting assessments, students were able to rise to the challenge. The improved student performance was regardless of gender, race, ethnicity or socioeconomic status.

A similar study that built on Newmann et al.'s study found significant improvement in the quality of student work in response to the high intellectual demands of the assessment tasks (Koh, Tan, & Ng, 2012). However, unlike the former, the latter employed a quasi-experimental design in which teachers in the intervention group were involved in ongoing and sustained professional development over two years to learn how to craft and refine AA. The control group of teachers were given one/two-day workshops on AAs. The researchers reported that in all three subject areas (English, science and mathematics), the intervention group produced higher quality assessment tasks, characterised by an emphasis on higher-order thinking skills (such as generation of new knowledge), sustained writing and real-world application. The student performance in these three areas was better from the intervention group who also saw an improvement over the two years. Based on their findings, the writers suggested that AAs could help create thinking schools where students "confidently demonstrate higher-order thinking" (p. 135) such as critical thinking and problem solving.

More direct evidence of the impact of authenticity came from a study by Murphy, Lunn and Jones (2006) who looked at the impact of authentic learning on 10 classes of Year 11 (age 15–16) students. It was conducted against the backdrop of piloting a new curriculum ("Twenty-First Century Science") using the module on "Radioactive materials", which attempted to include authenticity in terms of:

- *Cultural authenticity* (p. 232) interpreted as presenting and discussing the science behind radioactivity in relation to the professional practices (e.g., technicians using radiation in medicine). Assessment included students role-playing nuclear medicine professionals discussing how they would advise a patient on the benefits and risks of having a scan involving radioactive iodine.

- *Personal authenticity*, which refers to "the learners' ability to perceive value and meaning in what they are asked to do and learn" (p. 232). For example, radiation was introduced through a case-study of a patient diagnosed and being treated for cancer. The intention was to help students see the relevance of the scientific content to their lives. One assessment included student debates round power production.

Based on data from questionnaires and interviews, the findings found in the intervention group:

- Increased student engagement in the subject. Specifically, they reflected their learning "benefited from visualising complex issues and having access to world views that made the classroom walls permeable for them" (p. 244). In particular, the quantitative findings showed a very significant shift in the girls' interest in physics. In the interviews, the girls attributed this change to the approach in which science was embedded in real-life situations, and they had opportunities to consider different perspectives (e.g., reflect on positive and negative aspects of science).
- A significant increase in student understanding (measured through a knowledge probe included in the student questionnaires) which was "largely attributable to the very significant increase in girls answering the questions correctly" (p. 238).

Another study that found positive outcomes on learning disposition from the use of AA involved Secondary 4 students (aged 15–16) who completed two tasks: one that was a conventional paper-and-pen short essay and the other, an equivalent task set in a real-world context of a live online forum (Tay, 2015). In both cases, participants were required to read a text and give a written response, evaluating the writer's arguments and providing their own insight into the issues raised. The difference between the two tasks lay in the authentic context of a live online forum in which the participants would be writing for a real-world audience and their responses would be subjected to feedback from other readers. Data from individual interviews of 13 participants found the forum task was more engaging because they could choose to comment on a topic that was part of their daily lives. However, the real-life setting was not preferable per se but was preferable only if it offered something of personal interest or relevance to the participants. They also reported using the online comments as a model or reference for their own answers. In other words, the situational factors in a real-world context provided the feedback in real time to help a learner to self-appraise and self-manage. Such an ability to "look again" is key to learning in complex settings: learners must learn to monitor their performance, see their learning in context and to respond with awareness to the tasks (Boud, 2007).

Conclusion

While our understanding of learning has evolved, assessment practices in schools have remained largely unchanged over the years. Often, the blame is laid at the door of the backwash effect of high-stakes national examinations. Because of the examination board's need for high reliability and quick turnaround time in marking, they tend to test decontextualized isolated knowledge which is easier to score. As a consequence, teachers, who have generally been consumers rather than constructors of tests (Goldstein, 2015), replicate these for class tests or practice in order to ensure better performance by their learners.

I argue that the issue may be deeper than teachers' assessment practices. It could be in the teachers' empiricist view that learning comprises students passively acquiring externally transmitted knowledge. Hence, assessment is almost like applying a litmus test: something to be introduced externally (and in as objective and neutral way as possible) to the student to measure how much knowledge has been acquired.

The contemporary view is that learning is neither passive nor are assessments "neutral" (Elwood & Murphy, 2015, p. 189). Learning occurs in the interactions between the individual and the social environment (p. 192). A corollary is that learning also occurs when the learner interacts with the assessment. So, when the assessment is contextualized and designed to harness the learner's socio-cultural experiences, the assessment can enhance learning not just measure it. In that sense, assessment can be seen as more than just measurement but as a catalyst to promote learning, especially the kind that we value.

Summary

This chapter presented a theoretical basis for AA with

- important work from the past (Dewey's theory of an educative experience); and
- more contemporary perspectives (social cultural and social cognitive theories).

It also included a quick overview of seminal pieces of AA research. They all seem to suggest that AA has led to significant improvement in student work especially those that require higher order thinking.

Quick quiz

1. What did Dewey say with reference to AAs?
    Answer: He did not write about AA. But he did support any educative experience (presumably including that of assessments) that would grow out of the child's past (Principle of Continuity) and the child's interaction with the environment (Principle of Interaction). These principles align with contexts involved in AA.
2. In what way(s) do AA offer greater validity?
    Answer: Learners' performance in a real-world context gives a better indication of their ability to apply that learning in the future. Also, when learners see meaning in the tasks and invest in them, their performance is a more accurate indication of their true ability.

3. What seems to be a common finding in AA studies?
   a. Schools using AA found evidence of better performance in higher-order skills.
   b. Students were more engaged.
   c. AA can be used in a variety of subjects.
   d. All of the above.

Answer: All of the above.

Reflection questions

- Refer to the two examples given at the beginning of the chapter. In what way are the claims supported by the learning theories/research presented in this chapter.
- Similarly, reflect on your own perspectives about assessments (including that of AAs). In what way are they supported by the learning theories/ research presented in this chapter.

References

Atherton, J. S. (2005). *Learning and Teaching: Piaget's Developmental Theory* [Electronic Version]. Retrieved 15 March 2007, from http://www.learningandteaching.info/learning/piaget. htm

Biggs, J. (1996). Assessing learning quality: Reconciling institutional, staff and educational demands. *Assessment and Evaluation in Higher Education, 21*(1), 5–15.

Birenbaum, M. (2003). New insights into learning and teaching. In M. Segers, F. Dochy, & E. Cascallar (Eds.), *Optimising New Modes of Assessment: In Search of Qualities and Standards* (pp. 13–36). the Netherlands: Kluwer Academic Publishers.

Black, P., Harrison, C., Lee, C., Marshall, B., & Wiliam, D. (2004). Working inside the black box: Assessment for learning in the classroom. *Phi Delta Kappan, 86*(1), 9–21.

Boaler, J. (1993). The role of contexts in the Mathematics classroom: Do they make mathematics more real? *For the Learning of Mathematics, 13*(2), 12–17.

Boaler, J. (1998). Open and closed mathematics approaches: Student experiences and understandings. *Journal for Research in Mathematics Education, 29*(1), 41–62.

Boud, D. (2000). Sustainable assessment: Rethinking assessment for the learning society. *Studies in Continuing Education, 22*(2), 151–167.

Boud, D. (2007). Reframing assessment as if learning was important. In D. Boud & N. Falchikov (Eds.), *Rethinking Assessment for Higher Education: Learning for the Longer Term* (pp. 14–25). London: Routledge.

Bransford, J. D. & Schwartz, D. L. (1999). Rethinking transfer: A simple proposal with multiple implications. *Review of Research in Education, 24*, 61–100.

Bruner, J. (1966). *Toward a Theory of Instruction.* Cambridge, MA: Harvard University Press.

Butterworth, G. (1992). Context and cognition in models of cognitive growth. In P. Light & G. Butterworth (Eds.), *Context and Cognition* (pp. 1–7). Hillsdale, NJ: Lawrence Erlbaum.

Creswell, J. W. (1998). *Qualitative Inquiry and Research Design: Choosing Among Five Traditions.* Thousand Oaks, CA: Sage Publications.

Cronin, J. F. (1993). Four misconceptions about authentic learning. *Educational Leadership, 50*(7), 78–80.

Darling-Hammond, L., Ancess, J., & Falk, B. (1995). *Authentic Assessment in Action: Studies of Schools and Students at Work.* New York: Teachers College Press.

Dewey, J. (1902). *The Child and the Curriculum.* Chicago: University of Chicago Press.

Dewey, J. (1938). *Experience and Education.* New York: Touchstone.

Elwood, J. & Murphy, P. (2015). Assessment systems as cultural scripts: A sociocultural theoretical lens on assessment practice and products. *Assessment in Education: Principles, Policy & Practice, 22*(2), 182–192, DOI:10.1080/0969594X.2015.1021568.

Engeström, Y. (1999b). Expansive visibilization of work: An activity-theoretical perspective. *Computer Supported Cooperative Work, 8*(1–2), 63–93.

Goldstein, H. (2015). Validity, science and educational measurement. *Assessment in Education: Principles, Policy & Practice, 22*(2), 193–201.

Gulikers, J., Bastiaens, T., & Kirschner, P. (2004). A five-dimensional framework for authentic assessment. *Educational Technology, Research and Development, 52*(3), 67–87.

Hadwin, A. F., Winne, P. H., Stockley, D. B., Nesbit, J. C., & Woszczyna, C. (2001). Context moderates students' self-reports about how they study. *Journal of Educational Psychology, 93*(3), 477–487.

Johnson, L. F., Smith, R. S., Smythe, J. T., & Varon, R. K. (2009) *Challenge-Based Learning: An Approach for Our Time.* Austin, TX: The New Media Consortium. Retrieved June 7, 2016, from http://files.eric.ed.gov/fulltext/ED505102.pdf.

James, M. & Lewis, J. (2012). Assessment in harmony with our understanding of learning: Problems and possibilities. In J. Gardner (Ed.), *Assessment and Learning.* (2nd ed., pp. 187–206). London: Sage Publications.

Koh, K. H., Tan, C., & Ng, P. T. (2012). Creating thinking schools through authentic assessment: The case in Singapore. *Educational Assessment, Evaluation and Accountability, 24*(2), 1–15.

Kreber, C. (2013). Authenticity in and through Teaching in Higher Education. London: Routledge.

Lave, J. & Wenger, E. (1991). *Situated Learning: Legitimate Peripheral Participation.* Cambridge: Cambridge University Press.

McAlister, B. (2000). The authenticity of authentic assessment: What the research says … and doesn't say. In R. Custer (Ed.), *Using Authentic Assessment in Vocational Education* (ERIC Information Series No. 381, pp. 19–31), Columbus, OH: ERIC Clearinghouse on Adult, Career, and Vocational Education.

Messick, S. (1994). The interplay of evidence and consequences in the validation of performance assessment. *Educational Researcher, 23*(2), 13–23.

Murphy, P; Lunn, S., & Jones, H. (2006) The impact of authentic learning on students' engagement with physics. *The Curriculum Journal, 17*(3), 229–246, DOI:10.1080/09585 170600909688.

Newmann, F. M., Brandt, R., & Wiggins, G. (1998). An exchange of views on semantics, psychometrics, and assessment reform: A close look at 'authentic' assessments. *Educational Researcher, 27*(6), 20–21.

Newmann, F. M., Marks, H. M., & Gamoran, A. (1995). Authentic pedagogy: Standards that boost student performance. *Issues in Restructuring Schools, 8*, 1–4.

Newmann, F., Secada, W., & Wehlage, G. (1995). *A Guide to Authentic Instruction and Assessment: Vision, Standards and Scoring.* Madison: Wisconsin Center for Education Research.

Shepard, L. A. (1992). What policy makers who mandate tests should know about the new psychology of intellectual ability and learning. In Gifford, B. R. & O'Connor, M. C. (Eds.), *Changing Assessments: Alternative Views of Aptitude, Achievement, and Instruction.* Boston: Kluwer Academic Publishers.

Shepard, L. A. (2000). The role of assessment in a learning culture. *Educational Researcher, 29*(7), 4–14.

Tay, H. Y. (2015). Setting formative assessments in real-world contexts to facilitate self-regulated learning. *Educational Research for Policy and Practice, 14*(2), 169–187.

Terwilliger, J. (1997). Semantics, psychometrics, and assessment reform: A close look at "authentic" assessments. *Educational Researcher, 26*(8), 24–27.

Vygotsky, L. S. (1978). *Mind in Society*. Cambridge, MA: Harvard University Press.

Wiliam, D. (2008). Balancing dilemmas: Traditional theories and new applications. In A. Havnes & L. McDowell (Eds.), *Balancing Dilemmas in Assessment and Learning in Contemporary Education* (pp. 267–283). New York: Routledge.

Wolf, D., Bixby, J., Glenn, J. III, & Gardner, H. (1991). To use their minds well: Investigating new forms of student assessment. *Review of Research in Education, 17*, 31–74.

3

HOW DO YOU DESIGN QUALITY AUTHENTIC ASSESSMENTS?

Introduction

Conventionally, crafting assessments begin with reference to lesson or unit objectives. In the case of authentic assessment, teachers typically take a task-centred approach: that is, they often conceptualise the assessment task first and then inject a real-life context to it, mostly as a way to make it more engaging to students. However, this approach can lead to validity issues (see the example below). This chapter proposes using Messick's construct-based approach (1994) as a way to design quality authentic assessments (AAs).

Example 3.1

Subject: Science
Topic: Physical properties of materials
Target group: 9-year-olds (Primary 3)

Background
Students have learnt the physical properties (hardness, strength, flexibility, ability to sink/float and waterproof) of materials such as plastics, wood, rubber and metals.

Desired student outcomes

1. Identify suitable materials for creating a boat.
2. Justify the use of chosen materials and their physical properties.
3. Create a boat by applying understanding of physical properties of materials.

Task

1. Students are given a week to create, in groups of three, a boat that would be able to travel a distance of 1.5 m with the aid of a battery-operated fan, in the shortest time possible.

2. At planning stage, students will be given a list of suggested materials. They can then design and create a boat using chosen materials.

3. They have to design a poster that includes a sketch with labels of the identified materials for the respective parts of the boat.

4. At the end of the week, groups have to give verbal presentation of their boat using the poster. After the verbal presentation the boat test will be conducted to see how long it takes to travel 1.5 m.

5. Finally, depending on the outcome of the boat test, the teacher will pose questions to the group to get them to critically evaluate and reflect on their chosen materials, and explain how these choices have contributed to the success or failure of the boat. Groups will be given three minutes to deliberate before giving their group response. The teacher will then assess them based in the rubrics provided.

Self-check questions

1. Referring to Chapter 1, in what ways is this series of assessment tasks authentic to

    *   the working world;
    *   the student's world;
    *   the discipline?

2. What do you think is the rationale for the different parts of the assessment task?
3. What are some possible issues in

    *   implementing the assessment;
    *   interpreting assessment results?

Issues with a task-centred approach

Problematic AAs such as Example 3.1 are often the result of teachers merely adding on the real-world (or simulated real-world) conditions to the task. The task may have been initially well conceived to test the domain of interest, e.g., knowledge of physical properties of materials through the choice of materials that will float. But along with this intended or first-order expectation of the task, there is a second-order expectation of being able to build an aerodynamically sound boat that can race well. The danger of such a task-centred approach is that the expectations, which relate to the underlying or core concepts, understanding and skills (first-order expectations), risk being overwhelmed by expectations relating to the specific context of the task (the second-order expectations). Rather than bridging the gap between the world within and beyond the school walls, additional task demands can distract the students from the underlying expectations of the assessor.

As such, teachers should guard against such *camouflage* as explained by Cumming and Maxwell (1997) as the dressing up of tasks with token "real-world" elements thrown in to appear authentic. While one can reduce the distraction by making the intention of the assessment clear, the camouflage adds an extra hurdle to the learner because beneath the gloss of authentic simulation, the tasks are not, in fact "real life" and students are still required to respond in a certain prescribed way.

An example of camouflage is when students are asked to role-play a situation for language activity but are then penalized if they use colloquial terms.

Try critiquing this authentic assessment suggested by Wiggins (1993, p. 202) before reading Cumming and Maxwell's critique presented below:

Example 3.2

Subject: History
Topic: Revolutionary war

Task

You are a prosecutor or a defence attorney in a trial brought by a parent group seeking to forbid purchase by your high school of a U.S. history textbook, excerpted below. (The book would be used as a required supplement to your current text, not in place of it.) You will present a 10-minute oral case (supported by a written summary of your argument), in pairs, to a jury, taking either side of the question: Is the book appropriate for school adoption and required reading? You will be assessed on how well you support your claim about the accounts in the text, in response to the question, Are the accounts biased, inaccurate, or merely different from our usual viewpoint?

You will be judged on the accuracy, aptness and convincing qualities of your documentation and on the rhetorical effectiveness of your case. Be fair, but be an effective speaker and writer! A six-point scoring scale will be used for each dimension to be assessed: Persuasiveness of evidence, persuasiveness of argument, rhetorical effectiveness of speech and support material.

Critique by Cumming and Maxwell (1999):

The intent was to assess students' historical knowledge, understanding and analysis.

The first-order expectation of the task was for students to develop a historical argument about the appropriateness of the textbook's historical interpretation and accuracy. However, the task was embedded within a second-order expectation of performance within the simulated context of a courtroom (thus requiring emulation of legal forms, procedures and arguments). The second-order expectation dominates the assessment criteria: persuasiveness and rhetorical effectiveness are "characteristics of audience or reader reaction rather than characteristics of historical understanding per se" (p. 187).

Messick's construct-centred approach

In contrast to merely layering on superficial authentic elements in the task-centred approach, Messick suggests a "construct-centred" approach. This approach focuses on the most salient aspects of knowledge and skill that should be tested in the task for the assessor to make a valid inference about the learner with regards to the construct. Care must be taken to ensure that the construct is not underrepresented (that is, nothing of importance is left out) while minimizing construct-irrelevant variance (Messick, 1994).

> The things we measure in education are really "hypothetical constructs". They are hypothesized variables that we cannot observe directly, e.g., mathematical competence, spelling ability (Popham, 2010). Thus, we infer the existence of such traits when we observe behaviour that exhibits the knowledge, skills and attitudes associated with the variable.

Examples of construct under-representation include:

- The use of multiple-choice questions to test mathematical reasoning:
  Unless the learner presents his working before he arrived at the correct answer, the test does not give adequate evidence of the process involved. For all we know, the student got the correct answer not from sound mathematical reasoning but from pure luck.
- The slow pace of examiners' reading during the listening comprehension tests:
  Generally, in real life, people do not speak at the pace presented in these tests. Hence, the tests can be said to underrepresent the listening skills needed for everyday life.

> See more examples of construct under-representation, see Example 3.4 and elsewhere in Part II of the book (e.g., Example 6.1).

Examples of construct-irrelevant variance include

- Including aesthetics as a criterion in research work:
  Teachers often reward students for making an effort to make their research presentation more visually engaging. This additional criterion is irrelevant to the intended object of the task that is to assess if students can conduct sound research.
- Including a penalty for late or untidy work:
  This practice is rationalized as a form of instilling the proper work ethic in learners. While one can understand that they play many roles (including that of nurturing character), teachers need to be mindful as assessors what the task

was designed to measure (not character) and that the mark given for the task should be an accurate reflection of the learners' ability in that area.

More illustrations in the next section: Examples 3.3 and 3.4.
For a more elaborated contextualized example, see Example 8.2.

Here are some examples of how teachers revised AAs using Messick's approach.

Example 3.3

Subject: Social studies (SS)
Contributed by Nithiyah d/o Subramaniam
Level: 8-year-olds (Primary 2)
Topic: National symbols

- To learn and appreciate the history, identity and significance of the National Orchid Garden (NOG).
- To learn and appreciate the significance of the national flower, Vanda Miss Joaquim, as a national symbol.
- To learn and understand significance, role and use of national symbols.

Task

Background: Prior to the field trip, students are shown a PowerPoint presentation about the NOG as a key place of interest in representing Singapore's history, identity and significance. They also learn a simple "RIUU framework" (Represents, Identity, Unique and Unifies) to understand why the Vanda Miss Joaquim is a national flower. Students go on the field trip, guided by teachers who facilitate, share information at various pit-stops and answer students' questions.

After the trip, using "Think-Pair-Share", pupils are tasked to look at other national symbols (e.g., national anthem, pledge) and explain why they are national symbols guided by the "RIUU framework" (regardless of race and religion).

Strength of task

- Learner engagement through immersive experience through the field-trip.
- Learner's understanding is scaffolded through teacher's modelling of RIUU. Represents, Identity, Unique and Unifies (regardless of race and religion).

Weakness

- Students had difficulty explaining the coat of arms as a national symbol. Some responses were limited because of their lack of proficiency in language especially in explaining an abstract concept like national identity.

Language thus became a construct-irrelevance variance. A possible revision is to ask students to design a class symbol using RIUU. The more immediate references and concrete examples drawn from class community may be more authentic to the lives of the young learners.

Example 3.4

Subject: Science
Contributed by Ivin Chan
Target Group Level: 13-year-olds (Secondary 1)
Topic: Scientific inquiry

Learning objectives

1. Understand the scientific inquiry process.
2. Apply the scientific inquiry process to protect the egg from breaking.

Synopsis

The Egg-Drop Project is a six-week long group project. The project involves students, in groups of three to four, designing and creating a product that would support and protect a chicken's egg when it is dropped from the third floor of the school block. The students are expected to carry out experiments to determine the most effective materials and structure design to utilize when coming up with their product. They would also have to demonstrate the workability of the product and produce a project report and a personal reflection.

Task

Students are required to:

- Work in groups of three to four and develop a hypothesis and identify the independent, dependent and control variables in their experiments.
- Design a product and carry out experiments to determine the best possible materials and structure design to protect the egg when it is released from the specified height.
- Build and demonstrate the workability of the product.
- Write a report and reflection.

Strength of task

- Learner engagement through the hands-on activity culminating in the egg-drop.

Weakness

- The original rubric deviated from assessing the scientific enquiry process, with focus only on identifying variables and forming hypothesis. In Part 2 of the Task, which involved the actual egg-drop, is also irrelevant to the construct. The criteria used in the rubric involved assessing where the egg landed, the condition of the egg after the drop and the choice of materials.

- To address this under-representation of the construct (scientific inquiry), the rubrics was revised to better reflect the five stages of the scientific inquiry process:

  ○ Observation or questioning
  ○ Hypothesis making
  ○ Experimentation
  ○ Data collection
  ○ Evaluation and review

(See Example 3.4.1 for revised rubric.)

EXAMPLE 3.4.1 Rubrics for scientific inquiry task

Components	Points awarded		
	1	*2*	*3*
Hypothesis making	Able to define what is an independent variable, dependent variable, and controlled variables.	Able to relate correctly the IV and DV and controlled variables for the Egg drop project.	Able to justify why their hypothesis is better than their classmates'
Experiment	Able to describe the basic steps in conducting the experiment: procedures, materials, etc.	Able to show a clear relationship between the proposed hypothesis and how the experiment can test the hypothesis.	Able to design not just one experiment but multiple experiments with different perspectives to give more reliable data so as to test the hypothesis
Data collection	Able to collect a basic set of data and present it properly using tables: with correct units, decimal points.	Able to show the relationship between the data collected, and use of derived values where necessary to express relationship between IV and DV.	Able to present data in a form easily understandable showing the relationship between the IV and DV. Data collected appears to be precise and accurate.

(continued)

EXAMPLE 3.4.1 Continued

Components	Points awarded		
	1	*2*	*3*
Evaluation	Able to express the basic information obtained by the data collected, simple reporting of IV and DV, and other meaningful values.	Able to evaluate the proposed hypothesis and give reasons supported by data.	Able to evaluate the proposed hypothesis and give reasons supported by data. In addition, able to give a detailed error analysis of the experiment and possible adjustments to the experimental procedures for a better collection of evidence.

Example 3.5

Subject: Special needs education
Contributed by S. Thilagavathi
Target group:

- Students with profound hearing loss.
- Chronological age – 12.
- Developmental (cognitive and communication) age – 9.

Learning objective

- Communicate and interact well with others.
- Analyse, make predictions and solve problems.
- Manage and care for themselves independently.

Task

- Practical performance (prepare hot coffee) and oral questioning.

Teacher's reflections

Traditional paper-and-pen assessment is inadequate and inappropriate to assess students, especially those with diverse learning needs. Such assessment requires situations and behaviours that are "divorced from the children's natural developmental ecology" (Bagnato, 2007, p. 117). Observing students perform in their natural settings provides authentic information that is much more descriptive of them, which is then used to decide what is next for the students. Assessment must accommodate individual differences. Force fitting conventional teaching and assessments to atypical students is a clear-cut injustice done to them.

This assessment is designed around students' functional skills in daily routine to assess the constructs of safety and hygiene, which are important life skills. The teacher first demonstrates how to make a cup of coffee safely and hygienically, and simultaneously explains processes verbally. The students then perform the task (make coffee). They will be assessed using a rubric (see Example 3.5.1 Rubric Assessment 1 – Performance Assessment) and answer verbal questions posed by the teacher (see questions in Example 3.5.2 Rubric Assessment 2 – Oral). This oral interaction is an important step in assessing students' real understanding. Students may be just reproducing the teachers' actions without clear understanding. For example, they should be able to understand the rationale behind wiping their hands before turning on the switch. Thus, with oral questioning, the assessor is better able to ascertain students' understanding of the target constructs. In the design of this task, it was important not to include "second-order expectation" (Cumming & Maxwell, 1999). The criteria and rubrics for both assessments (performance and oral questioning) have been formulated with the threats to validity in mind. The behaviour indicators are carefully thought through to ensure that they are closely linked to the two constructs – safety and hygiene, without construct under-representation or construct irrelevant variance (Messick, 1994).

EXAMPLE 3.5.1 Rubric assessment 1 – performance assessment

2 – *Student consistently meets criterion*	1 – *Student inconsistently meets criterion*	0 – *Student does not meet criterion*
• Performs the task as specified in the criterion. • Performs the task independently. • Uses the skill across time, materials, settings and people.	• Does not consistently perform the task as specified in the criterion. • Performs the item with assistance. • Does not perform all components of the item or does not meet all aspects of the criterion (emerging behaviour). • Performs the task only under specific situations or conditions (with certain people or setting).	• Does not yet perform the task as specified in the criterion when given repeated opportunities or assistance or when modifications and adaptations are made.

Tasks	*Assessment criteria* *(refer to guidelines above)*		
Behaviour indicator 1 – use equipment safely (S) and hygienically (H)	**2**	**1**	**0**
H Wash hands at the sink.			
S, H Check jug for damage and wash jug before collecting water.			

(*continued*)

EXAMPLE 3.5.1 Continued

Tasks	Assessment criteria (refer to guidelines above)		
Behaviour indicator 1 – use equipment safely (S) and hygienically (H)	2	1	0
S Hold jug with two hands and bring jug to water dispenser.			
S, H Gently place jug on the table and dry hands with towel (cloth or paper).			
S Open dispenser's top and pour water from jug into dispenser.			
S Remove finger from the switch after turning on the switch.			
S Remove finger from switch after turning off the switch when water gets hot.			
S Check cup and teaspoon for damage.			
H Wash cup and teaspoon.			
S Keep scissors away after cutting the sachet.			
Behaviour indicator 2 – obtain information on safety (S) and hygiene (H) of 3-in-1 coffee sachet	2	1	0
H Check if sachet is not tampered.			
H Dispose sachet if tampered.			
H Check for expiry date.			
H Dispose sachet if expired.			

Tasks	Assessment criteria (refer to guidelines above)		
Behaviour indicator 3 – prepare 3-in-1 coffee safely (S) and hygienically (H)	2	1	0
S Hold sachet away from the perforated line as you cut.			
H Without dipping finger into the sachet, pour 3-in-1 coffee from sachet into cup.			
H Wipe off spillage (not to be scooped and placed into the cup) and wash hands before returning to the cup.			
S Place cup in dispenser and press dispense button with one hand and keep the other hand away from cup while hot water is being dispensed.			
S Stir cup gently with teaspoon to avoid splashing of hot coffee onto hand.			
H Wash teaspoon after tasting coffee, before putting it back into the cup.			
Final outcome	2	1	0

EXAMPLE 3.5.2 Rubric assessment 2 – oral

2 – Student consistently meets criterion	1 – Student inconsistently meets criterion	0 – Student does not meet criterion
• Performs the task as specified in the criterion. • Performs the task independently. • Uses the skill across time, materials, settings and people.	• Does not consistently perform the task as specified in the criterion. • Performs the item with assistance. • Does not perform all components of the item or does not meet all aspects of the criterion (emerging behaviour). • Performs the task only under specific situations or conditions (with certain people or setting).	• Does not yet perform the task as specified in the criterion when given repeated opportunities or assistance or when modifications and adaptations are made.

Tasks		Assessment Criteria (refer to guidelines above)		
Behaviour Indicator 1 – use equipment safely (S) and hygienically (H)		2	1	0
S, H	What is the first thing you would do when you want to make a cup of coffee?			
	Why?			
S	Why do you have to dry your hands before turning on/off switch?			
S	Why do you have to check the cup for damages?			
Behaviour Indicator 2 – obtain information on safety and hygiene of 3-in-1 coffee sachet		2	1	0
H	What could have possibly happened to a tampered sachet?			
H	What does it mean when the date on the coffee sachet is expired?			
H	What happens if you consume expired coffee?			
Behaviour Indicator 3 - Prepare 3-in-1 coffee safely and hygienically		2	1	0
H	Why can't you use your teeth to open the sachet?			
H	What is the reason for washing teaspoon after tasting coffee?			
H	If you spill the coffee mixture from the sachet, why can't you scoop and put it back into the cup?			
Final Outcome		2	1	0

Example 3.6

Subject: English language
Contributed by Toh Ji Rong
Target Group: 15-year-olds (Secondary 3)
Topic: Persuasive speech

Relevant standards

- Write a persuasive speech using at least two persuasion techniques (appeal to emotion, credibility and reason) and two speech features (parallelism, rule of three, antithesis).
- Deliver the speech clearly and effectively, showing awareness of purpose, audience and context (PAC) through varying appropriate rhythm and fluency.

Tasks

1. After being taught the text structure, PAC, language features and persuasion techniques of a persuasive speech through the use of a video of an authentic speech, the transcript of the speech is then analysed to identify the parts of the text organizational structure, language features and persuasion techniques.
2. Students then work in groups of three to improve a speech prepared by the teacher to make it more persuasive. They could edit or insert new sentences/ paragraphs. They must be able to explain what persuasion technique and speech feature they are using when presenting to the class. The teacher facilitates class discussion on the effectiveness of the changes.
3. Students proceed to write their speech individually as a situational writing task. The topic of the speech is different from the two they have previously worked on. They are also given a checklist (see Table 3.1) at the start so that they know what to look out for. Students are expected to do a self and peer evaluation using the checklist once they are done with their individual speech, edit accordingly, and submit to the teacher for marking.
4. After getting feedback from the teacher, students will create a podcast recording using their corrected speech. They will self-evaluate their recording using the rubric before submitting it for grading.

Teacher's reflections

The major component of this task is the podcast as it constitutes the students' summative grade. Students are assessed on the quality of the podcast, but this quality might be affected by the quality of the written speech. For example, language mistakes might interfere with the fluency of the oral recording. While the teacher would have marked and provided feedback for students to improve on their written speech, the quality of the eventual speech used for recording is not guaranteed. This may even make the assessment unfair. While the construct is to assess students' ability to communicate effectively and in particular to persuade, there is under-representation in the scoring rubric in terms of the ability to form the written exposition. There is overlap in the criteria of the original scoring rubric (which included pronunciation and articulation, rhythm and fluency; and awareness of purpose, audience and context). For example, if the student shows full awareness of PAC, he would have read with appropriate rhythm and fluency to good effect. The rubric also does not help students understand fully the criteria for success. Hence it was revised. It was decided that a holistic rubric (See Example 3.6.1 rubric) might be more relevant than an analytical one. The criteria should also be unpacked if they are to help students self-evaluate their podcast.

TABLE 3.1 Checklist for speech

Items	*Peer*	*Self*	*Teacher*
Format & structure			
The speech is organised in **at least five paragraphs.**			
The **title** of the speech is present.			
The speech starts with the **greeting** and ends with the **closing**.			
The **purpose and stand** are clearly shown by the end of the first paragraph.			
The **stand is restated** in the last paragraph.			
Task fulfilment			
All the points in the task are addressed.			
All the points in the task are sufficiently elaborated on.			
Information given in the task and visual stimulus are used relevantly.			
Own words are used whenever possible.			
PAC			
Use of first-person pronouns (highlight in yellow).			
Use of active voice.			
Use of connectors (highlight in pink).			
Persuasion techniques			
At least two persuasive appeals used (appeal to reason/credibility/emotion). ★Indicate in left margin.			
At least two persuasive language features used (parallelism/antithesis/rule of three). ★Indicate in left margin.			
Language			
Spelling is accurate.			
Full stops are used to separate sentences.			
Tenses are accurate.			
Subject-verb agreement is accurate.			

EXAMPLE 3.6.1 Podcast Rubric (revised)

	1–2	3–5	6–8	9–10
Effective communication through **1. Clear pronunciation & articulation.**	Message is not communicated effectively at all and there is distortion of meaning due to very weak pronunciation and articulation.	Message is not communicated effectively, and understanding is hampered due to weak pronunciation and articulation.	Message is communicated effectively, and understanding is established due to generally clear pronunciation and articulation.	Message is communicated very effectively, and full understanding is established due to very clear pronunciation and articulation.
2. Awareness of purpose, audience and context with appropriate:	Reads with little awareness of purpose, audience and context.	Reads with some awareness of purpose, audience and context.	Reads with good awareness of purpose, audience and context.	Reads with full awareness of purpose, audience and context.
(i). **rhythm, stress,** (ii). **fluency/pace,** (iii). **volume.**	There is no attempt to vary voice qualities. Reading is monotonous, too fast or too slow, and too loud or too soft.	Variation of rhythm, stress, pace and volume is inappropriate and thus ineffective.	Variation of rhythm, stress, pace and volume is generally appropriate and effective.	Variation of rhythm, stress, pace and volume is fully appropriate and effective.

Summary

This chapter contrasted two approaches to designing AA:

- The task-centred approach – that may lead to validity issues because of second-order expectations due to additional task demands.
- The construct-centred approach – that will help designers avoid issues of construct under-representation and construct-irrelevance.

Quick quiz

1. To assess if students have memorized the mathematical formulae taught during the term, the teacher designs an AA where the students have to create rhyming poems that will include elements of the formulae. Identify the first- and second-order expectations.
    Answer: First-order expectation refers to core concept, that is mathematical formulae; second-order expectations refer to the rhyming structure, which is the context in which the core concept is being demonstrated.
2. In what way is a project that allows learners to cut-and-paste information from internet sources under-representing the skill of evaluation?
    Answer: Evaluation requires that learners be required to show discernment and critique of the information gathered. These skills are not demonstrated if students are allowed to merely lift from sources.
3. When would a penalty for illegible handwriting *not* be considered construct irrelevant? When the task is assessing:
    (a) penmanship;
    (b) reading comprehension;
    (c) summary skills?

Answer: (a) because legible handwriting is directly related to penmanship skills.

Reflection questions

Reflect on the AA that you are currently using.

- Are there issues of construct under-representation or construct irrelevance?
- What do you need to do to improve the AA so that the assessment results accurately reflect the core concepts/skills that it is supposed to measure?

References

Bagnato, J. S., Neisworth, T. J., & Pretti-Frontczak, L. (2010). *Linking Authentic Assessment & Early Childhood Intervention: Best Measures for Best Practices.* (2nd ed.). Baltimore, MD: Paul H. Brookes Publishing.

Cronbach, L. J., & Meehl, P. E. (1955). Construct validity in psychological tests. *Psychological Bulletin, 52,* 281–302.

Cumming, J. J., & Maxwell, G. S. (1999). Contextualising authentic assessment. *Assessment in Education: Principles, Policy and Practice, 6*(2), 177–194.

McAlister, B. (2000). The authenticity of authentic assessment: What the research says … and doesn't say. In R. Custer (Ed.), *Using Authentic Assessment in Vocational Education.* (ERIC Information Series No. 381, pp. 19–31). Columbus, OH: ERIC Clearinghouse on Adult, Career, and Vocational Education.

Messick, S. (1994). The interplay of evidence and consequences in the validation of performance assessment. *Educational Researcher, 23*(2), 13–23.

Popham, W. J. (2010). *Everything School Leaders Need to Know about Assessment.* Thousand Oaks, CA: Corwin.

Tay, H.Y. (2014). Authentic assessment. In W.S. Leong, Y. S. Cheng, & K., Tan (Eds.), *Assessment and Learning in Schools.* Singapore: Pearson.

Tay, H.Y. (2015). Conclusion. In Tan, K. H. K., Koh, K. H., & Tay, H.Y. (Eds.), *Authentic Assessment in Schools.* Singapore: Pearson.

Wiggins, G. P. (1993). Authenticity, context, and validity. *The Phi Delta Kappan, 75*(3), 200–208, 210–214.

4

HOW DO YOU DESIGN RUBRICS TO ACCOMPANY THE AUTHENTIC ASSESSMENT?

Pam Hook

Introduction

In Chapter 3, we examined how to craft an authentic assessment (AA). However, in itself, the AA is incomplete as an assessment tool because it still needs a rubric as an evaluative guide. This chapter starts with an overview of the role of a rubric – how it functions as an evaluative tool and how it can also fulfil formative purposes. Next, after highlighting the different parts of a rubric, the chapter focusses on rubric standards, before presenting "Structure of Observed Learning Outcomes" (SOLO) as a framework to guide and to describe these standards. The explanation is supported with examples, many of which have been created by teachers and written with an aim to facilitate student self-assessment.

The summative and formative roles of rubrics

> The indispensable conditions for improvement are that the student comes to hold a concept of quality roughly similar to that held by the teacher, is continuously able to monitor the quality of what is being produced during the act of production itself, and has a repertoire of alternative moves or strategies from which to draw on at any given point.
>
> *(Sadler, 1989, p. 121)*

Rubrics measure learner performance – the level of task performance, the learning process itself, self-regulation and/or self (Hattie, 2009). They are "a scoring tool for qualitative rating of authentic or complex student work" (Jonsson & Svingby, 2007, p. 131). Rubrics tell the assessor what is considered important and what to look for when assessing: criteria (for rating important dimensions of performance); and standards of attainment for those criteria. Oftentimes in practice, when used with a score (e.g., out of ten) or a grade, rubrics have an "administrative" function (to categorise or classify students) or a "diagnostic" function (to represent a competency or capability). Typically, they use the number of factually correct or incorrect answers or frequency of occurrence.

When shared with students, rubrics help clarify learning intentions (learning objectives, learning outcomes) and success criteria for learning progress. With an "outcomes based", "constructive alignment" or "backwards design" planning process (Biggs, 1996; Biggs & Tang, 2007; Wiggins & McTighe, 2005), the rubric is also a framework for progress – providing a process of formative assessment that can be used to adapt students' learning experiences to support their progress from prior knowledge to the learning goal.

Among their many uses in teaching and learning, rubrics help teachers and/or students to:

- **plan learning experiences** (questions, discussion prompts and tasks) to provide evidence of progress in student learning;
- **give effective feedback and feedforward** (teacher to student, student to teacher and student to student) to assist learners to reach identified learning goals;
- **engage in dialogue for feedforward** ("Where to next?" conversations) for deeper learning;
- **develop learner agency** by enabling students to self-monitor the quality of their work, to self-direct and self-regulate their actions, and to take ownership of their own learning and how they share it through their thoughts and actions during, for example, peer-assessment, reciprocal teaching and collaborative learning; and
- **act as a learning resource in collaborative group work** when giving and receiving feedback with group goals and individual accountability.

What makes up a rubric?

A rubric is a grid with the following elements (see Figure 4.1):

- **Learning task description** states the learning intention or intended learning outcome. It consists of a learning verb, content and in some circumstances a context and clarifies the explicit nature of the learning task.
- **Standards** cover the possible levels of learning outcome. The columns indicate differentiated levels of success – each representing a curriculum level, scale of marks, given grade, etc.
- **Criteria** are the characteristics on which the learning task is to be judged. They indicate the different elements the student needs to do to complete the task. They can be weighted to indicate their relative importance to the whole learning performance.
- **Descriptors** describe the qualities the student needs to demonstrate they have achieved each standard within each criterion, from highest to lowest. Descriptors outline success criteria or the level of performance outcome expected to attain a given grade or level of knowledge. They are benchmarks for achievement.

- **Effective strategies** are the strategies that best help students meet expectations in the various criteria and descriptors. These may be categorised as cognitive, metacognitive, motivational or management strategies (Boekaerts, 1997; Dignath, Buettner, & Langfeldt, 2008, cited in Hattie & Donoghue, 2016). They support formative assessment. Both teacher and students can suggest effective strategies for achieving the standard. This row is not typical of rubrics that are used for summative purposes but adding this row enhances its usefulness as formative assessment.

Rubric standards

Rubric standards play a powerful role in clarifying our thinking, helping us to structure and detail classroom observations of student performance. Effective standards encourage teachers to notice student performance thoughtfully and critically, slowing closure, the rush to judgement that a simple assessment of correct and incorrect might bring.

However, standard descriptions do more than clarify goals. When aligned with a reliable and valid standard, they provide explicit, differentiated feedback on progress in learner performance.

In identifying different levels of success, the differentiated descriptions in a standard helps students monitor progress in the quantity and quality of their work. Comparing the level of their own work with the "quality work" or "deep learning" described in a standard identifies the gap between a student's learning outcome and the desired goal. In this way, a rubric's standard clarify feedback – indicating how a student might modify their work and close the gap.

There are two common approaches to developing rubric standards to discriminate learner performance (Nitko, 2004). The first is a *top down* approach using a

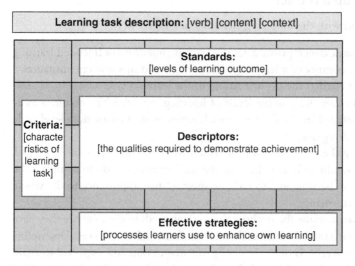

FIGURE 4.1 Rubric template.

framework designed by "curriculum experts" to serve as a standard for differentiating developmentally appropriate and comparable measures of student growth in learning and achievement. The second involves teacher practitioners in examining artefacts of student learning to induce a rubric standard – a *bottom up* approach to developing rubric standards. It has been assumed that when teachers are directly involved in building the rubric standards in bottom up approaches it might enhance teacher ability to use rubric assessments and, thus, make the rubric assessment more instructionally useful (Wei, Schultz, & Martin, 2014). It might also be argued that the bottom up approach sits more comfortably with notions of best fit within AA.

Regardless of who has created the standard, teachers (and students) discuss the implication and nuance in rubric standards extensively. It is important that both approaches seek discriminators and descriptors to make learning visible in ways that will enthuse and upskill students to make learning progress. To use the rubrics without this goal is, as Kohn (2006) opines, simply to create a new way to grade, rank and categorise students and does not represent authentic learning. However, educators wishing to use bottom up approaches for AA must take extra care to seek standard discriminators that have a high degree of inter-rater reliability and an internal consistency so that "bottom up" assessment decisions made using the standards can be replicated – they are both reliable and valid. Both top down and bottom up approaches should make time to ask the questions shown in Figure 4.2.

Using SOLO five-level framework for rubrics

SOLO taxonomy is a five-level model of learning developed by academics Biggs and Collis (1982) based on their research into surface and deep-learning outcomes. It can be used to independently assess the cognitive complexity of the learning task and the cognitive complexity of the learning outcome of that task.

The SOLO model describes a hierarchical standard where each SOLO level provides the platform for further learning and/or next steps. Each ascending SOLO level describes an outcome with an increase in structural complexity – an increase in knowledge (quantitative) or a deepening of understanding (qualitative). Table 4.1 gives a quick outline of SOLO, with a brief characterisation and associated observable outcomes at each level (see row on SOLO verbs). A more detailed description of each of the five levels (prestructural, unistructural, multistructural, relational and extended abstract) is also provided.

Prestructural level of understanding

In the rubric standard, the SOLO *prestructural* level of understanding describes an outcome where the student has approached the learning task or intended learning outcome inappropriately and has missed the point or needs help to start. The prestructural level reminds students that everyone will at different times nudge up against something they know very little about. With a SOLO standard, "knowing

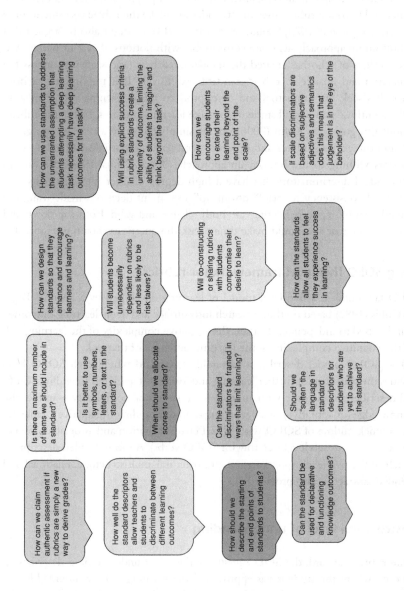

FIGURE 4.2 Common questions teachers ask about rubrics.

TABLE 4.1 The SOLO five-level framework for rubric standards

SOLO prestructural level	SOLO unistructural level	SOLO multistructural level	SOLO relational level	SOLO extended abstract level
		SOLO symbols		
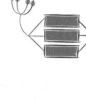				
	← Quantitative phase →		← Qualitative phase →	
	(Shows **how much** a student knows.)		(Shows **how well** a student knows about a topic and how well the students can apply the information into new as well as current contexts.)	
No engagement with the learning task or intended learning outcome.	Acquiring surface understanding.	Consolidating surface understanding.	Acquiring and consolidating deep understanding.	Extending deep understanding – conceptual understanding.
Learning outcomes show unconnected information and no organisation.	Learning outcomes show simple connections but importance is not noted.	Learning outcomes show connections are made but significance to overall meaning is missing.	Learning outcomes show connections are made and parts are synthesised with the overall meaning.	Learning outcomes go beyond the subject and make links to other concepts.
No relevant idea.	One relevant idea.	Many relevant ideas.	Related ideas.	Extended ideas.
		SOLO verbs		
	Identify, define, do simple procedure.	Enumerate, describe, list, combine, do algorithms.	Classify, sequence, compare, contrast, explain causes, analyse, relate, apply.	Theorise, generalise, hypothesise, reflect, evaluate, predict.
		SOLO hand signs[1]		

[1] Essential Resources Educational Publishers Ltd. Reproduced with permission.

nothing" is not a moment of embarrassment but rather a moment of anticipation and learner celebration. "So many of us know very little about [X], just imagine how much progress we are going to make in our learning about [X] this term. How shall we start?"

The next two levels in the rubric standard, SOLO *unistructural* and *multistructural*, are associated with outcomes at surface levels of understanding – bringing in information.

Unistructural level of understanding

At the SOLO *unistructural* level, the rubric describes an outcome where the student picks up one aspect of the task and their understanding is disconnected and limited. This step up from prestructural understanding is achievable – it is an advance but not too far in advance, just above the level the student is working at; it is explicit, proximal and hierarchical. Learning strategies that help students acquire surface understanding (and thus progress from a prestructural to unistructural level) can be included in the effective strategy component of the SOLO rubric enhancing its use in formative assessment. Strategies include looking at the object, event or idea and defining it (asking "What is it?"). Hattie and Donoghue (2016) suggest effective strategies to support acquiring surface understanding include: Integrating with prior knowledge (ES 0.93), outlining and transforming (ES[1] 0.85), mnemonics (ES 0.76), summarisation (ES 0.66), organising (ES 0.60), record keeping (ES 0.54), underlining and highlighting (ES 0.50), note taking (ES 0.50) and imagery (ES 0.45).

Multistructural level of understanding

Progress along the standard to the SOLO multistructural level is quantitative. At the *multistructural* level, the rubric standard describes an outcome where the student knows several aspects of the task but misses their relationships to each other and the whole. Again, this step up from unistructural understanding is achievable, just above the level the student is working at; it is explicit, proximal and hierarchical. In the effective strategy component of the SOLO rubric, learning strategies that help students acquire and consolidate surface understanding (and thus progress from a unistructural to multistructural level) may include describing the object, event or idea (asking "What is it like?"). Hattie and Donoghue (2016) suggest the following strategies are effective when consolidating surface understanding: Deliberate practice (ES 0.77), effort (ES 0.77), rehearsal and memorisation (ES 0.73), giving/receiving feedback (ES 0.71), spaced versus mass practice (ES 0.60), help seeking (ES 0.60), time on task (ES 0.54), reviewing records (ES 0.49) and practice testing (ES 0.44).

The progression along the standard to SOLO *relational* and *extended abstract* outcomes is qualitative.

Relational level of understanding

At the SOLO *relational* level, the rubric describes an outcome where the student links and integrates aspects of their learning, which contributes to a deeper level of understanding – a more coherent understanding of the whole. This step up from multistructural understanding is achievable but arguably more challenging than the previous steps on the rubric standard. It represents a significant shift from surface to deep understanding and an increase in cognitive load for the student as they make connections by integrating loose ideas. Once again using SOLO means the standard descriptor is explicit, proximal and hierarchical. Learning strategies for the effective strategy component of the SOLO rubric, which help students acquire and consolidate deep understanding (and thus progress from a surface multistructural level to a deep relational level), may include sequencing ("What is the order?"), classifying ("What is the group?"), compare and contrast ("How is it similar? How is it different?"), causal explanation ("What is the cause?") and analysis ("What are the parts and how do they work together?"). Hattie and Donoghue (2016) identify the following as effective strategies when acquiring and consolidating deep learning: Seeking help from peers (ES 0.83), classroom discussion (0.82), evaluation and reflection (ES 0.75), elaboration and organisation (ES 0.75), self-consequences (ES 0.70), problem-solving teaching (ES 0.68) and self-verbalisation and self-questioning (ES 0.64).

Extended abstract level of understanding

At the SOLO *extended abstract* level, the rubric standard describes an outcome where the student rethinks their new relational-level understanding at another conceptual level: They look at it in a new way and use it as the basis for predicting, generalising, reflecting, wondering or creating new understanding. This step up from relational understanding is often challenging for students and teachers. How can we best represent a level that goes beyond what we already know – that looks at the content or idea in a new way; that extends student thinking at the conceptual level of abstraction? For the effective strategy component of the SOLO rubric, learning strategies that help students extend their level understanding may include generalising, predicting, evaluating, wondering, creating new connections and so on. Hattie and Donoghue (2016) identify finding similarities and differences (ES 1.32), seeing patterns to new situations (ES 1.14) and far transfer (transfer between contexts that, initially, appear to have very little connection) (ES 0.80) as effective strategies for transferring understanding to new contexts.

Application of SOLO to rubrics

The SOLO levels of increasing cognitive complexity (quantitative and qualitative) – prestructural, unistructural, multistructural, relational and extended abstract – make a cohesive and well-grounded framework for discriminating the different standard descriptors when constructing rubrics. They provide the foundation needed to create rubric descriptors with specific, proximal and hierarchical criteria descriptions.

SOLO taxonomy thus provides a powerful, reliable and consistent framework for top down rubric creation. For example, in a top down approach the New Zealand NCEA[2] achievement standards for achievement, merit and excellence in mathematics and statistics are framed by a standard using the multistructural, relational and extended abstract levels of cognitive complexity in SOLO taxonomy.

More significantly, the SOLO levels provide a simple, reliable and robust standard for teachers and students creating "bottom up" rubrics where they induce a standard from the level in SOLO taxonomy and artefacts of student learning. The standard moves through quantitative and qualitative progress. Using SOLO as the framework ensures its construct validity. It also ensures every student experiences success and a new learning challenge; every student regardless of their entry point can access a proximal, hierarchical and explicit next step. See Table 4.2.

Some examples of rubrics created by teachers using SOLO levels for standards are shown in Tables 4.3, 4.4 and 4.5. Notice that they are written in the voice of the learner.

TABLE 4.2 Questions for teachers (and students) to consider when writing bottom up SOLO–based rubric criteria

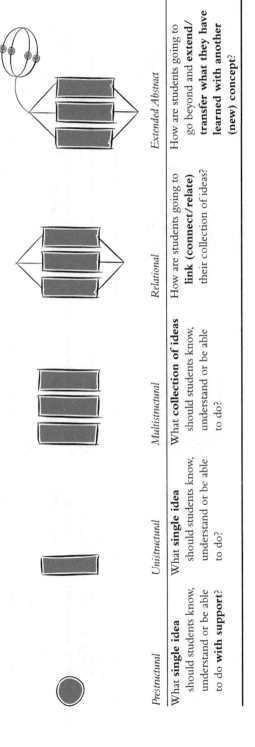

Prestructural	Unistructural	Multistructural	Relational	Extended Abstract
What **single idea** should students know, understand or be able to do **with support**?	What **single idea** should students know, understand or be able to do?	What **collection of ideas** should students know, understand or be able to do?	How are students going to **link (connect/relate)** their collection of ideas?	How are students going to go beyond and **extend/ transfer what they have learned with another (new) concept**?

TABLE 4.3 Develop a brief in technology

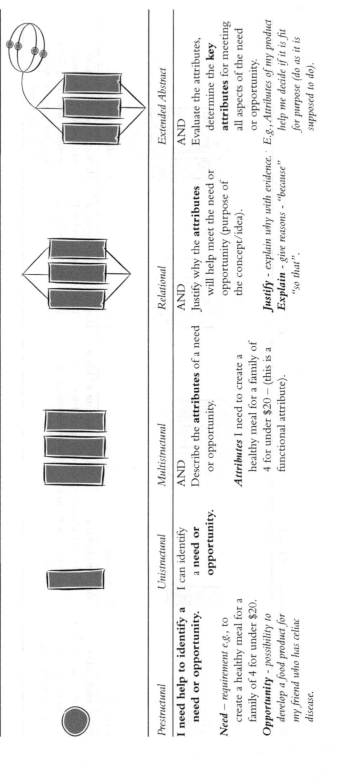

Prestructural	Unistructural	Multistructural	Relational	Extended Abstract
I need help to identify a need or opportunity. *Need – requirement e.g., to create a healthy meal for a family of 4 for under $20.* *Opportunity - possibility to develop a food product for my friend who has celiac disease.*	I can identify **a need or opportunity.**	AND Describe the **attributes** of a need or opportunity. *Attributes I need to create a healthy meal for a family of 4 for under $20 – (this is a functional attribute).*	AND Justify why the **attributes** will help meet the need or opportunity (purpose of the concept/idea). ***Justify** - explain why with evidence.* ***Explain** - give reasons - "because" "so that".*	AND Evaluate the attributes, determine the **key attributes** for meeting all aspects of the need or opportunity. *E.g., Attributes of my product help me decide if it is fit for purpose (do as it is supposed to do).*

		AND	AND	AND
I need help to identify key attributes. – These are the attributes that are key for our design from stakeholder feedback.	I can identify **one key attribute** of the design (product).	Describe **several key attributes** of the prototype.	I can explain why the key attributes will make the product fit for purpose.	Make suggestions (predictions) about how I could adapt the product to improve its fitness for purpose (do what it is suppose to now and in the future.
		AND	AND	AND
I need help to write a conceptual statement. *What must be done and why?* The Issue, brief and stakeholders needs and wants are described and any opportunities for the project.	I can write a statement identifying what I need to do for my project using a sentence starter.	Describe what I will do for my project and describe some key attributes from the given brief and specifications in my group folder and my personal blog. (Say what it is like.)	Justify why the key attributes will make sure the product meets the purpose. ***Justify*** *– explain why with evidence.* ***Explain*** *– give reasons – "because" "so that".*	Modify my justification to take into account: • Maggi kitchen show down competition in which the prototype will be used. • Resources available (kitchen, blog, tv).

Contributed by Suzette Ipsen and Irma Cooke Rototuna Junior High School New Zealand.

TABLE 4.4 Draw a précis sketch or map

Drawing a Précis Sketch or Map
(Functional knowledge)

	I can apply strategies in any situation to draw an accurate and detailed précis map or sketch. I could teach someone else how to as well.	
	My map or sketch includes all appropriate conventions: • Title, scale, orientation, key, frame, labels I use a range of strategies to ensure accuracy. Such as: • drawing a grid, drawing to scale, planning out shapes before drawing the outline, looking for reference points as a guide, drawing the shape of objects, colour	
	In my map or sketch I can include some conventions but I am unsure of what strategies I am using for accuracy	
	I can draw a map or sketch but have no strategies for accuracy or including correct conventions	
	I need help	

My current level is _____. I say this because ....

My next step for improvement is ....

Note: The last column is a visual example of the text description – an annotated drawing that can replace what is communicated in the text.

The SOLO rubrics try to reduce the amount of text needed to communicate the different levels.

"This is how you … because …" are the equivalent of "sentence starter" or "sentence frames" to help students start to respond – in this case it is showing what it might sound like – look like if the student was to teach another.

Contributed by Craig Perry, Lincoln High School, Canterbury, New Zealand.

TABLE 4.5 Interact spontaneously with others in junior French

Interact spontaneously with others

	I need help to [interact spontaneously] with others.	I can do it if I repeat what I hear others say. *[Unconsciously incompetent]*	I can do it on my own but I sometimes make mistakes and cannot correct them. *[Consciously incompetent]*	I can do it – I know what to say and when to say it. *["on to it"]* *[Consciously competent]*	I can do it without thinking and if I am not sure I can come up with something that will do the job. Do this in a range of contexts. *[Unconsciously competent]*
Strategies: • ask questions • seek clarification • justify ideas • using fillers • interjection • fluent conversation • new ideas generated • interaction with myself • interaction with others.					
Effective strategies *[insert strategies suggested by students and teachers.]*	**To move up a level:** Rote learning formulaic phrases and expressions; "Phrase of the week"; "Question for the week" etc. Modelling; text book – page X; role play – scripted play.	**To move up a level:** Starter prompts; round the table thing; build fluency in recall; times when only French is spoken; songs; repetition. Language perfect.	**To move up a level:** Repetition; practice; visualising.	**To move up a level:** Flexibility. Trying different contexts. Elaborating. Revisiting.	**To move on:** Habitual –spontaneous; intuitive; original use

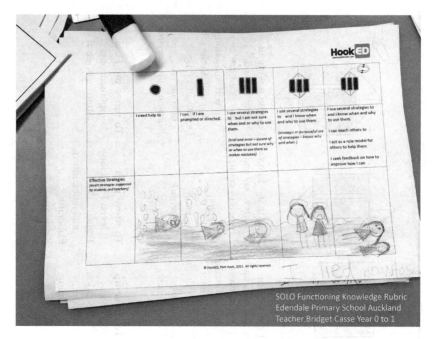

FIGURE 4.3 Co-constructed rubric: Learning to put my face in the water.

Source: Co-constructed with a five-year-old student at Edendale School, Auckland, New Zealand.

In my experience, students quickly familiarise themselves with using SOLO as a rubric standard so that even five-year-olds can help co-construct criteria in a SOLO rubric (refer to the rubric on "learning to put my face in the water" when learning to swim, shown in Figure 4.3).

Wiliam (2011) claims that being involved in the co-construction process encourages students to apply the rubrics to their own work. Of note, however, is that all parties are not equal in the co-construction process for a SOLO rubric. As Wiliam and Leahy (2015) argue, a teacher's professional expertise must provide the final guide to any interpretation of increasing competence – this is certainly the case with a rubric using SOLO as a standard.

The examples shown in Tables 4.6, 4.7 and 4.8 show how rubrics can be created to help students self-assess declarative (knowing about) and functional knowledge (knowing how to) outcomes using SOLO Taxonomy. For more examples and support in developing a declarative knowledge rubric in any curriculum area, go to the HookED Declarative Knowledge Rubric Generator: http://pamhook.com/solo-apps/declarative-knowledge-rubric-generator/. The app will generate a SOLO declarative knowledge rubric with or without content and context. Examples of rubrics for declarative knowledge

The generic rubric in Table 4.7 is used in the context of various subject areas in the following examples.

TABLE 4.6 Self-assessment rubric for declarative knowledge, built from SOLO Taxonomy

Declarative knowledge					
	SOLO prestructural level	SOLO unistructural level	SOLO multistructural level	SOLO relational level	SOLO extended abstract level
Descriptor	[needs help]	[one relevant idea]	[several relevant ideas]	[linked ideas]	[extended ideas]
Learning intention [verb] [content] [context]	I need help to start.	My [learning outcome] has one relevant idea.	My [learning outcome] has several relevant ideas.	My [learning outcome] has several relevant ideas and links these ideas.	My [learning outcome] has several relevant ideas, links these ideas and looks at them in a new way.

Note: For a comic strip example of this rubric, see Pam Hook's digital edition (http://issuu.com/pamhook/docs/solo_declarativerubric).

TABLE 4.7 Describe [something] for a language class

Describe a feral cat SOLO *rubric standard*

SOLO Levels

	Prestructural	Unistructural	Multistructural	Relational	Extended abstract
			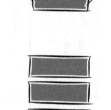	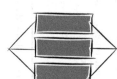	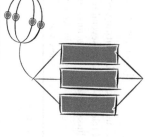
Text criteria	I need help to describe [X].	My description of [X] has one relevant attribute.	My description of [X] has several relevant attributes.	My description of [X] has several relevant attributes, and my description links these attributes. (*Link – sequence, classify, compare and contrast, explain causes, explain effects, analyse (part whole).*)	My description of [X] has several relevant attributes and links these attributes, and my description looks at these attributes in a new way. (*New way – generalises, evaluate, predict, and create.*)
Example		*The feral cat has a torn ear.*	*The feral cat has a torn ear, matted fur, a bent tail and a furtive manner.*	*The feral cat has a torn ear **because** it has not been neutered and gets into fights for territory and mates. It has matted fur **because** it is living outside and struggles to shelter where it can groom itself. It has a bent tail and a furtive manner **because** people often throw objects at it to hurt it and make it go away.*	*… In my opinion the best thing we can do for the cat is to capture the cat and euthanise it. Removing the feral cat from the environment is the best option because the cat is hunting and killing native species for food and mating with other wild cats, adding to the feral cat population. Research supports this claim, showing us that feral cats have devastated wildlife*

TABLE 4.8 Classify fractions for mathematics

(Which of these things go together?)

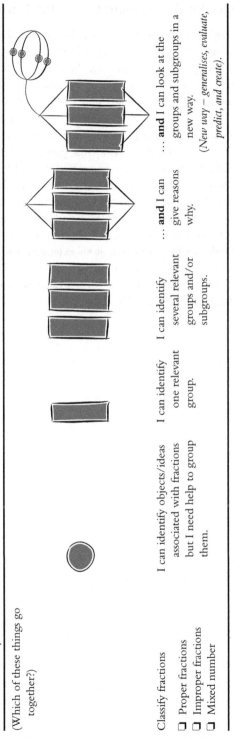

Classify fractions

☐ Proper fractions
☐ Improper fractions
☐ Mixed number

I can identify objects/ideas associated with fractions but I need help to group them.

I can identify one relevant group.

I can identify several relevant groups and/or subgroups.

... **and** I can give reasons why.

... **and** I can look at the groups and subgroups in a new way.
(*New way – generalises, evaluate, predict, and create*).

SOLO as stages for the learning task vs the learning outcome

Recall that in Table 4.1, different verbs may be associated with different levels of SOLO. For example, classify is a relational level task because it requires students to categorise or group objects or ideas on the basis of their similarities. However, though the task is at one level of SOLO, the outcome can be at another level. Students who are attempting to classify may identify only one group, hence demonstrating only a unistructural level learning outcome for the relational task. Or the students may identify several groups and or sub groups giving them a multistructural outcome. If they can explain the basis for the groups and sub groups they have a relational outcome. If they can make a generalised claim about the extent or importance of the groups and sub groups, then they have an extended abstract outcome.

In short, unlike Bloom's taxonomy where there is an unwarranted assumption that task and outcome are at the same level, with SOLO, the cognitive complexity of the student learning outcome can differ from the SOLO level of the task. A multistructural task can be completed at an extended abstract level; an extended abstract task can be completed at a unistructural level. Tables 4.9, 4.10 and 4.11 show examples of how students can perform a relational task (classify or compare and contrast) at any of the levels of SOLO.

TABLE 4.9 Compare and contrast [the structure of] [plant cells and animal cells]

(How are they similar? How are they different?)

| Compare and contrast plant cells with animal cells. | I can identify the objects/ideas associated with plant cells and animal cells but I need help to compare and contrast them. | I can identify one relevant similarity and one relevant difference between plant cells and animal cells. | I can identify several relevant similarities and differences between plant cells and animal cells. | ... **and** I can give reasons why. | ... **and** I can look at them in a new way. (*New way – generalises, evaluate, predict, and create.*) |

TABLE 4.10 Explain the effects of globalisation

(What happened as a result?)

Explain the effect/s of globalisation.

I can identify globalisation but I need help to identify a relevant effect.

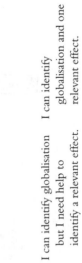

I can identify globalisation and one relevant effect.

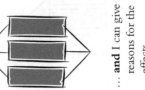

I can identify globalisation and several relevant effects.

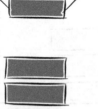

... **and** I can give reasons for the effects.

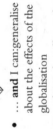

- ... **and** I can generalise about the effects of the globalisation.
- evaluate the effects of the globalisation.

TABLE 4.11 Analyse a piece of music

(What are the parts and how do they work?)

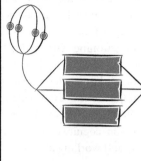

| Analyse a piece of music. | I can identify the piece of music but I need help to identify the relevant parts. *e.g, melody, harmony, lyrics, form, texture, tempo, metre, timbre, dynamics, mix, groove.* | I can identify the piece of music and one relevant part. | I can identify the piece of music and several relevant parts. | 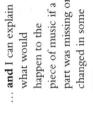 … **and** I can explain what would happen to the piece of music if a part was missing or changed in some way. | 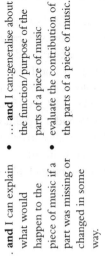 • **and** I can: generalise about the function/purpose of the parts of a piece of music • evaluate the contribution of the parts of a piece of music. |

Examples of rubrics for functioning knowledge

Table 4.12 presents a generic SOLO rubric for self-assessing surface and deep levels of *functioning knowledge* outcomes. A range of examples based on specific performance tasks follows. For support in developing a functioning knowledge rubric in any curriculum area, go to the Hooked Functioning Knowledge Generator at http://pamhook.com/solo-apps/functioning-knowledge-rubric-generator/

The following examples of SOLO functioning knowledge rubrics (Tables 4.13, 4.14, 4.15, 4.16, 4.17, 4.18 and 4.19) illustrate just some of the wide range of curriculum areas and different rubric structures in which they can be used.

The examples that follow are rubrics for non-cognitive areas: Time management (Table 4.20), active listening (Table 4.21) and working in groups (Table 4.22).

TABLE 4.12 Self-assessment rubric for functioning knowledge, built from SOLO Taxonomy

Functioning knowledge

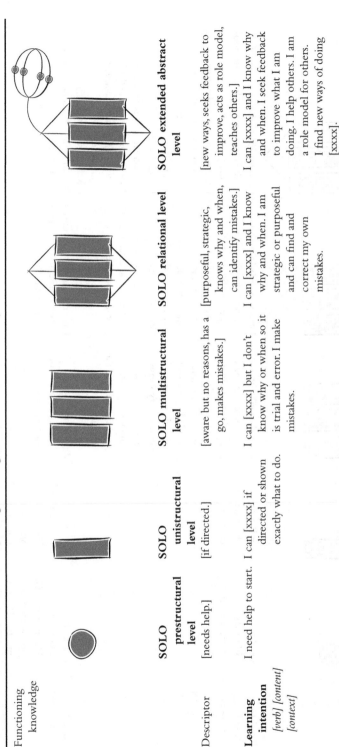

	SOLO prestructural level	SOLO unistructural level	SOLO multistructural level	SOLO relational level	SOLO extended abstract level
Descriptor	[needs help.]	[if directed.]	[aware but no reasons, has a go, makes mistakes.]	[purposeful, strategic, knows why and when, can identify mistakes.]	[new ways, seeks feedback to improve, acts as role model, teaches others.]
Learning intention [verb] [content] [context]	I need help to start.	I can [xxxx] if directed or shown exactly what to do.	I can [xxxx] but I don't know why or when so it is trial and error. I make mistakes.	I can [xxxx] and I know why and when. I am strategic or purposeful and can find and correct my own mistakes.	I can [xxxx] and I know why and when. I seek feedback to improve what I am doing. I help others. I am a role model for others. I find new ways of doing [xxxx].

Note: For a comic strip example of this rubric, see Pam Hook's digital edition (http://issuu.com/pamhook/docs/solo_functioningrubric).

TABLE 4.13 Respond to characters as part of reading comprehension

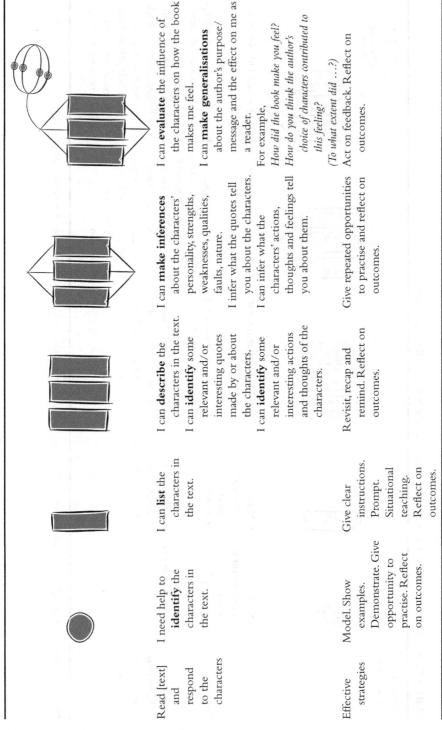

| Read [text] and respond to the characters | I need help to **identify** the characters in the text. | I can **list** the characters in the text. | I can **describe** the characters in the text. I can **identify** some relevant and/or interesting quotes made by or about the characters. I can **identify** some relevant and/or interesting actions and thoughts of the characters. | I can **make inferences** about the characters' personality, strengths, weaknesses, qualities, faults, nature. I infer what the quotes tell you about the characters. I can infer what the characters' actions, thoughts and feelings tell you about them. | I can **evaluate** the influence of the characters on how the book makes me feel. I can **make generalisations** about the author's purpose/message and the effect on me as a reader. For example, *How did the book make you feel? How do you think the author's choice of characters contributed to this feeling? (To what extent did ...?)* |
| Effective strategies | Model. Show examples. Demonstrate. Give opportunity to practise. Reflect on outcomes. | Give clear instructions. Prompt. Situational teaching. Reflect on outcomes. | Revisit, recap and remind. Reflect on outcomes. | Give repeated opportunities to practise and reflect on outcomes. | Act on feedback. Reflect on outcomes. |

TABLE 4.14 Make connections using number

Number

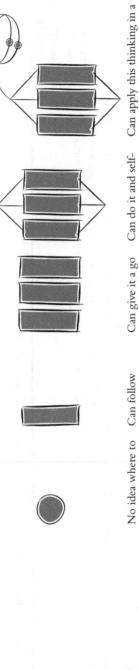

	No idea where to begin.	Can follow a pattern someone else starts.	Can give it a go BUT make mistakes.	Can do it and self-correct mistakes.	Can apply this thinking in a real world situation

Transfer:
I can make connections between:
- *math and math*
- *math and self*
- *math and world.*

FRACTIONS
Finding equivalents.
Simplifying
Converting to decimal.

No idea where to begin.

Can follow a pattern someone else starts.

Can give it a go BUT make mistakes.

Can do it and self-correct mistakes.

Can apply this thinking in a real world situation
Can create examples for others
Can zoom out
Can transfer.

Contributed by Greg Patel, Flanshaw Rd School, Auckland, New Zealand.

TABLE 4.15 Use strategies in mathematics

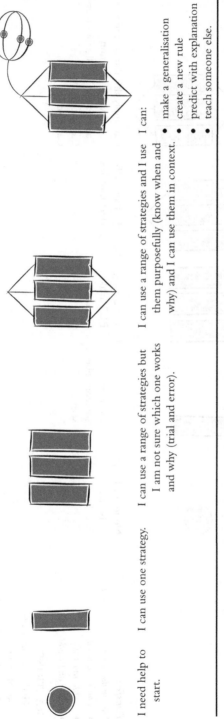

I need help to start.	I can use one strategy.	I can use a range of strategies but I am not sure which one works and why (trial and error).	I can use a range of strategies and I use them purposefully (know when and why) and I can use them in context.

I can:
- make a generalisation
- create a new rule
- predict with explanation
- teach someone else.

Contributed by Dean McKenzie St Andrews College, Christchurch New Zealand.

TABLE 4.16 Think like a historian

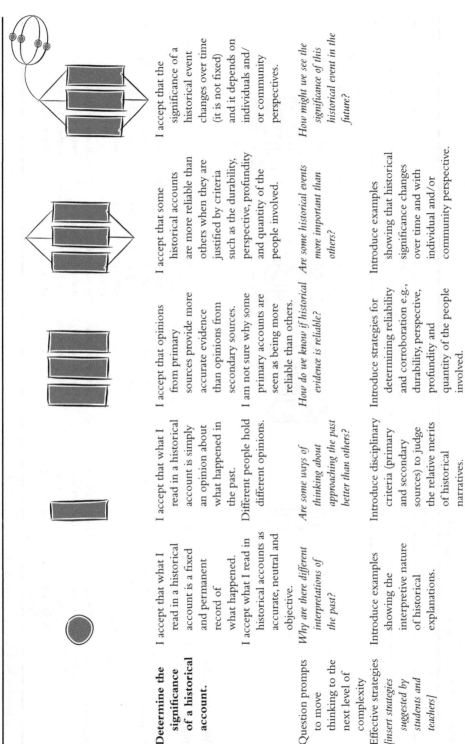

Determine the significance of a historical account.	I accept that what I read in a historical account is a fixed and permanent record of what happened. I accept what I read in historical accounts as accurate, neutral and objective.	I accept that what I read in a historical account is simply an opinion about what happened in the past. Different people hold different opinions.	I accept that opinions from primary sources provide more accurate evidence than opinions from secondary sources. I am not sure why some primary accounts are seen as being more reliable than others.	I accept that some historical accounts are more reliable than others when they are justified by criteria such as the durability, perspective, profundity and quantity of the people involved.	I accept that the significance of a historical event changes over time (it is not fixed) and it depends on individuals and/or community perspectives.
Question prompts to move thinking to the next level of complexity	*Why are there different interpretations of the past?*	*Are some ways of thinking about approaching the past better than others?*	*How do we know if historical evidence is reliable?*	*Are some historical events more important than others?*	*How might we see the significance of this historical event in the future?*
Effective strategies *[insert strategies suggested by students and teachers]*	Introduce examples showing the interpretive nature of historical explanations.	Introduce disciplinary criteria (primary and secondary sources) to judge the relative merits of historical narratives.	Introduce strategies for determining reliability and corroboration e.g., durability, perspective, profundity and quantity of the people involved.	Introduce examples showing that historical significance changes over time and with individual and/or community perspective.	

Source: Based on presentation at ICOT 13 by Mark Sheehan, Victoria University of Wellington, New Zealand.

TABLE 4.17 Functioning rubric for music composition

Learning intention(s)

- To be able to compose a piece of music using the elements of music.

Context of learning Scary music

Success Criteria					
Pitch	I can use high, low or middle pitches *with teacher support*.	I can use high, low or middle pitches.	I can use high, low *and* middle pitches.	I can use high, low and middle pitches *which make the music sound scary*.	I can use high, low and middle pitches *which build up, climax and resolve*.
Tempo	I can use a fast or slow tempo *with teacher support*.	I can use a fast or slow tempo.	I can use fast *and* slow tempos.	I can use fast and slow tempos *which gradually build up to make the music sound scary*.	I can use fast, slow and gradual tempos *which build up, climax and resolve*.
Timbre	I can play *an* instrument, or use my voice, differently *with teacher support*.	I can play *an* instrument, or use my voice, differently.	I can play at least two instruments and use *my voice differently*.	I can play at least two instruments and use *my voice differently to make the music sound scary*.	I can use a variety of instrument and vocal timbres *which build up, climax and resolve*.

Contributed by Nikki Booth, Wolgarston High School, Staffordshire.

TABLE 4.18 Use programming principles to meet a brief

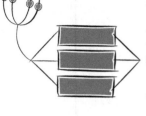

Programming principles may include:

- adding sprites
- creating sprites
- moving sprites
- resizing a sprite
- changing the background
- editing a sprite costume
- using audio
- using a start flag event
- making sprite react to key presses or mouse clicks
- using loops (such as forever or number of times)
- using wait time
- using variables to store info (score, questions and answers etc)

I can use programming principles if prompted and directed. Like following a guided tutorial. I am not able to create these programs by myself yet.

I can use programming principles on my own. However, the program does not always work as it should.

Some parts of my program work properly. I often make mistakes and there are many errors and problems.

I need help to identify and fix my mistakes.

I can write a computer program using several programming principles and I know when and why to use them.

I am strategic and purposeful in understanding which programming principles to use why, how and when.

I can find my mistakes and solve these problems on my own.

My programs work properly when tested.

I can effectively and efficiently use programming principles in creative ways to meet complex briefs.

I can write a computer program using several strategies to implement the program effectively and efficiently.

I know when and why to use particular programming principles to meet the complexities of a brief.

I can teach others to write programs to meet a brief and act as a role model.

(continued)

TABLE 4.18 (Continued)

• broadcasting and receiving messages from other sprites to control sprites • debugging – finding and fixing problems • other _____	I seek feedback on how to improve my outcomes and how I can improve my programming skills and knowledge. I can apply these programming principles in other computer languages and environments.
Question prompts	• Can I try to write some of the code by myself?	• How can I use my skills and knowledge in another programming environment or with a different programming language? • What other programs can I write that could benefit other stakeholders? • How can I extend my programming to meet more complex needs and opportunities?
	• How can I practise more so that I can eventually write code accurately and independently on my own? • Who could help me and what could I do to get better at identifying and fixing more of my mistakes? Who can I ask or what can I do when I get stuck?	

Contributed by Sandra Silcock, Rototuna Junior High School, Hamilton, New Zealand.

TABLE 4.19 Demonstrate game sense when striking

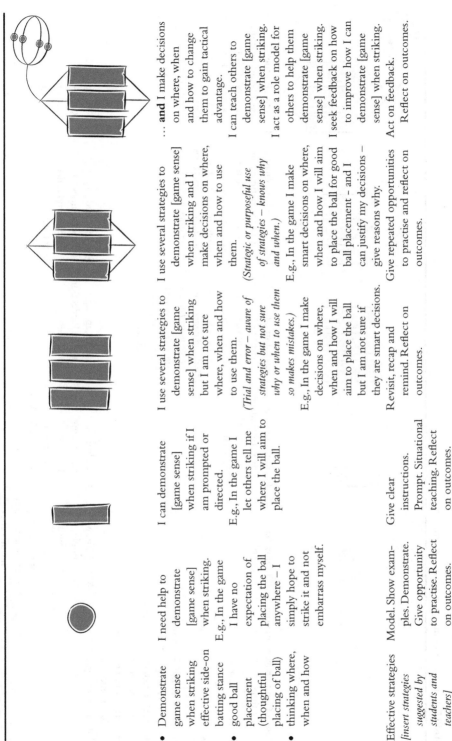

• Demonstrate game sense when striking effective side-on batting stance • good ball placement (thoughtful placing of ball) • thinking where, when and how	I need help to demonstrate [game sense] when striking. E.g., In the game I have no expectation of placing the ball anywhere – I simply hope to strike it and not embarrass myself.	I can demonstrate [game sense] when striking if I am prompted or directed. E.g., In the game I let others tell me where I will aim to place the ball.	I use several strategies to demonstrate [game sense] when striking but I am not sure where, when and how to use them. *(Trial and error – aware of strategies but not sure why or when to use them so makes mistakes.)* E.g., In the game I make decisions on where, when and how I will aim to place the ball but I am not sure if they are smart decisions.	I use several strategies to demonstrate [game sense] when striking and I make decisions on where, when and how to use them. *(Strategic or purposeful use of strategies – knows why and when.)* E.g., In the game I make smart decisions on where, when and how I will aim to place the ball for good ball placement – and I can justify my decisions – give reasons why.	... **and** I make decisions on where, when and how to change them to gain tactical advantage. I can teach others to demonstrate [game sense] when striking. I act as a role model for others to help them demonstrate [game sense] when striking. I seek feedback on how to improve how I can demonstrate [game sense] when striking.
Effective strategies *[insert strategies suggested by students and teachers]*	Model. Show examples. Demonstrate. Give opportunity to practise. Reflect on outcomes.	Give clear instructions. Prompt. Situational teaching. Reflect on outcomes.	Revisit, recap and remind. Reflect on outcomes.	Give repeated opportunities to practise and reflect on outcomes.	Act on feedback. Reflect on outcomes.

TABLE 4.20 Use a Gantt chart to manage my time

			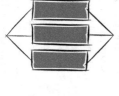	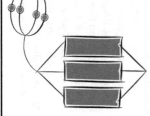	
Use a Gantt chart to manage my time: • break down inquiry into steps • estimate time taken for each step • put start and finish times for each step on chart • mark actual start and finish times on chart • reflect on use of time during inquiry.	I do not manage my time.	I can use a Gantt chart to manage my time if I am directed.	I can fill in a Gantt chart but I am not sure how, when and/or why it helps to manage my time. (*Trial and error – aware of strategies but not sure why or when to use them so make mistakes.*)	I can use a Gantt chart to manage my time and I know how, when and why to use them. (*Strategic or purposeful use of strategies – knows why and when.*)	I can teach others to use a Gantt chart to manage their time. I seek feedback on ways to improve how I can use a Gantt chart to manage my time.
Effective strategies	Model. Show examples. Demonstrate. Give opportunity to practise. Reflect on outcomes.	Give clear instructions. Prompt. Situational teaching. Reflect on outcomes.	Revisit, recap and remind. Reflect on outcomes.	Give repeated opportunities to practise and reflect on outcomes.	Act on feedback. Reflect on outcomes.

TABLE 4.21 Demonstrate active listening when with others

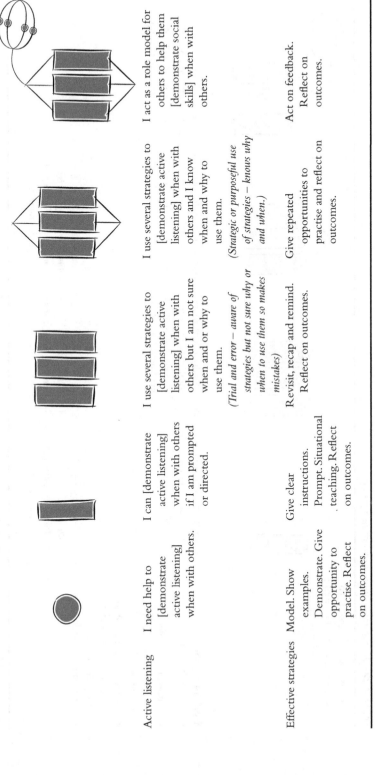

Active listening	I need help to [demonstrate active listening] when with others.	I can [demonstrate active listening] when with others if I am prompted or directed.	I use several strategies to [demonstrate active listening] when with others but I am not sure when and or why to use them. *(Trial and error – aware of strategies but not sure why or when to use them so makes mistakes)*	I use several strategies to [demonstrate active listening] when with others and I know when and why to use them. *(Strategic or purposeful use of strategies – knows why and when.)*	I act as a role model for others to help them [demonstrate social skills] when with others.
Effective strategies	Model. Show examples. Demonstrate. Give opportunity to practise. Reflect on outcomes.	Give clear instructions. Prompt. Situational teaching. Reflect on outcomes.	Revisit, recap and remind. Reflect on outcomes.	Give repeated opportunities to practise and reflect on outcomes.	Act on feedback. Reflect on outcomes.

TABLE 4.22 Demonstrate ability to work in a group

To work in a group to
[insert verb] [insert content]
[insert context]

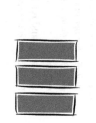

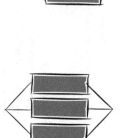

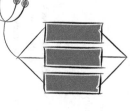

Work in a group It matters that you … • maintain your role, • stay on task, • ask for help, • assume good faith (AGF), • accept the consequences of a group decision.	I can [work in a group] if someone tells me what to do.	I can usually [work in a group] but sometimes things go wrong and I don't know how to fix it.	I can successfully [work in a group]. I can explain how and why.	… **and** I can lead a group. I can teach others to work effectively as a group.
Question prompts – Ask yourself …	*Am I involving myself in the group?* *Am I respectful when listening to others' ideas?* *Am I on task?*	*… **and*** *Am I asking for help?* *Am I working through group issues?*	*… **and*** *Am I supporting others?* *Am I leading the group in the right direction?*	

Contributed by Rototuna Junior High School, Hamilton, New Zealand

Visual rubrics

SOLO functioning knowledge rubrics commonly use images, annotation or animation to replace text when describing rubric criteria at different SOLO levels. Figure 4.4 shows a visual rubric where a generic sketch accompanies the level of detail proportion annotation required at each level of SOLO. Figure 4.5, however, is a SOLO spiderdiagram. It is used to reflect a student's achievement in the separate criteria, rather than aggregate it in a single score. Feedback that is based on the sum of several separate criteria is not as helpful.

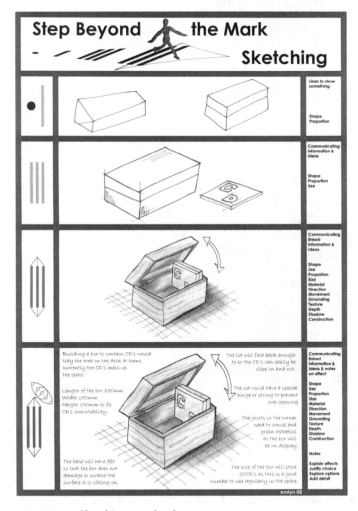

FIGURE 4.4 Sketching – technology.

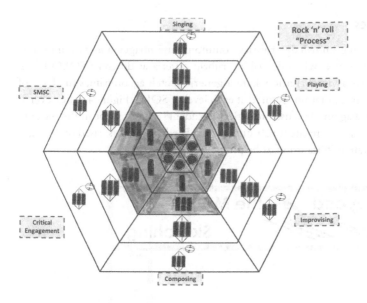

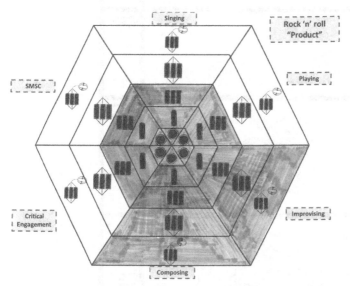

FIGURE 4.5 Spiderdiagram. Contributed by Nikki Booth, Wolgarston High School, Staffordshire.

Summary

SOLO taxonomy is a model of learning based on surface and deep learning outcomes (Biggs and Collis, 1982). When shared with students SOLO provides a common language and framework for conversations about learning progress. When SOLO is used as a standard in a rubric to measure learner performance they clarify: where the learner is going, where the learner is in their learning, how the learner will get there (Hook 2016).

Using SOLO levels ensures a rubric with specific, proximal and hierarchical standards for both declarative and functioning knowledge outcomes. What students know, understand and are able to do fits well with the context of the SOLO Taxonomy. SOLO levels identify the cognitive complexity of each learning task and the cognitive complexity of the success criteria for each task. In this way, SOLO rubrics make learning visible to students and teachers. The simplicity and explicit nature of the SOLO levels are easily acquired and embedded by primary and secondary students. This makes SOLO based rubrics easy to co-construct with students. When an extra row is included in the rubric, teachers and students can add suggestions for effective strategies allowing rubrics to function as a tool for ongoing formative assessment. The examples provided in the chapter give an indication of the wide use of SOLO rubrics in primary and secondary schools to engage (and enthuse) students in learning. SOLO rubrics are used in authentic learning when planning, giving feedback, engaging in learning conversations, developing learner agency and acting as a learning resource. In classrooms across the world SOLO rubrics are represented in innovative ways – by visual maps, spiderdiagrams, writing templates, SOLO shapes, comic strips, annotated diagrams as well as matrices.

Quick quiz

1. What is a rubric?
   Answer: A scoring tool used to measure task performance.
2. What are the levels in SOLO?
   Answer: Prestructural, unistructural (one idea), multistructural (many ideas), relational (linked ideas) and extended abstract (extended ideas). Surface understanding is developed in the unistructural and multistructural levels. Deep understanding is developed in the relational and extended abstract levels.
3. How does the addition of an effective strategies row enable a rubric to become a formative assessment?
   Answer: Rubrics provide students have a clear understanding of what success on a task looks like. The addition of a range of effective strategies students can choose to apply at different stages of the learning process enables students to monitor and control their own learning process.
4. Does a rubric always have to be represented by a matrix?
   Answer: A scoring tool used to measure task performance can be created using multiple modalities – text, images, video, symbols, shapes etc.

Reflection questions

- How are students advantaged when their model of learning (SOLO Taxonomy) is also a default standard for the rubrics they use to measure learning progress?
- How are students disadvantaged when their model of learning is also a default standard for rubrics they use to measure learning progress?

Notes

1 The *effect-size method* described by Hattie in "Visible Learning for Teachers" is a process for calculating the effect of the intervention within a cohort of students rather than by comparing differences in outcome between two groups of students (Hattie, 2012, appendix E).
2 National Certificates of Educational Achievement (NCEA) are New Zealand's national qualifications for senior secondary students. NCEA is part of the National Qualifications Framework.

References

Biggs, J. B., & Collis, K. F. (1982). *Evaluating the quality of learning: The SOLO taxonomy.* New York: Academic Press.

Biggs, J. B. (1996). Enhancing teaching through constructive alignment. *Higher Education, 32*(3), 347–364. http://dx.doi.org/10.1007/bf00138871.

Biggs, J. B., & Tang, C. (2007). *Teaching for Quality Learning at University: What the Student Does* (3rd ed.). Berkshire: Society for Research into Higher Education & Open University Press.

Black P., & Wiliam, D. (1998). Assessment and classroom learning. *Assessment in Education, 5*(1), 7–74.

Cizek, G. J. (2010). An introduction to formative assessment: History, characteristics, and challenges. In H. Andrade & G. Cizek (Eds.), *Handbook of Formative Assessment* (pp. 3–17). New York: Routledge.

Fraile, J., Panadero, E., & Pardo, R. (2017). Co-creating rubrics: The effects on self-regulated learning, self-efficacy and performance of establishing assessment criteria with students. *Studies in Educational Evaluation 53,*: 69–76.

Hattie, J. A. C. (2009). *Visible Learning: A Synthesis of over 800 Meta-Analyses Relating to Achievement.* London: Routledge.

Hattie, J. A. C., & Donoghue, G.M. (2016). Learning strategies: A synthesis and conceptual model. *Nature Partner Journals Science of Learning Review.* Article Number 16013.

Hook, P. (2016). *First Steps with SOLO Taxonomy. Applying the Model in your Classroom.* New Zealand: Essential Resources Educational Publishers.

Jonsson, A., & Svingby, G. (2007). The use of scoring rubrics: Reliability, validity and educational consequences. *Educational Research Review, 2*(2), 130–144.

Jönsson, A. & Panadero, E. (2017). The use and design of rubrics to support assessment for learning. In D. Carless, S. Bridges, C. Chan, & R. Glofcheski (Eds.), *Scaling up Assessment for Learning in Higher Education* (pp. 99–111). New York: Springer.

Kohn, A. (2006). The trouble with rubrics. *English Journal, 95*(4), http://www.alfiekohn.org/article/trouble-rubrics/

Nespor, J., & Barber, L. (1996). Abolishing marking systems. In K. Watson, S. Modgil, & C. Modgil (Eds.), *Educational Dilemmas: Debate and Diversity* (pp. 459–465). London: Cassell Publishers.

Nitko, A. J. (2004). *Educational Assessment of Students* (4th ed.). Columbus, OH: Pearson.

Panadero, E., & Jönsson, A. (2013). The use of scoring rubrics for formative assessment purposes revisited: A review. *Educational Research Review, 9,* 129–144.

Sadler, R. (1989). Formative assessment and the design of instructional systems. *Instructional Science, 18,* 119–144.

Wei, R. C., Schultz, S., & Martin, D. (2014). *Top-Down versus Bottom-Up Innovation: The Relative Merits of Two Approaches to Designing Performance Assessments.* Paper presented at the Annual Meeting of the American Educational Research Association Philadelphia, PA. April 2014.

Wiggins, G., & McTighe, J. (2005). *Understanding by Design* (expanded 2nd ed.). Alexandria, VA: ASCD.

Wiliam, D. (2011). What is assessment for learning? *Studies in Educational Evaluation, 37,* 3–14.

Wiliam, D., & Leahy, S. (2015). *Embedding Formative Assessment: Practical Techniques for K-12 Classrooms.* Learning Sciences International.

5

WHAT IS THE PLACE OF AUTHENTIC ASSESSMENT IN 21ST CENTURY COMPETENCIES?

Introduction

We are well into the new century but the term "21st century competencies" (21CC) is still very much a buzzword in educational circles. Most countries claim they value these skills but there are "few specific definitions of these skills and competencies at national or regional level and virtually no clear formative or summative assessment policies for these skills" (OECD, 2009, p. 4). This chapter begins with a brief review of suggested definitions of 21CC and its component skills. The section that follows proposes the relevance of authentic assessment (AA) in this area before presenting examples of how some teachers have designed AA to assess 21CC.

Defining Critical 21CC

The arguments for 21CC are typically premised on how the world has changed at the turn of the century. This present world is characterised as volatile, uncertain, complex and ambiguous (VUCA), a result of constant challenges brought about by rapid technological advancements and globalized, information-based knowledge economies. Consequently, both governments and employers are concerned about whether school leavers have been adequately equipped to enter a working world that is characterized by "an infinite, dynamic and changing mass of information" (Dochy, Segers, Gijbels, & Struyven, 2007, p. 87) and where they need to "navigate change and diversity, learn-as-they-go, solve problems, collaborate, and be flexible and creative" (Kalantzis & Cope, 2001, pp. 2–3).

So, what would be the skills that students must acquire in school to succeed in such a world as described? Among the many suggestions, there appear to be some common themes (see Table 5.1). As part of an assessment and teaching of 21st-century skills project (ATC21S), Binkley and her colleagues (2012) analysed

TABLE 5.1 Examples of 21CC frameworks and component skills

ATC21S	National Research Council	OECD
Ways of thinking: • Creativity and innovation. • Critical thinking, problem-solving, decision-making. • Learning to learn/metacognition. **Tools for working:** • Information literacy. Information and communication technology (ICT) literacy. **Ways of working:** • Communication, collaboration (teamwork). **Ways of living:** • Citizenship, life and career, personal and social responsibility.	**Cognitive competencies:** • Cognitive Processes and Strategies (e.g., critical thinking, problem solving, analysis, reasoning/argumentation, interpretation, decision making). • Knowledge (e.g., information literacy, oral and written communication; active listening). • Creativity (others may use terms like "innovation"). **Interpersonal competencies:** • Teamwork and collaboration. • Leadership. **Intrapersonal competencies:** • Intellectual openness. • Work ethic/conscientiousness (e.g., citizenship). • Positive Core Self-Evaluation (self-regulation).	**Information dimension:** • Information as source: searching, selecting, evaluating and organising information. Relevant skills include information literacy, research and inquiry and media literacy. • Information as product: Restructuring and modelling of information and development of own ideas (knowledge). Relevant skills include creativity and innovation, problem solving and decision making. **Communication dimension:** • Information and media literacy, critical thinking and communication. • Collaboration/team working and flexibility and adaptability. **Ethics and social impact dimension:** • Social responsibility and social impact.

national education curricula frameworks from a number of countries including those in the European Union, United Kingdom, United States, Japan and Australia. Their research identified 10 skills which they grouped into four categories. Another group of researchers defined 21CC as the blend of content knowledge and related skills that can be "transferred or applied in new situations" (National Research Council, 2012, p. 23). Their first step toward describing 21CC was to argue for three distinct domains of competence: Cognitive, interpersonal and intrapersonal. They then reviewed literature to identify 21CC that corresponded to these three areas. However, researchers at the Organisation for Economic Co-operation and Development (OECD), adopting the working definition of 21CC as "those skills and competencies young people will be required to have in order to be effective workers and citizens in the knowledge society of the 21st century" (p. 8), suggested three dimensions: Information, communication and ethics and social impact.

As can be seen from the table, the common themes appear to be what some writers term as "the 4Cs": Critical thinking, creativity, collaboration and communication (P21, n.d.). One also notes that the four themes are not mutually exclusive, with some overlaps. For example, creativity in innovations (e.g., product design) also involves critically evaluating the problem (e.g., purpose, cost) and arriving at an ethically acceptable solution (e.g., ecologically sound). In addition, critical and creative thinking are arguably best served by the collaboration of different individuals.

Perhaps, special mention should be made about the place of technology in the 21st century, given how the use of digital devices has changed how we work and interact. Our young people should be equipped to know how to use information technology wisely and responsibly. At the same, we should leverage technology for opportunities for students to develop and demonstrate 21CC-like critical thinking and collaboration.

Assessing 21CC

Having a clearer idea of 21CC still begs the question of how they are best assessed. Darling-Hammond (2012) argues that while there is a place for short item on-demand tests for demonstration of certain skills (perhaps grasp of isolated bits of knowledge), they are not adequate for 21CC. In other words, the use of tests for decontextualized isolated bits of knowledge under-represents the 21CC construct (see explanation of construct-based approach by Messick (1994) in Chapter 3). Instead, 21CC "must be examined in contexts that allow larger-scale tasks to be tackled over a longer period of time" (Darling-Hammond, 2012, p. 304). Because the resources and time required may be too formidable for large-scale testing, which requires quick turnaround time, these more open-ended and extended performance-based demonstrations are best situated in classroom-based, curriculum-embedded assessments. In other words, teachers are best placed to be designing the assessments for 21CC.

Teachers doing so can get guidance from some principles proposed by Binkley et al. (2012):

- Be aligned with the development of significant, 21st-century goals.
- Incorporate adaptability and unpredictability.
- Be largely performance-based.
- Add value for teaching and learning.
- Make students' thinking visible.
- Be fair.
- Be technically sound.

> As you read the examples in the next section, look for evidence of these principles.

One notices that much of what has been recommended echoes the descriptions of AA in the earlier chapters. For example, Wiggins had described AA to be "engaging worthy problems" (1993, p. 229) which gave students opportunities to show their understanding through non-routine and multi-stage performance tasks. Advocates of AA also recommended situating these performance tasks in the relevant real-world contexts of the working world, the child and the discipline (see Chapter 1). One can see how these contexts are not only advantageous but even necessary to ascertain the extent of a learner's critical thinking, creativity, collaboration and communication. As argued in Chapter 2, assessments in such settings can do double duty: they measure the competencies of interest but also promote the development of such qualities.

Examples of 21CC AA in Singapore

Like in many other countries, the educational authority in Singapore has identified key skills and competencies for the 21st century. They are largely similar to the themes described earlier.

Critical and inventive thinking

It is argued that to thrive in a fast-changing world, school leavers "need to be able to think critically, assess options and make sound decisions. They should have a desire to learn, explore and be prepared to think out of the box. They should not be afraid to make mistakes and face challenges" (MOE, 2016, annex C).

Relevant Standards: Sound reasoning and decision making; reflective thinking; curiosity and creativity, managing complexities and ambiguities (Liew, 2013).

Communication, collaboration and information skills

With the internet revolution, students must know "what questions to ask, how to sieve information and extract that which is relevant and useful ... be discerning ...

while adopting ethical practices in cyberspace". It is also argued that in the workplace of the 21st century, our young must be able to "work together in a respectful manner to share responsibilities and make decisions with one another to meet group goals. Importantly, they should also be able to communicate their ideas clearly and effectively" (MOE, 2016, annex C).

Relevant standards: Openness, management and responsible use of information, communicating effectively (Liew, 2013).

Civic literacy, global awareness and cross-cultural skills

In an increasingly cosmopolitan world, school leavers need "a broader worldview, and the ability to work with people from diverse cultural backgrounds, with different ideas and perspectives" (MOE, 2016, annex C). At the same time, they should remain committed to play their role in the community and as a citizen.

Relevant standards: Active community life, national and cultural identity, global awareness, socio-cultural sensitivity and awareness (Liew, 2013).

In the following section, you will see examples of how teachers have tried to unpack and design AA to assess 21CC. Notice that the assessment tasks may assess more than one particular 21CC (see Table 5.2).

TABLE 5.2 Summary of the examples of AA

Example	21CC	Topic/Context	Task
5.1	Critical thinking.	Design and technology.	Plan and complete a design project.
5.2	Critical thinking & citizenship.	Character and citizenship education.	Plan and execute a project to meet community needs.
5.3	Critical and inventive thinking.	Music composing.	Compose music to accompany a photo montage.
5.4	Communication, collaboration & information skills.	Water conservation.	Creating an animated video clip e-portfolio.

Example 5.1

21CC Focus: Critical thinking in design and technology (D&T)
Contributed by Ng Joon Yong
Target group: 15-year-olds (Secondary 3)

Relevant standards for Secondary 3 D & T

- identify a situation that requires a design solution;
- define a need by considering appropriate human, functional and aesthetic factors;

- gather and use relevant information for design decision making;
- generate and develop ideas using appropriate methods;
- test and evaluate their design ideas, making appropriate modifications;
- apply appropriate communication techniques to inform and justify ideas.

Relevant standards for critical and inventive thinking

- generate ideas and explore different pathways that are appropriate for responding to an issue/challenge;
- use evidence and adopt different viewpoints to explain his/her reasoning and decisions;
- reflect on his/her thoughts, attitudes, behaviour and actions during his/her learning experiences and determine the modifications require;
- identify essential elements of multiple tasks/roles, stay focused on them and persevere when he/she encounters difficulties and unexpected challenges;
- accept different perspectives, solutions and/ or methods, even in the face of uncertainty.

Context

Design and technology is a subject offered at secondary school. It aims to develop students as a person holistically (Chia & Tan, 2012) through nurturing their ability to solve real-life problems (Cross, 2007). At the age of 12 and beyond, advanced cognitive skill, such as reasoning about the basis of knowing in relationship to ill-structured problem solving, can be developed by involving students in solving ill-structured problem (Kitchener, Lynch, Fischer & Wood, 1993) and problem solving is regarded as one of the most important cognitive activities in everyday life and workplace context (Jonassen, 2000).

An example of such an ill-structured problem would be for students to investigate the issue of bicycle theft and propose an innovative design solution that create value. This also provides opportunities for students to take intellectual risk and encourage student to try, fail and learn from mistakes as they navigate through the design process of solving real-life problems, working with local entrepreneurs and with their teacher.

Example 5.1 shows how the context is designed to create ambiguity for the students as the events unfold. Teacher facilitation is key not only to ensure that the students learn the generic design process but also help them identify the contextual knowledge of the project.

A simplified instruction procedure also helps students organize themselves their learning more efficiently in an unfamiliar context. The evidence of success is seen in the observable outcomes as students demonstrate the skills while completing the required tasks that are often complex and mirror real-life situations (see Examples 5.1.1 and 5.1.2).

EXAMPLE 5.1.1 Task and lesson plan

Week	Learning objective: Students should be able to	Task with Context	Contextual Knowledge required by teacher	Instructional Procedure	Evidence of success
1	Prepare a Gantt chart with detailed stages based on the design model.	An average of 100 bicycles was stolen each month in 2014. You are to prepare a detailed plan using Gantt Chart before you embark on this design–and–make project.	Background information on the issue in Singapore and other countries.	Student are to brainstorm what needs to be done in the given context with reference to the design model.	Ghatt chart with rows for updating of progress showing generic design stages taking into consideration of iterative process of design.
2	Consider the relationship among scope of project, time, quality of solution and safety when planning and monitoring the project.	Mr Francis, co-founder of LoveCyclingSG will be ready to answer your questions about the project to solve the problem on bicycle theft. The purpose of this on-line conference is to gather information so that you can decide on the scope of the project. You are to refine your Gantt chart after the conference and upload into google drive. Write a short paragraph of fewer than 50 words on refinement made and why.	Background of Mr Francis How bicycle is usually stolen and existing solutions etc. Expectation of quality of proposed solution (from prototype to actual functional product).	Students are to prepare questions before conference call with Mr Francis.	Ghatt chart with rows for updating of progress showing context-specific design stages based on interview with Mr Francis. Reflection could show considerations of time and demand of projects.

(continued)

EXAMPLE 5.1.1 (Continued)

Week	Learning objective: Students should be able to	Task with Context	Contextual Knowledge required by teacher	Instructional Procedure	Evidence of success
3–4	Identify and select design problem which existing solutions cannot fully address the problem.	Research and review the effectiveness of existing solutions to prevent bicycle theft and the latest trends in design of lock, parking space, bicycle accessories that prevent or deter thief.	Existing systems to prevent bicycle theft and its effectiveness.	In groups of three to four, students are to decide on an area of focus such as the design of lock, parking lot, bicycle and systems beyond the product.	Critical analysis of existing solutions and the extent they solve the problem and make recommendations or draft specifications to guide design.
5–7	Generate solutions from using various ideation techniques. Evaluate and select best idea.	IDEO designers at work: Watch the video on how designers at IDEO generate their ideas. Consider how designers generate idea using brainstorming. Use also other techniques such as SCAMPER as well as computational thinking such as Morphological Analysis to help you in divergent thinking. CEO of a local bicycle producer, Mr Alan, and Mr Francis will be on the judging panel to listen to your best idea and provide insights for development.	Application and example of brainstorming, SCAMPER & Morphological Analysis by practicing designers.	In groups of 3–4, students are to generate idea individually to contribute to the group, and then select and defend the best idea for development.	Sketches of exploration of ideas and selected idea with information to defend the best idea.

8–12	Develop chosen solution by considering various design factors such as function, aesthetic, construction, material and ergonomic considerations.	Mr Alan has kindly allowed a visit to his workshop to see how bicycle concepts are developed. Study how a local manufacturer of bicycles develops and manufactures quality and affordable bicycles for all types of cyclists and apply the learning to develop your own design.	Manufacturing requirements (such as safety, material and processes) in Singapore in the area of bicycle related product.	Students are to develop the chosen idea individually and make improvements by comparing their work with those in the theme.	Sketches of development of ideas and how ideas are built on with information from the teammate.
13	Resolve tensions among dimensions of project management.	Mr Francis is interested in your idea and wishes to mass produce your design. However, his condition is that you need to produce a prototype within the next month. Will you agree with his request? Why? How will you make adjustment to your schedule?	Knowledge on patent issue, students' other commitment that could affect students' work progress.	Discuss with students about the risk involved in taking up the offer and how to plan a schedule with limited time to complete the project. (For students with promising ideas for mass production.)	Ghatt chart with rows updated with more reflections of adjustment independently. Adjusted schedule considers allowance for unknown and contingency plans.

(continued)

EXAMPLE 5.1.1 (Continued)

Week	Learning objective: Students should be able to	Task with Context	Contextual Knowledge required by teacher	Instructional Procedure	Evidence of success
14–16	Refine solution in consultation with experts related to the context of the problem and apply necessary information for realization of solution.	As your idea has the potential to be marketed, Mr Alan has agreed to be your project advisor to connect you to other expert in this field so that your idea can be fully developed for mass production.	Background of experts in the following area: defined group of end user, designers and manufacture of the field.	Students are to identify knowledge gap that requires expert support for mass production.	Sketches of detailed refinement with consultation from experts.
14–20	Make the prototype and present the solution to potential clients.	You are to present your prototype and sketches on the product to Mr Fancis and Mr Alan for final approval of your design to be mass produced. In case the final design is rejected, you are to reflect on the mistakes made and learn from this experience.	Criteria for mass production.	Students are to plan and make a prototype taking into consideration the limitation(s) of the school workshop in fabrication as compared to industrial workshop.	Prototype made from resistance material and rendered sketch using free-hand and marker or computer-aided drawing.

EXAMPLE 5.1.2 Rubrics

	Novice (1–2)	Developing (3–5)	Capable (6–8)	Exceptional (9–10)
Project management (10%)	Produced a broad plan.	Produced a detailed plan with a list of activities required for monitoring of project, plan updated.	Considered the relationship among scope of project, time, quality and safety when planning and monitoring project.	Resolve tensions among dimensions of project management.
Problem identification (10%)	Problem defined is too specific or too broad.	Problem is defined from multiple perspectives such as user, context, time and space with comprehensive specifications.	Problem is defined with justification, causes and its implications with relevant specifications that guide the direction of the project.	Critical problem defined has influence over a larger problem with important and measurable specifications that could be used to evaluate the success of the project.
Research (30%)	Gathered information from one source for one design stage.	Gathered information from different sources for each design stage to make decision.	Information gathered from multiple sources is relevant for use at the various design stages or across stages of design to support decision making.	Critically review various types of information to make sound decision.
Idea generation (10%)	Few ideas generated.	Many ideas generated from multiple perspectives or using various techniques.	A wide range of interconnected ideas generated to solve the problem through integration of ideation techniques and perspectives.	A wide evolving range of ideas generated to solve the problem through adaption of ideation techniques and new techniques.
Development of idea (20%)	Idea is developed by considering one factor.	Idea is developed by considering design factors such as aesthetics, functionality, material, use and construction in isolation.	Creative idea is developed with consideration of interdependency of design factors: aesthetics, functionality, material use and construction.	Innovative ideas or idea developed thoroughly and thoughtfully with further considerations such as sustainability, social, cultural and economic factors.
Refinement of solution (10%)	Refine solution by testing prototype.	Refine solution by testing prototype against design factors.	Improve solutions by testing against relevant design factors and specifications.	Improve solutions for optimal use by testing against critical design factors and important specifications.
Communication (10%)	Communicate ideas using one graphical media.	Communicate ideas using multiple graphical media.	Select most appropriate graphical media for different purpose of communication.	Strategic use of most appropriate graphical media to effectively and purposefully communicate the idea.

Example 5.2

21CC Focus: Critical thinking and citizenship
Contributed by Wong Yu Kai, William
Target group: 17-year-olds (Junior College 1)

Relevant standard(s)
For Civic Literacy:

- the student is able to independently initiate, plan and organise school and community activities/ programmes to address social issues.

For critical and inventive thinking:
The student is able to:

- generate ideas and explore different pathways that lead to solutions;
- use evidence and adopt different viewpoints to explain his/her reasoning and
decisions, having considered the implications of the relationship among different viewpoints;
- suspend judgement, reassess conclusions and consider alternatives to refine his/
her thoughts, attitudes, behaviour and actions;
- identify essential elements of complex tasks, stay focused on them, take on
diverse roles and persevere when he/she encounters difficulties and unexpected challenges; and
- manage uncertainty and adapt to diverse demands and challenges in new and
unfamiliar contexts.

Context

As part of "character and citizenship education" (CCE), schools in Singapore create opportunities for students to contribute to the community through "values in
action" (VIA) activities. The aspiration is that VIA fosters student ownership over how
they contribute to the community and critical reflection on their experience (MOE,
2017). And it is usual t o see schools segmenting a VIA activity into three stages: Pre-
VIA, VIA and post-VIA. The activities that make up these stages of VIA consist of, e.g.,
preparation for special performance, logistical preparation, the actual visit to the site
of service followed by reflection.

The conventional form of VIA grossly simplifies the complexity of defining and
resolving community issues; this form of VIA is superficially complex because the
form fulfils both requirements of involving the student in deciding what needs to
be done and is layered in stages. On closer scrutiny, VIA that is implemented in this
manner does not aid in the cultivation of authentic social/community problem-
finders and solvers who mingle in the community, conduct research and analyse
complex data to determine the true needs and problems of the people. Because
there is no deliberate opportunity for students to produce new knowledge and

understanding of and for the community during the learning experience, there is a high tendency to reproduce established understanding of the stakes and nature of the problem; this makes the experience inauthentic. Thus, in attempting to streamline VIA lessons so that the whole learning experience can be neatly compartmentalized, slotted into limited curriculum space (and "ending" with a reflection), teachers might have provided (excessive) scaffolding that make VIA inauthentic/superficially authentic.

This redesigned VIA AA rides on existing CCE curriculum structure and resources in schools to develop learners who are finders and solvers of social problems. Specifically, this task aims to support pre-university level CCE in the pursuit of one of the learning goals: "[for students to] demonstrate social responsibility and make meaningful contributions to the community by leading through service" (MOE, 2016). One specific programme in the CCE curriculum is VIA, which is framed as "learning experiences that support students' development as socially responsible citizens who contribute meaningfully to the community, through the learning and application of values, knowledge and skills" (MOE, 2015).

Task

You will be embarking on a two-week attachment to a voluntary welfare organization (VWO) of your choice. The focus of this task is to gain a deeper understanding of the inner workings of the VWO and, especially, the social/community problem the VWO is trying to ameliorate. The focus of this task is not so much providing a working solution in order to resolve the social/community problems you will define during the attachment as the problems that you probably will identify are often complex and take more than your attachment period in order to be resolved/improve in situation. A rubrics is shown in Example 5.2.1.

Assignment intention

We are interested in how you gather evidence from various sources, consider diverse human perspectives and synthesize your own understanding of what are some root causes of the problem. You are, of course, free to propose and explain why your suite of solutions that might work to improve the problem situation.

EXAMPLE 5.2.1 Rubrics

Appreciation of diversity in communities and cultures	Evaluates and applies diverse perspectives to community problems in the face of multiple and even conflicting positions. Demonstrates evidence of adjustment/change in own point of view and beliefs because of working within and learning from a diverse range of stakeholders. Demonstrates evidence of appreciation of diversity in the community.	Synthesizes multiple perspectives in trying to understand community problems. Reflects on how own attitudes and beliefs are different from community. Exhibits curiosity in wanting to learn from the diversity in the community.	Identifies and explains multiple perspectives in trying to understand community problems. Exhibits little curiosity in wanting to learn from the diversity in the community.	Identifies multiple perspectives while maintaining a position that a singular factor is the key to understanding the community problem. Expresses attitudes and beliefs that are one-sided.
Ability to analyse the "Big Picture"	Organizes and synthesizes evidence to reveal insightful community trends, variations, or similarities related to focus topic. Focuses on and explains clearly how different segments of the community come to function as a whole.	Organizes evidence to reveal important community trends, variations, or similarities related to focus topic. Focuses on and explains how different segments of the community come to function as a whole.	Organizes evidence but struggles to reveal trends, variations, or similarities. Identifies and explains parts of the community but struggles to explain the mutual interaction of parts.	Listing of evidence with minimal organization. Gets stuck with details. Unable to go beyond one point of view.
Ability to analyse interdependencies and consequences	Identifies and explains cause and effect as happening in cycles. Describes how causes and effects repeat over extended period. Identifies/predicts and clearly explains how and why specific action can cause specific short and long-term results (intended and unintended).	Explains cause and effect as happening in cycles. Identifies/predicts and explains how and why specific actions cause specific short and long-term results (intended and unintended).	Explains cause and effect as part of a system directly causing a change in a second part; linear causal relationship/ compartmentalized perspective of community. Identifies and explains how a specific action can affect the community in short-term.	Explains events/problems but unable to identify causes. Understands that actions can have consequences but explains in a generic manner; no specific examples.
Ability to define the problem	Demonstrates the ability to construct a clear and insightful problem statement (or multiple strongly linked statements) with strong evidence of contextual factors.	Demonstrates the ability to construct an adequately clear problem statement (or multiple linking statements) with evidence of contextual factors.	Able to construct a problem statement (or multiple weakly related statements) with evidence of contextual factors, but the problem statement is superficial.	Able to construct a simple problem statement (or multiple disparate statements) with limited contextual factors. Problem statement is superficial.

Task 1 (Individual)	Before the start of the attachment, please send me a short write-up/reflection about why you want work with a particular VWO. You can write about your expectation and apprehension about the attachment.
Task 2 (Individual)	One week after the attachment, please send me another short write-up/reflection on the experience. Ideally, you would have the chance to talk to many people so do reflect on at least one of the interviews. It is also timely to read what you've written for the first reflection and think about whether the experience so far has met your expectation. If it hasn't, is there anything you might consider doing differently? Was it as scary as you imagined it to be?
Task 3 (Group)	During the attachment, you will be working in a group of four. At the end of the two-week attachment, you have another week to synthesize the findings and orally present your work as a group to the management of the VWO and me.
Task 4 (Individual)	You will have your own ideas and thoughts even though you are working in a group. As such, you will also submit an individual portfolio (photos, short reflection essays)/essay/report/website/ short film chronicling the attachment. There is no word limit, but an appropriate word count is from 1,500–2,000 (if opting for short film option, a suggested film length is 3–5 minutes with a 500 word essay); this will ensure that you adequately provide evidence for all competency areas.

Example 5.3

21CC focus: Critical and inventive thinking through music composition
Contributed by Joanne Tan
Target group: 13-year-olds (Secondary 1, music elective programme (MEP))

Relevant standards for higher music

- compose a complete piece that is built on a chosen musical concept/ genre/style/form;
- reflect on musical decisions made in the composing process.

Relevant standards for critical and inventive thinking

- generate ideas and explore different pathways that are appropriate for responding to an issue/ challenge;
- use evidence and adopt different viewpoints to explain his/her reasoning and decisions;
- reflect on his/her thoughts, attitudes, behaviour and actions during his/ her learning experiences and determine the modifications required;
- identify essential elements of multiple tasks/roles, stay focused on them and persevere when he/ she encounters difficulties and unexpected challenges;
- accept different perspectives, solutions and/ or methods, even in the face of uncertainty.

Context

The music elective programme at secondary level in Singapore is a talent programme that offers musically inclined students to pursue the subject at a deeper and more comprehensive level. The authentic music task described here is designed for Secondary One MEP students. It involves composing music for a photo montage, focusing especially on designing the form or structure of the music. Students have to consider macro and micro aspects in their design, so that their music ideas cohere with the photos in the montage. Additionally, to focus their attention on the composing process, students will be guided to reflect periodically using visible thinking routines (Ritchhart, Church & Morrison, 2011), so that they may develop insights into their own thinking. The many skills involved (ability to generate and consider multiple solutions; to imagine and perceive various outcomes; and to purposefully pursue goals while remaining flexible) bear transferability to other areas of music students' lives, and when consistently developed, can become positive lifelong dispositions. Assessment of the music composing process must harness its potential for such authenticity to students' lives.

Task

You are to compose music for a photo montage

1. Put together a photo montage of up to two minutes in duration, based on a theme of your choice (e.g., family holiday, school event, friendship, planets, environment).

[The themes are merely suggestions and you are reminded that the main focus of the task is the music you compose, rather than the photos.]

2. Compose music for your photo montage, focusing particularly on the *structure* of the music in relation to your photos and theme.
3. Consider the macro and micro aspects of your music (i.e. the sections of music and the individual music phrases) and how they relate to the different sections and the individual photos in your montage.

[Refer to the assessment rubrics and exemplars.]

4. The task is to be completed over nine weeks. To facilitate the composing process, we will be doing the following in class:
   • Week 1 – Explore the task requirements and assessment rubrics as a class, in relation to different exemplars.
   • Week 4 – Clarify the task requirements and assessment rubrics as a class; share your composition draft with the class; complete a guided self-reflection.
   • Week 7 – Share your composition draft with the class; further clarify assessment rubrics as a class and provide feedback on one another's drafts; complete a guided self-reflection.
   • Week 9 – Share your final work with the class; complete a final self-reflection to distil your learning from the composing process.

5. You are required to submit a final e-portfolio that includes the following in Week 9:
   • completed work for assessment;
   • at least two composition drafts (dated);
   • self-reflections (Weeks 4, 7, 9).

Notice how the contributor used SOLO (see Chapter 4) as a framework to design the rubrics shown in Example 5.3.1.

Example 5.3 Rubrics (Part 2: Sample exemplars)

It is helpful to accompany rubrics with exemplars, especially in areas that are unfamiliar or perceived as abstract to students.

Extended abstract (7–8 marks)

https://www.youtube.com/watch?v=uBGnMF1jsLM

There is careful control of macro and micro aspects of structure throughout the montage, with central musical ideas carefully developed in juxtaposition of both short and long music phrases. These are carefully coordinated with the duration of each visual frame to pique the viewer's interest at the start of the advertisement and lengthening to the ending frames that allow the viewer to then take in information on where the product is to be purchased.

Relational (5–6 marks)

https://www.youtube.com/watch?v=2PUVyixT6F0

The different music phrases generally coordinate with the change between photos and text, with some consideration at the micro aspect of using single music phrases or combination of several music phrases to facilitate viewer's reading of the text. However, the music structure does not demonstrate metacognitive understanding to serve the impact that the photo montage intends to have on the viewer. Impact on the viewer is the result of the storyline itself, not the result of the music structure.

Multistructural (3–4 marks)

https://www.youtube.com/watch?v=N5xnyfBkmjo

Consideration has been given to design of the macro aspect of music structure. Different sections of the music coordinate with different parts of the story, so that the overall mood of one section of music matches the message relayed at that part of the

EXAMPLE 5.3.1 Rubrics (Part 1).

Criterion	Uni-structural (1–2 marks)	Multi-structural (3–4 marks)	Relational (5–6 marks)	Extended Abstract (7–8 marks)
Designing the structure of the music	Overall duration of the music matches the overall duration of the photo montage.	Consideration is made of the macro aspect of music structure, so that different sections of music cohere with the different sections of the photo montage.	Consideration is made of the macro and micro aspects of music structure, so that different music phrases develop musical ideas to cohere with different photos in the photo montage.	Consideration is made of the macro and micro aspects of music structure, so that different music phrases develop musical ideas to aesthetically cohere with different photos in the photo montage. The structure of the music serves to illustrate the theme/mood/purpose/impact/message of the photo montage.
Reflecting on the process of designing music structure	Some reflection has been made using some components of the visible thinking routines.	Reflection has been made using all components of the visible thinking routines.	Reflection has been made using all components of the visible thinking routines, and the insights facilitate decisions for the design of music structure in the composition.	Reflection has been made using all components of the visible thinking routines, and the insights facilitate decisions for the design of music structure in this composition and for future music compositions.

story (e.g., transitions from one section to another at 0:21, 1:04, 2:29 according to the meaning of the inspirational story). At the micro aspect, however, the coordination of music phrases with individual photos is not always coherent.

Unistructural (1–2 marks)

https://www.youtube.com/watch?v=YTW2-r7dOeA (0:00 to 1:07)
https://www.youtube.com/watch?v=Ue8RSDMZVOQ

Music is provided with the photos, but music phrases and sections do not coordinate with the photos, even if the mood evoked by the music is suitable for the theme. The music serves merely as background sound, and there is little understanding of how the macro and micro structure of the music could relate with the images.

Example 5.4

21CC Focus: Communication, collaboration and information skills
Contributed by Maria Bhavani Dass
Target group: 11-year-olds (Primary 5)

Relevant standard in Pri 5 water cycle

• Show concern for water as a limited natural resource and the need for water conservation.

Relevant standards for communication, collaboration and information skills

• convey information and ideas clearly;
• interact with others to explore and assess information and ideas;
• work in a respectful manner with others in a group setting to meet the group's goals;
• conduct internet searches and organise the digital information for ease of retrieval; while recognising copyright regulations governing the use of digital information; and
• verify the accuracy, credibility and currency of a piece of information.

Context

This AA has three overarching benefits. First, it presents a real scenario where knowledge is produced. Pupils have opportunities to understand Singapore's water dependency issues and its conservation efforts in whole and not in fragments through this task. Second, this AA reflects the kinds of mastery demonstrated by experts who create new knowledge that depends on pupils' prior knowledge, in depth understanding and integration of the knowledge. The design creates opportunities for pupils to look into what they know, learn more and organize their understanding to create an animated clip. Third, the AA brings about aesthetic and utilitarian value. Pupils' end product

EXAMPLE 5.4.1 Rubrics *Collaborative Learning Domain*

	Exemplary	Proficient	Developing	Emerging
Task focused	I/My member … consistently stay/s focused on the task and am/is self-motivated to put in a lot of effort to complete task by discussing only the relevant subject matter.	I/My member … focus/es on the task and put/s in adequate effort to complete the task by discussing the subject matter.	I/My member … focus/es on the task at times and put/s in little effort to complete the task by rarely discussing the subject matter.	I/My member … have/has no focus on the task and put/s in no effort to complete the task.
Respectful	I/My member … listen/s attentively and interact/s respectfully with all the members in the group, which helps to direct the discussion and decision making.	I/My member … listen/s and interact/s respectfully to all the members in the group to engage in a discussion and decision making.	I/My member … attempt/s to listen and interact with the members in the group but tend/s to dominate/s the discussion.	I/My member … do/does not listen and arugue/s with the members in the group and am/is unwilling to consider other opinions.
Team player	I/My member … share/s useful ideas and perform/s all assigned roles. to positively contribute to the project goals.	I/My member … share/s helpful ideas and perform/s most of the assigned roles. to contribute to the project goals.	I/My member … share/s helpful ideas and makes the minimal effort to participate.	I/My member … show/s no evidence of sharing helpful ideas.

when viewed by the peers sends a message across – to conserve water. See example
5.4.1 for a rubrics on collaborative learning.

Task

Students work in groups of four to produce an animated video clip that promotes
water conservation.

A. **Scenario**

Singapore is facing a water shortage. You need to promote water conservation
at home and school.

B. **Task Requirement**

You are to create an animated video-clip advertisement that includes the following:

- water conservation at home or at school;
- a clip less than two minutes;
- digital music in the background;
- a 10-minute oral presentation of your group's learning in doing this project work which includes the advertisement.

C. **Online Portfolio**

Your group must keep an online portfolio that will include your research, ideas
generated, digital images, digital music and your reflections about the project.
The portfolio will also capture your online group discussions.

D. **Roles**

- You need to take on the following roles:
- Group Leader – encourages and leads members to achieve objectives.
- Time Manager – reminds the members of the timeline.
- Turn Taker – reminds one another to take turns to talk and listen.
- Note Taker – takes notes of discussions.

Technology offers an added advantage here because an online portfolio can
store and present photos, music, unlike a paper-and-pen version.

In addition, it captures the group's collaboration in a visible form.

Summary

As pointed out in Chapter 1, the concept of AA has been mooted and discussed
since the 1990s. However, it continues to be relevant even now in the 21st century.

The literature in 21CC highlights four main themes of critical thinking, creativity, collaboration and communication. This chapter argues that these competencies

are best assessed in performance tasks set in contexts that are authentic to the real world outside of school, as well as real world of the child and the discipline.

In designing these performance tasks, the teachers in this chapter each started by unpacking the competency in terms of relevant standards before designing tasks that would elicit the behaviours that would meet these standards. Concomitantly, the rubrics are also crafted to address the relevant standards.

Quick quiz

1. What are the common skills included in 21CC?
   Answer: They may be labelled differently by various writers, but the common skills appear to be critical thinking, creativity, collaboration and communication.
2. How are 21CC best assessed?
   Answer: Open-ended, performance-based assessments that will allow learners the extended time and context to demonstrate these complex competencies.
3. In what way can AA be said to be doing double-duty when used for assessing 21CC?
   Answer: AA measure the competencies of interest and also promote the development of these competencies.

Reflection questions

While there is little debate about the promotion of 21CC, the difficulty may lie in assessing them. Does your institution face this concern? How have the content and examples included in this chapter apply to your context?

References

Binkley, M., Erstad, O., Herman, J., Raizen, S., Ripley, M., Miller-Ricci, M., & Rumble, M. (2012). Defining Twenty-First Century Skills. In P. Griffin, B. McGaw, & E. Care (Eds.), *Assessment and Teaching of 21st Century Skills.* (pp. 17–66). Dordrecht: Springer.

Chia, S. C. & Tan, S.C. (2012). Teaching Design & Technology to Develop Students as Persons: A Singapore Vision. Paper presented at the 74th Annual ITEEA Conference, Long Beach, CA. Retrieved from http://www.iteea.org/Conference/PATT/PATT26/Chin%20&%20Chong.pdf.

Cross, N. (2007). The nature and nurture of design ability. In N. Cross (Ed.), *Designerly Ways of Knowing.* Basel: Birkhäuser.

Darling-Hammond, L. (2012). Policy frameworks for new assessments. In P. Griffin, B. McGaw, & E. Care (Eds.), *Assessment and Teaching of 21st Century Skills.* (pp. 301–339). the Netherlands: Springer.

Dochy, F., Segers, M., Gijbels, D., & Struyven, K. (2007). Assessment engineering: Breaking down barriers between teaching and learning, and assessment. In D. Boud & N. Falchikov (Eds.), *Rethinking Assessment for Higher Education: Learning for the Longer Term* (pp. 87–100). London: Routledge.

Jonassen, D. H. (2000). Toward a design theory of problem solving. *Educational Technology Research and Development, 48*(4), 63–85. doi:10.1007/BF02300500.

Kane, M. (2012). Validating score interpretations and uses. *Language Testing, 29*(1), 3–17. doi:10.1177/0265532211417210.

Kalantzis, M. & Cope, B. (2001). *New Learning: A Charter for Australian Education.* Canberra: Australian Council of Deans of Education.

Kitchener, K. S., Lynch, C. L., Fischer, K. W., & Wood, P. K. (1993). Developmental range of reflective judgment: The effect of contextual support and practice on developmental stage. *Developmental Psychology, 29*(5), 893. doi:10.1037/0012-1649.29.5.893.

Liew, W. L. (2013, 15 Jan). Development of 21st century competencies in Singapore. Presentation at OECD-CCE-MOE Educating for Innovation Workshop. Singapore. Retrieved on May 26, 2017, from https://www.oecd.org/edu/ceri/02%20Wei%20 Li%20Liew_Singapore.pdf.

Messick, S. (1994). The interplay of evidence and consequences in the validation of performance assessment. *Educational Researcher, 23*(2), 13–23.

Messick, S. (1995). Validity of psychological assessment. *American Psychologist, 50*(9), 741–749.

MOE. (2016). 21st Century Competencies. Retrieved on 16 May 2017, from https:// www.moe.gov.sg/education/education-system/21st-century-competencies and https:// www.moe.gov.sg/docs/default-source/document/education/21cc/files/annex-21cc-framework.pdf.

MOE. (2016). *Character and Citizenship Education Syllabus Pre-university.* Singapore: Ministry of Education (MOE).

MOE. (2017). *Values in Action.* Retrieved 8 June 2017, from https://www.moe.gov.sg/ education/secondary/values-in-action#sthash.XS6TEvDT.dpuf.

National Research Council. (2012). *Education for Life and Work: Developing Transferable Knowledge and Skills in the 21st Century.* Committee on Defining Deeper Learning and 21st Century Skills, J. W. Pellegrino and M. L. Hilton, Editors. Board on Testing and Assessment and Board on Science Education, Division of Behavioural and Social Sciences and Education. Washington, DC: The National Academies Press. Retrieved 25 May 2017, from http://www.p21.org/storage/documents/Presentations/NRC_ Report_Executive_Summary.pdf.

OECD. (2009). 21st century skills and competences for new millennium learners in OECD countries, *OECD Education Working Papers,* No. 41, OECD Publishing.

P21. (n.d.). 4Cs Research Series. Retrieved 16 May 2017, from http://www.p21.org/ component/content/section/9.

Ritchhart, R., Church, M., & Morrison, K. (2011). *Making Thinking Visible: How to Promote Engagement, Understanding, and Independence for All Learners.* San Francisco: Jossey-Bass.

Wiggins, G. (1993). *Assessing Student Performance.* San Francisco: Jossey-Bass.

PART II

Theory into practice

6

AUTHENTIC ASSESSMENTS IN HUMANITIES

Introduction

This chapter will feature history and geography, as well as social studies and English literature, which are some of the subjects included in the humanities curriculum in Singapore schools. A unique feature of this chapter is presenting how teachers revised the original task/rubrics. The intent is to show that a good authentic assessment (AA) is the result of a few rounds of revision by reflective practitioners.

Context

Singaporean students have often made headlines in the areas of mathematics and science, thanks to their consistently strong performance in the Trends in International Mathematics and Science Study (TIMSS). This is testament to the importance placed on mathematics and science education. However, the Singapore curriculum also emphasises that the humanities and the arts are as equally important.

Students in Singapore get introduced to social studies at the primary level. The aim of social studies is to develop students as informed, concerned and participative citizens, competent in decision-making with an impassioned spirit to contribute responsibly to the society and the world they live in (MOE, 2016). Social studies is also a compulsory subject at lower secondary, along with geography and history; two subjects that students can pursue at upper secondary as well. All three subjects (social studies, geography and history) take the inquiry approach with students working as a group to investigate a societal/geographical/historical issue. It is envisioned that the issue-based approach provides learners with the real-life opportunities to not just apply but be inducted into the discipline.

Examples from these three subjects are featured in the next section, along with English literature, which is also a compulsory subject at lower secondary. Table 6.1 shows a summary of the AAs presented in this chapter.

TABLE 6.1 Summary of the AA presented in this chapter

Examples	Level	Subject	Topic/Context	Task
6.1	Primary	Social studies	People and environment	Research and role-play
6.2	Lower Secondary	Geography	Geographical issue	Journal writing
6.3	Secondary 3	History	Rise of Stalin	Skit
6.4	Secondary 1	Literature in English	Poem	Performance Poetry

Example 6.1

Subject: Social studies
Contributed by Pang Peng Tiong
Target group: 11-year-olds (Primary 5)

Relevant standards from Primary 5 social studies

• Explain how people adapt to their environment (MOE, 2014b, p. 91)

Relevant standards for Primary 5 civic literacy, global awareness and cross-cultural skills

• Demonstrate sensitivity and acceptance of the customs, practices and behaviour of people from different socio-cultural and religious backgrounds within and beyond Singapore.

Context

The current conventional assessment task is to complete a table in the workbook. Pupils are to fill up the table with information about how communities adapted to the different environments in terms of food, shelter, clothing and transport. However, this under-represents the construct as students can just fill in information given in the textbook.

The assessment task was thus revised. It was decided that the learning would be enhanced if the children had opportunities to reflect on the content more deeply through role-play. Morris (2001) asserted the value of role-play in helping learners to explore places, times and situations that they may not have directly experienced (Daniels, 2010; Edwards & Craig, 1990; Fischer, 1989; Morris, 2001).

Lesson

Expert group and research questions

This assessment seeks to enhance learning through jigsaw activity (a co-operative learning strategy) a role-play.

1. Pupils from the home groups are each assigned a number. Pupils of the same number from different groups gather to form the expert groups.

2. Each expert group will be assigned an environment (rainforests, temperate forests, etc.) to research on "If your group is living in the [assigned environment] ... how would you have adapted in terms of food, shelter, clothing and transport?" This question is slightly modified to make it more open-ended to provide more opportunities for critical and inventive thinking.

3. Pupils will then research and evaluate information found on the list of recommended websites and other internet sources (e.g., YouTube). This gives them opportunities to evaluate information from multiple resources while developing their ICT skills which are also 21st-century learning skills and competencies.

4. Pupils will collaborate and discuss as a group the information that they will present to their classmates through a role-play.

5. The teacher will formatively assess the content accuracy while the rest of pupils are to make notes in their workbook while watching the role-play.

6. After the role-play, pupils go back to their home groups to check each other's understanding as reflected in what they had written in the workbook.

7. The teacher gives qualitative feedback to the groups.

This assessment certainly will be more engaging to the students, first because they get to play a more active role in finding out new information and presenting their learning. With the various opportunities for peer and teacher feedback, the assessment also gives more valid information about the extent of the learning. However, this is provided that the student performance is not subject to second-order expectations, e.g., credit for use of props and costumes (see critique of use of court trial to assess history in Chapter 3).

Example 6.2

Subject: Lower secondary (LS) geography
Contributed by Rita Yap Siu Li
Target group: 14-year-olds (Secondary 1–2)

Relevant standards for LS geography

• Students are able to support their personal opinion about a geographical issue with reasons and examples.

Context

Central to the 2014 LS geography syllabus is creating opportunity for students to appreciate the relevance of geography in the real world and to develop students' valuing of different perspectives, a key competency in the Ministry of Education (MOE) 21st Century Competencies (21CC) for geography education. Against this backdrop, a new assessment task where students write a response to a geographical issue (GR) has been introduced. An example of GR writing task is for students to respond to an excerpt from a newspaper report on plans to build a train tunnel under Singapore's largest nature reserve. As part of their response, students are required to write a summary of the issue and a personal response on the issue and support their opinion with reasons and examples.

The rationale for GR is that it provides an opportunity for students to examine current issues through global and local perspectives as informed, concerned and participative citizens. At the LS level, it is intended to enable students to apply what they have learned in their geography lessons to support their personal opinion about a geographical issue with reasons and examples.

With regards to literature on methods to facilitate and assess students' development of geographical thinking, one approach is "writing-to-learn" (Slinger-Friedman & Patterson, 2012). In two separate studies on the impact of writing-to-learn exercises on student attitudes and performance, they reported while students' grades in the intervention programme showed no significant difference compared to the non-writing class, the students believed writing helped them in learning geography well. Hence, they argue:

> [W]riting activities can help geography students with theoretical and real-world scenarios in which they can practice applying concepts and ideas learned in class through working through the writing activities which support authentic learning. In this way, students develop the habit of thinking spatially and get the importance of understanding concepts of space, place, environment, society and representation.
>
> *(p. 193)*

The current practices by geography teachers to integrate writing in geography include getting students to write critical analyses of articles, learning journals, narratives, etc. In relation to assessment, if the purpose of the geography assessment is to make valid inferences about the depth of students' level of thinking and conceptual understanding about geographical issues, then a fit for purpose, writing task that allows for elaboration of students' responses may be more authentic than assessment of a traditional mode such as multiple –choice or short answer questions.

Task

This task involves students writing journal entries on a specific geography topical issue during the course of studying the issue in class. A minimum of three 40-minute sessions is required for its full implementation. At the last session, the students will submit their personal response of 50–80 words on the issue and support their opinion with reasons and examples. See Example 6.2.1 for the lesson plan and Example 6.2.2 for the rubrics.

Reflection question

Note the use of Structure of Observed Learning Outcomes (SOLO) as guide to framework for lesson planning.

Go back to Chapter 4, if necessary, to see how the different lessons cohere with the SOLO levels.

EXAMPLE 6.2.1 Lesson plan

Sequence	Questions to guide journal entry	Other notes
Unistructural.		
After reading a selected article related to a topical geographical issue featured recently, students individually write a journal entry, drawing upon their prior knowledge and information gathered from the article.	• What is my opinion on the issue? • Why do I hold this opinion? • How can I support my opinion on the issue?	Class work. Submission required. Not graded. Teacher gives qualitative feedback.
Multistructural.		
Working in groups of three, students share their journal entries. Students then write their second journal entry which captures their peers' feedback and personal responses.	• What are my peers' views on the issue? • Why do they hold this view? • How did they support their opinions on the issue?	Class work. Group discussion. Not assessed. Peer feedback to check for clarity and accuracy in representing opinions.
Relational.		
Using the two journal entries, students write a final entry of their response to the issue.	• Which opinion(s) are of most worth about the issue? • Why do I value this opinion as most worth? • How do I support the opinion(s) with the most geographical worth?	Class work. Submission required. Graded using the rubrics.

EXAMPLE 6.2.2 Rubric

Level of valuing perspective-taking in geographical thinking

Unistructural	Multistructural	Relational
(1–4 marks)	*(5–8 marks)*	*(9–10 marks)*
At this level, the student is able to:	At this level, the student is able to:	At this level, the student is able to:
• state a general opinion about the issue, • use examples as support from article but may not always be successful,	• describe at least two opinions specific to a key geographical issue, • successfully use examples as support from article,	• compare opinions specific to a key geographical issue, • successfully use examples as support from the article and beyond,

(continued)

EXAMPLE 6.2.2 (Continued)

• construct an explanation with no or a failed attempt to bring in any geographical slant, resemblance of a description of the article or a summary.	• construct explanation with consideration of a geographical slant using any one geographical concept as a lens.	• construct explanation with consideration of a geographical slant using the idea of spatial representation.

Use this rubric to holistically assess students' level of valuing perspective-taking in thinking geographically.

The mark is discriminated by the qualitative descriptions at the specific level.

In the instance where a response bears at least one characteristic of the higher level, it is preferred that students be awarded the higher band if all the qualities of the lower level are fulfilled.

Example 6.3

Subject: History
Contributed by Melanie Lim Seok Yin
Target group: 15-year-olds (Secondary 3)

Relevant standards for Secondary 3 history

- Analyse the roles of key players in shaping particular forces and developments during that period of history.
- Understand that decisions and actions by people in the past were made and taken in the context of that time.

Context

In the Secondary 3 history syllabus, the rise of Communist Russia in the first half of the 20th century is used as a case study of totalitarian regimes and the roles of certain individuals that shaped the events of that time. To address the inquiry question, "What does it mean for Stalin to rise to power?", students were tasked to research the factors that led to the rise of Stalin and present their findings in a skit. After the performance, students were required to write an essay on the reasons why Stalin was able to rise to power. Also, they had to assess their peers on the extent of contribution, the degree of focus and how well each member worked with others. Students were also required to do a reflection on the process of carrying out the alternative assessment.

Before you read the next paragraph, can you see where there are possible issues with constructs?

However, this task was too narrow for the inquiry question. Students were only required to enact the process of how Stalin rose through the ranks to becoming a leader. However, the inquiry question, "What does it mean for Stalin to rise to power?", which entails more, e.g., the factors contributing to and impact (social, economic and political) of his rise to power.

Revised task

After the first introductory lecture on Communist Russia, students are tasked with researching Stalin, focusing on his character traits, ambition and background, so that they can better understand the motivation behind Stalin's rise to rule Russia. Research must also include the factors (social, economic and political) that led to his rise. The teacher can give feedback to the individual groups and highlight to students the areas they can work on before moving on to the script writing.

After the performance of the skit, the students will research the impact of Stalin's rule on Russia. They can give an oral presentation or a report of their findings. Teacher will give feedback. For their individual assignment, students are required to write an essay on the reasons why Stalin was able to rise to power as well as reflect on their new knowledge gained on the topic and their opinion on communism; allowing them to question their assumptions made prior to the teaching of topic.

Again, this task reminds us of the example from Chapter 3. So, what should not be included as criteria in the rubrics to avoid construct irrelevance?
(Consider the critique by Cumming and Maxwell in Chapter 3.)

Example 6.4

Subject: Literature in English
Contributed by Lily Chua and Jaime Chua
Target group: 13-year-olds (Secondary 1)

Relevant standards

- Speak with accurate pronunciation and appropriate intonation.
- Use appropriate voice qualities (i.e. pace, volume, tone and stress) to convey meaning.
- Convey the intended message effectively and with impact.

Context

Performance poetry uses the stage as the page, transforming poetry readings into theatrical events. We would like to create an enjoyable, risk-free environment for Secondary One students to be introduced to poetry. As they act out the language and experience the rhyme and rhythm, this provides them with an opportunity for better understanding of concepts. The inclusive, participatory and collective mode of performance poetry helps to ensure maximum participation as students try to engage the audience in the listening experience.

Lesson plan for teachers

1. View a YouTube video as an introduction to *The Highwayman* poem.
2. Go through *The Highwayman* poem: clarify difficult words, discuss the actions of the characters, etc.
3. Teach vocal techniques: Breathing, pause, pitch, articulation/diction, tone, emphasis and volume.
4. Teach students the poetic devices used in poetry: similes, metaphors, alliteration and onomatopoeia.

5. Choral reading performance:
    - A checklist will be given to the students to help them to prepare.
    - Students to be graded on their group performance of a few stanzas of the poem, making sure that they convey the intended message of the poetic devices effectively and with impact.
6. A reflection form introduced to ask the students how they could have improved on their performance.
7. Feedback given before the students perform the next task.
8. Individual poetry recitation:
    - Students to select a poem which has the components of the poetic devices taught to them. They have to convey the intended message of the poetic devices effectively and with impact.
9. A reflection form introduced to ask the students how they could have improved on their performance.
10. Feedback given to the students after this task

Issues with the original marking rubrics for choral reading

- Too many components.

  The original marking rubrics included the following ten components: volume, pronunciation, pitch, speed, pauses, facial expressions and body language, eye contact, posture, preparedness and uniqueness. There are too many items for a teacher to focus on during the few minutes of the choral reading of a few stanzas.

- Possible construct irrelevance.

  Some of the items such as volume, facial expressions and body language, eye contact and posture may not be critical in the assessment of the choral reading. Students should be aware of what they should do for a performance and they can be given a checklist to ensure that they incorporate such elements of volume, facial expressions and body language, eye contact and posture in their performance. Volume may not be critical as they are reading aloud as a group, and so they should be loud enough to be heard by the audience. Facial expressions and body language, eye contact and posture are important in a performance. However, as we do not expect the students to memorise the poem, so long as they can read the poem expressively. Hence it is probably construct irrelevant to expect students to "establish eye contact with the audience *throughout* the performance".

- Problem of weighting.

  There was equal weighting assigned to delivery and performance. In the revised rubrics, the allocation of marks was re-assigned to place more weighting on the delivery and less on the performance to emphasise the productive aspects of reading rather than on the performance aspects even though this is a performance poetry activity.

- Holistic versus analytic.

  The original criteria were also too discrete and could be more holistically integrated into the revised rubrics. In fact, the criteria were reduced to four items – pronunciation and articulation, fluency and rhythm, vocal intonation and expressiveness and engagement. The first three look into the mechanics of reading while the last item looks into the performance aspect.

See the revised rubrics in Example 6.4.1.

EXAMPLE 6.4.1 Rubric for choral reading (revised)

Criteria	16–20 marks	11–15 marks	6–10 marks	1–5 marks
Pronunciation & Articulation.	Clear pronunciation & articulation that effectively conveys meaning.	Pronunciation that gives the needed clarity & articulation with intermittent mistakes.	Moderately incorrect pronunciation of words with some effort at clear articulation.	Very uncertain pronunciation & articulation that misrepresents the meaning.
Fluency & Rhythm.	Reads with suitable pace & fluency using appropriate rhythm & stress.	Reading is largely effortless (fluent) with some errors in stress & rhythm.	Hesitant reading with numerous errors in stress & rhythm.	Reading is very uncertain with grave mistakes in stress & rhythm.
Vocal intonation & expressiveness.	Highly effective and expressive intonation used to reinforce change in mood, voice, setting, and/or characterization.	Effective and expressive intonation used to reinforce change in mood, voice, setting, and/or characterization.	Moderately effective and expressive intonation used with room for improvement and practice.	Limited effectiveness; intonation may not represent the meaning adequately.
Engagement.	Performance has a unique factor that captivates the audience (a song, a dance move, an interesting prop).	Performance is entertaining and able to engage most of the audience.	Performance is mediocre and not all the audience members are attentive.	Performance is not interesting and does not captivate the audience.

Adapted from http://www.readwritethink.org/files/resources/lesson_images/lesson1001/poetry.pdf, O-level rubrics for EL Paper 4.

> While this rubric is generally sound, consider the criteria on "engagement", which is often included to evaluate performances such as this. While it is true that a polished performance will result in an engaged audience, is the reverse always true? That is, if the audience is not engaged, could there be other factors?

Conclusion

Often, in order to help learners see the relevance of what they are studying in humanities, field trips are organized to bring students into the real world (e.g., Example 3.1 in Chapter 3). However, when that is not possible, an alternative approach is to bring the real world into the classroom, through role-play (Example 6.1), current issues in the news (Example 6.2), research (Example 6.3), performance (Example 6.4). One can appreciate that the teachers hope that through such engaging activities students will see how the humanities is part of their everyday lives. However, in doing so, there is a danger of introducing threats to validity, e.g., second-order expectations (Examples 6.1 and 6.3). The examples in this chapter show how teachers can guard against such threats through thoughtful refinement of the assessment tasks and rubrics.

References

Daniels, M. L. (2010). A living history classroom using re-enactment to enhance learning. *Social Education, 74*(3), 135–136.

Edwards, J., & Craig, T. (1990). A teacher experiments with drama as a teaching tool: A collaborative research project. *Alberta Journal of Educational Research, 36*(4), 337–351.

Fischer, C. W. (1989). Effects of a developmental drama-inquiry process on creative and critical thinking skills in early adolescent students (Doctoral dissertation, Kansa State University).

Ministry of Education. (2014a). 21st Century Competencies. Retrieved from http://www. moe.gov.sg/education/21cc/.

Ministry of Education. (2014b). Inquiring into our world 5: Teaching and learning guide. *Curriculum Planning and Development Division.* Singapore: Marshall Cavendish Education .

Morris, R. V. (2001). Drama and authentic assessment in a social studies classroom. *Social Studies, 92*(1), 41–44.

Ministry of Education (MOE) (2014). *Lower Secondary Geography Teaching Syllabus for Express and Normal (Academic).* Retrieved from http://library.opal.moe.edu.sg/library/slot/reslib/dc259/4a78db882_258514.pdf.pdf.

MOE. (2016). *Social Studies Syllabus.* Retrieved on 27 May 2017, from https://www.moe.gov.sg/docs/default-source/document/education/syllabuses/humanities/files/2016-social-studies-(upper-secondary-express-normal-(academic)-syllabus.pdf.

MOE. (2016). History Syllabus: Upper Secondary. Retrieved on 27 May 2017, from https://www.moe.gov.sg/docs/default-source/document/education/syllabuses/humanities/files/2017-history-(upper-secondary)-syllabus.pdf.

Slinger-Friedman, V., & Patterson, L. M. (2012). Writing in geography: Student attitudes and assessment. *Journal of Geography in Higher Education, 36*(2), 179–195. doi:10.1080/03098 265.2011.599369.

7

AUTHENTIC ASSESSMENTS IN LANGUAGES

Introduction

This chapter will feature authentic assessments (AAs) designed for assessing different language skills across different age and ability groups (see Table 7.1). Language teachers will find there is something to learn from the following examples, including the two AAs designed for Chinese language and Malay language learners. The other reason for the inclusion for these non-English language subjects is explained below.

Context

In Singapore schools, where the medium of instruction is in English language (EL), every child is required to learn EL at first-language level. They are also expected to study a second language that is their official mother tongue (MT): Chinese (for the ethnically Chinese), Malay (for the ethnically Malays) and Tamil (or a non-Tamil Indian language for those who are non-Tamil Indians). Exceptions are made only on a case-by-case basis (e.g., child has been abroad for some time). The rationale for the bilingual policy is that EL, being the lingua franca of the working world, gives school leavers a competitive edge in a highly globalised economy. At the same time, the MT helps them access their respective ethnic culture and retain a distinctive Asian identity (MOE, 2007). However, there has been a demographic shift in the language spoken at home, with more than half of school population coming from households where EL is used more than MT. Hence, there has been a push to adopt less didactic and more interactive approaches to engage students during MT lessons. At the same time, it is acknowledged that EL learning in a multilingual country presents challenges not present in a monolingual or near-native context. As such teachers adopt "a principled blend of first language (L1) and second language (L2) teaching methods" to achieve a balance between "systematic and explicit instruction" and "a contextualised and holistic approach to learning that will provide a rich language environment" to build a strong foundation in language skills, grammar and vocabulary (MOE, 2008, p. 8).

TABLE 7.1 Summary of the AA presented in this chapter

Example	Level	Subject	Task	Skills assessed
7.1	Primary 4	Chinese Language	Video recording of news report	Listening/Speaking
7.2	Secondary 1	Malay Language	Project-based performance	Reading/ Writing/Speaking/ Listening
7.3	Secondary 1 Normal Technical (High Support)	English Language	Interviewing tourists	Spoken communication
7.4	Polytechnic (Post-Sec)	English Language	Live presentation on new product	Research and oral presentation

Example 7.1

Subject: Chinese Language
Focus: Listening/speaking
Topic: News report
Contributed by Michelle Lim
Target group: 10-year-olds (Primary 4)

Relevant standards

- understand and identify the key theme of the audio message,
- critically process and comprehend information received through visual and audio forms, and
- connect prior knowledge and personal experiences to construct a coherent and focus utterance.

Context

The teaching of the Chinese language in Singapore used to focus on four language skills – listening, speaking, reading and writing. The four skills were, however, not allocated equal standing, with emphasis usually placed on the reading, especially reading comprehension, and writing. It was assumed, as this writer once had, that the primary school students innately possess listening and speaking skills, therefore, there is no need to conduct explicit teaching of the two skills. Teaching, usually teaching to the test, for the two skills typically intensified in the weeks leading up to the listening comprehension and oral communications examinations. The assessment of oral skills was conducted as a summative test, with students receiving the consolidated marks for their assessment, resulting in them not knowing which component of the oral skills assessment require improvement. Fortunately, the above-mentioned teaching and assessment of oral skills for the Chinese language is a thing of the past. The Mother Tongue Languages Review (MTLR) conducted in 2010 recommends an emphasis be returned to oracy – a term coined by Andrew Wilkinson (1965) which refers to an individual's general ability in using the oral skills of speaking and listening (cited in Goh, 2005). The committee recognises that language acquisition and learning occurs through listening and speaking, and recommends that oracy be systematically taught and developed. This is critical to ensure students learn to use oral language that is appropriate for the ever-increasing variety of purpose and contexts that they encounter.

The MTLR committee observed that effective learning takes place when students are taught to use the language actively and interactively in a variety of real-life settings, therefore, it introduced two additional language skills – interacting in spoken forms and interacting in written forms, in addition to the four skills of listening, speaking, reading and writing. Three communication modes – interpretive, interpersonal and presentational – were highlights for pupils to develop oracy competence.

In response to the recommendations, primary schools introduced show-and-tell, news-reporting, story-telling and other oral communication tasks that are purportedly situated in real-life or 'authentic' settings, to develop one's ability to interact in spoken form. Some benefits of authentic assessments that can add value to teaching and learning are:

1. Promoting higher-order skills such as critical thinking and connecting content knowledge with personal life experiences (Wiggins, 1993).
2. Motivating and engaging learners through a real-world context of authentic learning and assessment using intellectual worthy tasks (Wiggins, 1993).

Task

Students are to choose from three newsworthy incidents shortlisted by the Chinese Language department. Their task to be assessed consists of writing a news-reporting script based on that incident, before recording a two-minute video of themselves reading the news.

Lesson

To prepare students for the task, the teacher will model the expectations of this task, and highlight common mistakes that students may commit. The subsequent sessions will see the teacher model active listening and responsive speaking through feedback to the students.

There will be two mass screenings of the news report, after which the students will be given 15 minutes to write and organize their responses to the news report. Each student will be allowed three minutes to present his or her response, after which a two-minute question-and-answer session will follow. Last, there is a five-minute feedback for the student to reflect and suggest areas for improvement.

To ensure validity and reliability, the appropriate criteria for scoring will be emphasised and standardised (Wiggins, 1993). The validity of the assessment, which depends in part on whether the assessment stimulates real world "tests" of ability, is ensured through the design of the task of responding to a news report. Please see Example 7.1.1.

EXAMPLE 7.1.1 Rubrics

Construct	Excellent (9–10)	Good (7–8)	Fair (5–6)	Unsatisfactory (<5)
Active listening.	Student is able to summarize and paraphrase the key theme of the news report.	Student is able to summarize and identify the key theme of the news report.	Student is able to identify the key theme of the news report using keywords they heard in the news report.	Student is unable to identify the key theme of the news report.
Responsive speaking.	Student has a good hook and presents response in a logical and interesting order, which the audience can easily follow. A wide range of vocabulary and expression is used to present his/her response.	Student presents information in a logical order, which the audience can follow. He/she uses subject-specific language and speaks in complete sentences using correct grammar.	Student presents information in an ambiguous order, which the audience has some difficulty in following. He/she uses complete sentences and some connectives. He/she speaks without using filler words e.g., like, erm	Student does not present information in a logical order, therefore the audience are unable to understand the presentation. He/she uses a limited vocabulary and struggles with using complete sentences to articulate his/her response.

Example 7.2

Subject: Malay language
Focus: Narrative writing and effective communication
Contributed by Mislimah Binte Misti
Target group: 13-year-olds (Secondary 1)

Relevant standards

- Develop, organise and express ideas coherently and cohesively in writing and representing for a variety of purposes, audiences, contexts and cultures.
- Produce a variety of texts for creative, personal, academic and functional purposes, using an appropriate register and tone.
- Plan and present information and ideas for a variety of purposes.
- Use appropriate skills, strategies and language to convey and construct meaning during interactions.

Context

Since 2005, there has been a move towards aligning teaching and testing to achieve language proficiency via alternative modes of assessment such as authentic assessment. Portfolios, performance-based assessment, the use of rubrics as learning tools, research-based assessment were some of the alternative mode of assessments practiced in schools. Following that, the 2010 MTL Review Committee Report recommended greater use of authentic materials reflective of everyday situations and contexts, so as to better prepare pupils to actively use their MT in real-life situations.

In BaTuTa!,[1] the task is scoped as a real-world problem experienced by the Malay community today. Solving the problem by creating suitable story books by students themselves makes this task authentic to them as students. By allowing the students' choice to bring in their past experiences that are relevant, BaTuTa! can be seen to honour the students' experiences. In advocating educative experience proposed by Dewey (1938), BaTuTa! should bring into play the principle of continuity and interactivity, allowing students to see relevance and transferability of the experience. Through BaTuTa!, students can appreciate the relevance and importance of narrative writing when they write a type of narrative text that resembles those written by professionals in real life. Thus, there is a transfer of learning beyond the classroom.

In creating the story book, students will get to experience a writer's writing process, from deciding on the character, plot, setting, theme, language and style of writing giving a title to their story; illustrating key scenes of their story and even selecting suitable materials for the making of their big story book. Again, this shows that the task is situational and has contextual realism. At the same time, the task can be considered as non-routine and multi-stage as students will need to use a repertoire of knowledge about narrative writing and their good judgment throughout the process of creating their product, the story book.

Task

In groups of three to four members, students are required to create a big MT story book for the pre- schoolers in response to the shortage of appropriate MT story books for pre-schoolers, aged four to six years old, in the local pre-school centres. Students are encouraged to use their creativity to select a suitable theme for the story book. In writing the story, students need to apply the narrative writing structure and techniques learnt in MT class. Students are required to adhere to the instructions in the BaTuTa! Project Progress Timeline. On the project presentation day, students are required to submit the group's big MT story book and present the process of making it by sharing their group's project journal (not graded). Every member in the group must speak up during the presentation, which will be followed by a question and answer session (not graded). Questions will be asked by the teacher and non-presenting groups. A week after the presentation day, students are required to submit an individual write up narrating their experience accomplishing BaTuTa! See Example 7.2.1.

Reflection question

Here is a case where there are opportunities for formative feedback built into the authentic assessment.

Recall Chapter 1 that advised a distinction is made between the types (e.g., authentic assessment) and purpose of assessment (e.g., formative assessment).

Consider the rationale for assessing the students formatively without according marks as part of feedback.

EXAMPLE 7.2.1 Rubrics

Project BaTuTa! assessment

Rubrics

Narrative writing–big MT story book & personal narrative

	Beginning 0–5	Developing 6–11	Accomplished 12–15	Exemplary 16–20
Organization. The organization and focus of the narrative is clear and maintained throughout.	There is little or no discernible plot or there may just be a series of events Little or no attempt to establish setting and/or characters. Point of view is not clear or it frequently shifts, confusing the reader.	Inconsistent plot leading to uneven focus of the story/experience Unevenly or minimally maintains settings and develops characters. A few noticeable shifts from first-person point of view occur Uneven use of appropriate transitional strategies and/or little variety.	Evident plot helps to create a sense of unity and completeness, though there may be minor flaws and some ideas may be loosely connected Adequately maintains setting, develops characters and maintains point of view Adequate use of a variety of transitional strategies to clarify the relationship between and among ideas/events.	Clear and coherent plot to unifying events and create a sense of completeness Effectively establishes and maintains setting, develops characters and maintains point of view Consistent use of a variety of transitional strategies to establish strong connection between and among ideas/events.

Development.

The narrative provides thorough, effective elaboration using relevant narrative techniques (details, dialogue and description).	Experiences, characters, setting and events are vague and lack clarity, making it confusing for readers to understand the flow of events in the narrative writing. Use of narrative techniques are minimal, incorrect and irrelevant affecting the development of the story or experience.	Experiences, characters, setting and events are unevenly developed with a weak attempt to convince readers of the theme in the narrative writing. Use of narrative techniques are uneven and inconsistent, interfering with the development of parts of the story or experience.	Experiences, characters, setting and events are adequately developed and allow readers to relate to the theme of the narrative writing. Adequate use of a variety of narrative techniques that generally advance the story or illustrate the experience.	Experiences, characters, setting and events are clearly developed and allow readers to connect with larger issues beyond the narrative writing. Effective use of a variety of narrative techniques that advance the story or illustrate the experience.

(continued)

EXAMPLE 7.2.1 (Continued)

Project BaTuTa! assessment

Rubrics

Narrative writing–big MT story book & personal narrative

	Beginning 0–5	Developing 6–11	Accomplished 12–15	Exemplary 16–20
Language. Accurate and effective use of standard written Malay with audience in mind.	Minimal use of correct grammar and sentence structure, punctuation, capitalization, and spelling. Language has many grammatical errors and many sections that are too confusing. Vague words throughout the narrative making it difficult for the reader to picture any event.	Inconsistent use of correct grammar and sentence structure, punctuation, capitalization, and spelling. Language has grammatical errors and some sections are too confusing. Precise words are used occasionally, vague words prevent reader from picturing most events.	Use of correct grammar and sentence structure, punctuation, capitalization, and spelling. Language is understandable. Precise words used in most of the narrative to communicate specific ideas or create images in the reader's mind, but some vague words are used.	Adequate use of correct grammar and sentence structure, punctuation, capitalization, and spelling. Language is clear and concise. Relevant and precise words used throughout to communicate specific ideas or create images in the reader's mind.

Example 7.3

Subject: English language
Focus: Spoken communication
Contributed by Rachel Tan Jiahui
Target group: 13-year-olds (Secondary 1)

Relevant standards from Secondary 1

- Demonstrate knowledge of spoken grammar and register.
- Speak with accurate pronunciation and appropriate intonation.
- Plan and present information and ideas for a variety of purposes.
- Use appropriate skills, strategies and language to convey and construct meaning during interactions.
- Produce spontaneous and planned spoken texts that are grammatically accurate, fluent, coherent and cohesive.

Context

The target population of students for this authentic assessment is a class of 19 Secondary 1 Normal Technical students. These students are generally weak in English and had scored badly in English language in their Primary 6 Primary School Leaving Examinations (PSLE). As a result, they do not have much interest in English and are largely in the low readiness level for English. The main language they are fluent in is their MT, and most of the students display low confidence in speaking aloud.

The assessment task is situated within the unit of lessons that aims to develop students to become better communicators. The AA task in question involves students working in groups in a guided inquiry type of task, where they have to craft interview questions and subsequently interview different people in a particular destination. Prior to this, the teacher would have taught students how to craft questions using the 5W1H (Who, What, When, Where, Why and How) method, which is using the question stems of who, what, where, when, why and how. Students will then brainstorm in groups of threes and fours, and craft questions about the Botanic Gardens (their chosen destination). They will also include an appropriate introductory and closing paragraph that they will use during the actual interviews. The teacher would also share with students the criteria for success, in the form of the assessment rubrics.

Students will then be brought to the Botanic Gardens, where they will take turns in their groups to interview people there. They are required to interview a total of 15 people, whether tourists or locals visiting the Botanic Gardens. Students are also supposed to record their interviews on the iPads that the school will provide. Through this AA task, students will demonstrate the application of their knowledge of the positive interactions and sociolinguistic competence.

The intended subject matter for this AA task are the constructs of clear articulation and a focus on sociolinguistic competence in verbal interactions, where the desired outcomes for this AA task will be for students to be able to speak clearly with clear pronunciation and intonation, be able to communicate effectively using the appropriate register with the suitable audience, be able to maintain eye contact, be able to listen attentively to the speaker and practice turn taking in a verbal interaction. These skills are found in the Ministry of Education (MOE) 2010 English Syllabus for Normal Technical under Speaking and Representing (MOE, 2010, p.38). It is important for students to be competent in these oracy skills as one of the aims of the syllabus is to "equip students with the necessary skills for self-expression and social interaction that will allow them access to a wide range of job opportunities" (MOE, 2010, p. 38).

In the implementation of the assessment task, there is a good combination of teacher instruction and students' guided inquiry. While the earlier parts involve the teacher's instruction on crafting interview questions and the components of positive interactions, the latter part of the lessons involve students' exploration of their ideas and the teacher being the facilitator who gives timely feedback to help them improve. This is very much in line with Wiggins' (1993) definition of AA, where students are immersed in the real-world context and producing a quality product. They are not merely completing a task, but are involved in the creation and execution of the task. The teacher's role has also changed from the instructor to the facilitator, and through the discussions there will be opportunity for feedback and suggestions for improvement.

Task

In groups of three or four, students craft five interview questions about their chosen destination (Botanic Gardens), together with introductory and closing speeches. In this planning stage, students are given some question starters as a guide to help them craft their questions.

They take turns to interview 15 people about the Botanic Gardens during their learning journey.

They record the interviews using the iPads loaned to them during the learning journey. They submit the recordings of the interviews.

They are also required to review the recordings and present a short verbal reflection of their experience interviewing others. See Example 7.3.1.

EXAMPLE 7.3.1 Rubrics

	Novice 0–2 m	Apprentice 3–5	Expert 6–8	Master 9–10
Pronunciation and intonation.	Mispronounces many words and asks questions in monotone.	Some mispronunciation of words and some variation in pitch.	Mostly error-free pronunciation with variation in pitch.	Pronunciation free from error with variation in pitch to signal questions.
Register.	Uses an inappropriate register that does not take into account the audience.	Uses an appropriate register inconsistently – frequent lapses into informal register when speaking to strangers.	Uses an appropriate register inconsistently with some lapses into informal register when speaking to strangers.	Register is well matched to the audience in question: formal register used with strangers.
Purpose.	Purpose of the interview is not stated.	Purpose of the interview is briefly mentioned.	Purpose of the interview is stated in the introduction.	Purpose of the interview is clearly explained in the introduction.
Turn taking.	Interrupts the interviewee at many junctures in the interview.	Interrupts the interviewee at some points in the interview.	Interviewee largely uninterrupted when speaking.	Allows the interviewee to complete all he has to say before taking his turn to speak.
Eye contact.	Does not make eye contact with the interviewee; looks at the script when asking questions.	Makes limited eye contact with the interviewee.	Maintains eye contact with the interviewee; tries to look at the interviewee when asking questions.	Maintains appropriate eye contact with the interviewee when asking questions; looks at the interviewee when interviewee is speaking.

Example 7.4

Subject: English language
Focus: Research/oral presentation
Contributed by Ho Mei Yuen Rathi
Target group: 16-year-olds (Polytechnic)
Faculty: School of chemical and life sciences
Diploma/Level: Diploma in Perfumery & Cosmetic Science (Year 1)

Relevant standards

- Provide scientific information (ingredients and processes) about a new product that is appropriate to the purpose, audience and context (PAC).
- Use appropriate visuals/tools to organise and enhance the content.
- Demonstrate suitable non-verbal cues for effective communication (eye contact, body posture and hand gestures).
- Communicate in Standard English that is articulate and well-intonated, with the right stresses on key terms and phrases.

Context

The AA task is targeted at first-year students who have applied to be in a diploma programme that was recently set up in the polytechnic. Currently, the Diploma in Perfumery and Cosmetic Science (DPCS) is the only local diploma programme in Singapore that provides training in chemistry with applications in perfumery and cosmetic science. Therefore, the AA task that has been selected allows first-year students to present their findings of the chemical qualities and processes of various new cosmetic and perfumery products on the international market to a selected audience. This assessment is also chosen because it is integral to the students' long-term educational goal. After applying the chemical knowledge, they have gained through their research and findings to create new chemical formulations in their final year, students still need to convey the success of their new chemical formulations to various industry players. They need to do so in order to secure internships and employment opportunities. Therefore, the construct that is assessed in this AA task is "effectiveness" in oracy because students need to become well-versed in listening and speaking appropriately in a given professional context.

While there are competing and conflicting models of oracy in English, in the polytechnic, the dominance of a functional and competent model of oracy persists, where speaking is often privileged over listening. Students talk while their peers listen to them passively. In such an environment, the diversity and potential of class discourse and interaction are often neglected in the learning and assessment process (Hughes & Westgate, 1998). It is a traditional model of teaching and assessing oracy that perpetuates the idea that students have a limited role to play in asking questions, providing feedback and assessing their work and others, since the educators are the ones who control the transference of a prescribed bank of knowledge. Any oral presentation then becomes just another way to assess whether this transference has taken place. However, this way of assessing oracy is not constructively aligned for the long-term with how students in DPCS will eventually need to listen and speak effectively within their chosen professional context. In other words, the language in the classroom needs to become an instrument of learning and not simply one of teaching or for the giving of instructions (Britton, 1970). Therefore, the rationale for adapting a current language task is to shift the focus of assessment away from merely concentrating on the students' ability to speak well. Instead, what is more important is the need to contextualise the assessment in authentic tasks such as the application of knowledge to real-life cases (Dochy, 2001). Thus, AA provides a platform to assess the students' cognitive knowledge, understanding, thinking process, and capacity to communicate in relation to the scientific content that has been mastered and the professional context that is provided.

Task

- Research the industry and choose any three products. Each group is allowed the flexibility of having up to three choices so that no two groups end up presenting the same product.
- Present using various visual tools besides PowerPoint such as Prezi, infographics, models, samples, etc. or a combination to present the product as effectively as possible.
- Conduct a mock presentation in a seminar room.
- Listen to feedback from both their peers and lecturer on areas to improve.
- Conduct the final presentation during the annual faculty workshop, where representatives from various interested companies are usually present (presentations will be video-recorded). Conduct a formal 15 minutes presentation. See Example 7.4.1 for the rubrics.

EXAMPLE 7.4.1 Rubric for product presentation

Criteria	E (1–2)	D (3–4)	C (5–6)	B (7–8)	A (9–10)
Content (10%).	Provides a sketchy understanding of scientific information that may/may not be appropriate to the purpose, audience and context (PAC) of the presentation.	Provides a confused understanding of scientific information that may/may not be appropriate to the purpose, audience and context (PAC) of the presentation.	Provides a basic understanding of scientific information that is appropriate to the purpose, audience and context (PAC) of the presentation.	Provides an advanced understanding of scientific information that is appropriate to the purpose, audience and context (PAC) of the presentation.	Provides a penetrative grasp of scientific information that is appropriate to the purpose, audience and context (PAC) of the presentation
Visuals (10%) (e.g., diagrams, graphs, flowcharts, sketches, prototypes).	Superficial use of visuals with questionable links to content.	Random use of visuals with spurious links to content.	Evidence of some relationship between visuals and content.	Appropriate use of quality visuals to enhance content.	Masterful use of quality visuals to enhance and reinforce content.
Delivery Features (10%).	Unaware of the audience. Poor demonstration of appropriate non-verbal cues.	Vaguely aware of the audience Insufficient demonstration of appropriate non-verbal cues.	Somewhat aware of the audience. Occasional demonstration of appropriate non-verbal cues	Frequently aware of the audience. Maintains rapport through the consistent use of appropriate non-verbal cues.	Fully engaged with the audience. Maintains rapport through robust demonstration of non-verbal cues.
Language (10%).	Critical problems with articulation and intonation, with an obvious lack of word stressing. Weak grasp of Standard English.	Serious problems with articulation and intonation, with amateurish word stressing. Basic grasp of Standard English.	Some problems with articulation and intonation, with unclear word stressing at times. Evident grasp of Standard English.	Slight problems with articulation and intonation, with minimal unclear word stressing. Good grasp of Standard English.	Highly affective articulation and intonation, with proficient word stressing. Commendable grasp of Standard English.

Reflection question

Note that Examples 7.2–7.4 require that learners use the language with a real and live audience. How would that engage the learners more than if the audience was just the teacher for the purpose of grading?

Summary

In Chapter 1, it was argued that a real-life setting in AA is not inherently more authentic to the learners unless they find it personally interesting or relevant. Of course, the issue is that with the learners coming from different backgrounds, how can the teacher design AA that will be of meaning to each learner? In this chapter, we see the teachers offering the learners some choice of topic or flexibility in crafting their approach. When learners can choose a focus that appeals to them or they are more familiar with, they are more motivated. In addition, they are likely to have a better idea of how to go about planning and completing the task. In other words, they are more metacognitively and behaviourally active participants in the process (Tay, 2015). Hence, as argued in Chapter 2, AA such as the ones described in this chapter where learners have choice and a voice in their assessments can enhance learning, not just measure it.

Note

1 BaTuTa! refers to Baca Tulis Cipta, meaning read, write, create.

References

Britton, J. (1970). *Language and Learning*. Harmondsworth: Penguin.

Cumming, J. J. & Maxwell, G. S. (1999). Contextualising authentic assessment. *Assessment in Education*, 6(2), 177–194.

Dochy, F. (2001). A new assessment era: Different needs, new challenges. *Research Dialogue in Learning and Instruction* 10(1), 11–20.

Huges, M. & Westgate, D. (1998). Possible enabling strategies in teacher-led talk with young pupils. *Language and Education* 12(3), 174–191.

MOE. (7 March, 2007). Preparing Students for a Global Future: Enhancing Language Learning. Retrieved 6 June 2017, from https://www.moe.gov.sg/media/press/2007/pr20070307.htm.

MOE. (2008). English Language Syllabus 2010: Primary & Secondary (Express/Normal [Academic]). Retrieved 6 June 2017, from https://www.moe.gov.sg/docs/default-source/document/education/syllabuses/english-language-and-literature/files/english-primary-secondary-express-normal-academic.pdf.

Shank, P. (2009). Assessing Whether Online Learners Can DO: Aligning Learning Objectives with Real-world Applications. *Assessing Online Learning: Strategies, Challenges and Opportunities*, pp. 8–9.

Tay, H. Y. (2015). Setting Formative Assessments in Real World Contexts to Facilitate Self-regulated Learning. *Educational Research for Policy and Practice*, 4(2), 169–187.

Wiggins, G. (1993). *Assessing Student Performance*. San Francisco: Jossey-Bass Publishers.

8

AUTHENTIC ASSESSMENTS
IN MATHEMATICS

Introduction

This chapter will present examples of authentic assessments (AA) from a range of age groups: from Primary 4 when students are aged 10 to polytechnic students who are 17 years and above (see Table 8.1). Unlike other chapters, this one includes an example from New Zealand so that readers can compare and contrast how AAs are designed in different countries.

Context

Singapore has often been highlighted for consistently doing well at international assessments like Trends in International Mathematics and Science Study (TIMSS) and Programme for International Student Assessment (PISA). Perhaps because of that, there has been much interest in how mathematics is taught in Singapore. In fact, "Singapore maths" is a term known in at least 14 countries (Sin, 2017). Not only have the textbooks been adopted in other countries (Tang, 2014), the Singaporean mathematics mastery approach has also been the focus of research (Blalock, 2011; Ginsburg, Leinwand, Anstrom, & Pollock, 2005; Yeap, Ferrucci & Carter, 2006).

Nonetheless, the Ministry of Education (MOE) continues to review the mathematics curriculum especially with the view of better equipping students with the skills and competencies for the 21st century. Hence, there is an increased emphasis on the process of learning, with the latest syllabuses explicitly stating the learning experiences that should accompany the mathematical processes and skills being taught (MOE, 2012a and 2012b).

Similarly, in New Zealand (NZ), there is an increased focus on developing learners' competencies in increasingly complex and unfamiliar situations (MOE,

TABLE 8.1 Summary of the AA presented in this chapter

Example	Level	Topic/Focus	Task
8.1	Primary 4.	Mathematical problem-solving.	To solve given problem.
8.2	Secondary 2 Normal Technical (Low Progress).	Formulating a mathematical problem.	To help selection of athlete.
8.3	Polytechnic.	Mathematical modelling in engineering mathematics.	To determine the most cost-effective pipeline route.
8.4	NZ Year 11. NCEA Level 1.	Area, perimeter, volume and surface area of 3D figures.	To design packaging for Lindt chocolates.

2016). So, while there are the three-hour written examinations that students sit for in Years 11, 12, 13 as part of the National Certificate of Educational Achievement (NCEA) examinations, schools may craft AA as part of the internal assessments, with guidelines from NZ's examination board, New Zealand Qualifications Authority (NZQA). These AA enable assessment of skills that are not able to be assessed by external examinations alone. The example from NZ at the end of this chapter (Example 8.4) is an internal assessment task on the topic of measurement created by the mathematics department of Wellington Girls' College to get students go beyond formulaic calculations to solve a complex, real life problem.

Example 8.1

Focus: Mathematical problem solving
Contributed by Ong Shin Leei, Nathalie
Target group: 12-year-olds (Primary 6)

- Topic: Area and perimeter

Relevant standards

- Understand and apply the underlying principles on area and perimeter using dimensions of figures related to square, rectangles and circles.
- Use mathematical reasoning to analyse and interpret problems in everyday and mathematical situations, then select and apply a variety of problem solving strategies to arrive at a conclusion.
- Use mathematical language to communicate mathematical ideas and arguments effectively.

Task

Students are to work on a floor plan for the furniture arrangement for the school's charity dinner 2020. Students are to house the most number of guests given the stipulated measurements and considerations, while ensuring that their plans allow comfortable seating spaces amongst the guests. Students must discuss and make decisions on the choice of shapes to use to meet the objectives of the challenge. See Example 8.1.1 for the rubrics.

Lesson:

Task 1: Generating ideas

1 Introduction on the idea of generating number patterns using a visual approach:

1.1 In groups of four, group members will discuss and sketch possible ways to solve the challenge. They will come up with floor plans using symbols, brainstorm possible choice/s of furniture pieces (mathematical solution) in the context of planning the table arrangement for the charity dinner (real-world problem), taking into account the underlying considerations (existing length and breadth of the school hall, factsheet containing dimensions of square, rectangular and circular tables, and dimensions of the chairs to be used).

These questions are provided to guide students in their initial discussion:

- Why do we use floor plan? What are the important things a floor plan must adhere to?
- Calculate the total surface area of the table or chair tops of your chosen furniture pieces. Will the answer be more than, equal or less than the floor area of school hall? Explain your answer.
- Will the shape of the tables chosen be able to accommodate the most number of guests?
- Have you factored in the space amongst tables and chairs?

These are questions to generate deeper discussions on their tentative plans:

- What must be the same and why?
- What must be different and why?
- What are you trying to find?
- Which Mathematical concept(s) is the experience linked to?

[Linking length, breadth and radius to perimeter and area]

Task 2: Seeing the connection

2.1 Students are to write down their interpretations of the question:

- Should they use rectangular (200 cm by 60 cm) or square tables (100 cm by 100 cm)? Can square tables be combined to form rectangular ones?
- Is it better to use 12-seater round tables (diameter 210 cm) instead?
- Can the chosen pattern of tables and chairs be repeatedly arranged in the entire hall space given? Which mathematical concept is it linked to? Sufficient area? Sufficient lengths and breadths using perimeter concept?

Task 3: Representing the strategy

The teacher communicates success criteria using rubrics and leads the students to represent the listing in several forms, such as

1. Systematic listing by purely sketching every table and chair out.
2. Seeing number patterns or general rule and generating possibilities by forming one module and repeats the module in the given space, guided by perimeter and area concepts.

Each group will present their solutions on a butcher sheet, along with their answers to the following questions, written on the same butcher sheet:

- What is the approach you have chosen and why?
- Did you verify the answer using another approach or a different set of numbers?
- What is your intentional choice of words when presenting your solution?

Task 4: Presentation and gallery walk

One student in each group will stay back to explain/justify his group's solutions to other groups' students during gallery walk.

Task 5: Consolidating

- The student who stayed back in each group will relate and clarify with the other members in the group on the feedback given by others.

Guiding questions in task:

- Are there any other useful inputs raised by your classmates?
- How can you use the points raised to improve on your solution?
- Given such questions, which best method will you use to solve?

Task 6: Conclusion

- Every student will be given a few minutes to reflect on the above tasks. Get students to articulate the procedural steps to analyse, interpret and solve problems.
- Remind the students to think about how they make connections when attempting the task.
- Misconceptions will be elicited from the students.

Teacher gives feedback on the work of the group as a whole using rubrics.

EXAMPLE 8.1.1 Rubrics

Approach and reasoning: *The strategies and skills used to solve the problem and the reasoning that supports the approach.*

Level 1	Level 2	Level 3	Level 4
• Approach and reasoning do not work. • No approach and reasoning is evident.	• Approach and reasoning lead to solving only part of the problem.	• Approach and reasoning work but student does not explain or verify the solution.	• Verifies the solution by using a different mathematical process.

Solution: The answer(s) to the questions(s) asked in the task and the mathematical work that supports it.

(continued)

EXAMPLE 8.1.1 (Continued)

Level 1	Level 2	Level 3	Level 4
• No part of the solution is correct. • Some work is present but the work does not support the answer to the problem.	• Solution is appropriate but is incomplete. *E.g., correct shapes of tables chosen but does not maximise the space given.*	• Solution is appropriate, complete but contains minor flaws. *E.g., does not factor space between tables and chairs.*	• The solution is appropriate, complete and accurate.

Example 8.2

Focus: Formulating a mathematical problem
Contributed by Lawrence Koh
Target group: 14-year-olds (Secondary 2 Normal Technical)
Topic: Statistics and probability

Relevant standards
Applications and modelling

- Apply mathematics concepts and skills to solve problems in a variety of contexts within or outside mathematics, including:
  - Identifying the appropriate mathematical representations or standard models for a problem.
  - Using appropriate mathematical concepts, skills (including tools and algorithm) to solve a problem.
- Understand some elements of the mathematical modelling process, including:
  - Formulating a simple mathematical model to represent a real-world problem
  - Applying mathematics to solve the problem.
  - Interpreting the mathematical solution and making informed decisions.

Reasoning, communication and connections

- Use appropriate representations, mathematical language (including notations, symbols and conventions) and technology to present and communicate mathematical ideas.
- Reason inductively and deductively, including:
  - Explain or justify/verify a mathematical solution/statement.
  - Draw logical conclusions.
  - Make inferences.
- Make connections within mathematics, and between mathematics and the real world.

Context

This is an authentic task which I have designed using the guidelines of the Secondary 2 Normal Technical mathematics syllabus (MOE, 2012). It specifically calls for students to be exposed to problems derived from the real-world context of "everyday statistics" such as sports and games. The syllabus also advocates that students apply reasoning, communicating in mathematical language and make connections in between mathematics and the real world. As such, the task can be said to be authentic to the subject matter. The task is authentic to students because at their level, they would have already learnt the statistical concept of central tendencies (i.e. mean, median and mode) as well as statistical representations (such as graphs and charts). Also, the mathematical knowledge includes concepts that when extended, are found in upper secondary mathematics (such as outliers and inter-quartile range). Finally, students would be familiar with the context of a long jump in the sport of athletics. The task is largely reflective of the adult world in that the selection trial is conducted in a similar fashion, and while athletes are chosen based on their performance at events leading up to the major sports meet, a selection committee has the autonomy to select athletes based on factors such as consistency and extenuating circumstances that result in less than optimal performances. The task could be more authentic to the adult world if the data is not provided. However, I refrained from this practice as an online search for actual data turned up empty; the data reflects the actual performance of long jump athletes in the countries that took part in the 2015 games.

Reflection question

Recall the three referent contexts for authenticity mentioned in Chapter 1. How has the teacher unpacked them here?

The task does not require the full use of the mathematical modelling framework. Instead the construct focuses on "Formulating a mathematical problem". This is intentional for three reasons. First, as Normal Technical students may not be familiar with mathematical modelling, so exposure to a subset of the framework makes learning less daunting. Second, students are very familiar with solving problems, but find themselves in unfamiliar territory when it comes to problem formulation. The focus here is not just formulating a problem, but instead to formulate the problem based on the practical demands surrounding it in the real world. Finally, I argue that the formulation stage in the mathematical modelling framework is the most important. Ang (2009) remarks that a solution is only as good as the assumptions made to the problem, implying that if the question is phrased poorly, the solution, no matter how accurate it was, would be a poor solution such that it probably would be impractical to be used in a real-world scenario.

I have unpacked the construct of formulating a mathematics problem as the following: (1) understand the problem in the real-world; (2) make assumptions to simplify the problem; and (3) represent the problem in the mathematics world. The use of rubrics (see Example 8.2.1 Rubrics) is appropriate because formulation as a construct is complex and does not carry with it a "right answer".

Messick (1994) advocates a construct-driven approach to task design because "the meaning of the construct guides the selection or construction of relevant tasks as well as the rational development of scoring criteria and rubrics". He warns of the two main threats to validity issues: construct underrepresentation and construct irrelevance, which he precludes that the construct-driven approach will naturally surface. In the case of formulating a mathematics problem, understanding the problem requires students to make sense of the information provided, as well as collect additional information (or remove irrelevant ones) for the purpose for lending clarity to the problem. For example, although a winner is determined as the person who can jump the farthest, the decision of selecting a representative of the games may mean something else, such as the person who is most consistent in jumping a distance that is within a target limit rather than a one-time performance. Also, major games have a minimum distance that long jump athletes will need to meet at their regional trials, hence the best jumper in our trial may not be ultimately sent to the games.

Assumptions are critical to the process because of the need to establish relationships between variables and/or factors, which in turn needs to be defensible as assumptions are arguable and can nullify the "mathematization" process. For example, the data provided gives hint to the different styles found typically among long jump athletes. Students will need to decide if jumps which are "faulted" should be ignored or be attributed a distance of zero metres. The decision taken will greatly affect the decision-making process from a mathematical world perspective (since the data set is extremely small).

The final aspect of the formulation stage is the accurate representation of the problem in the mathematic world, otherwise known as the model. A model is a mathematical representation that can take the form of equations, tables and geometrical figures, or in the case of this example, statistical representation. A second aspect about models is that if well executed, the information can be represented in a simple and "beautiful" manner, as opposed to the same information represented in raw or in a lengthy manner, which complicates the later stages of the mathematical modelling process.

Reflection question

How does this add to your understanding of Messick's construct-centred approach (see Chapter 3)?

Task

Singapore plays host to the XXVIII South East Asian Games in 2015. The Singapore National Olympics Committee oversees the selection of athletes to the games. One of the events to be competed under athletics will be long jump. A trial was conducted recently to select an athlete to represent Singapore in the long jump event. Table 8.2 shows the results of the top three athletes.

TABLE 8.2 Real-world problem posed to Secondary 2 Normal (Technical) student

	Ahmed	Bala	Chee Keen
1st attempt	*fault*	7.28 m	7.32 m
2nd attempt	7.33 m	7.31 m	7.36 m
3rd attempt	7.27 m	7.34 m	*fault*
4th attempt	7.36 m	7.36 m	7.35 m
5th attempt	7.34 m	7.34 m	7.15 m

EXAMPLE 8.2.1 Rubrics for formulating a mathematical problem

Formulating a mathematical problem	Exceeding expectations	Meeting expectations	Approaching expectations	Not meeting expectations	Unacceptable work*
Understand the problem (in the *real* world).	Makes sense of all the information provided, and collected additional (and/or removed irrelevant) information to lend greater clarity to the problem.	Makes sense of most of the information provided, and collected additional (and/or irrelevant) information to lend some clarity to the problem.	Makes sense of some of the information provided, and collected additional information which may not have lent clarity to the problem, or may have removed some relevant information.	Makes sense of some of the information provided and may have removed some relevant information.	No attempt made to make sense of some of the information provided.
Assumptions Taken to simplify the problem *★Variables are quantifiable factors.*	Identifies appropriate variables/factors★ involved, and selects important ones to simplify the problem. Makes adequate and plausible assumptions for important variables/factors★ such that the relationship obtained is defensible.	Identifies appropriate variables/factors★ involved to simplify the problem. Makes some reasonable assumptions for variables/factors★ to obtain a relationship.	Identifies variables/factors★ involved to simplify the problem. Assumptions made for variables/factors★ to obtain a relationship may not be always feasible.	Identifies variables/factors★ involved to simplify the problem. No assumptions made for variables/factors★ to obtain a relationship.	No attempt to Identify or select variables/factors.★
Represent the problem (in the *math* world).	Accurately represented the problem in a simple/beautiful mathematical model.	Accurately represented the problem in an appropriate mathematical model.	Inadequate or inappropriate representation of the problem in mathematical model.	Inadequate or inappropriate representation of the problem in mathematical model.	Unable to represent the question in mathematical model.

*Do you think this standard is necessary or helpful?

Example 8.3

Focus: Mathematical modelling
Contributed by Jennie Ling
Target group: Above 16-year-olds (Polytechnic)
Topic: Calculus

Relevant standards

- Display mathematical thinking and problem-solving skills, and apply these skills to formulate and solve problems.
- Display the abilities to reason logically, to communicate mathematically.

Context

In engineering mathematics, model-eliciting Activity (MEA) has been identified as an effective learning experience which "support(s) deep learning of concepts and development of technical and professional skills through authentic engineering problems" (Diefes-Dux, Hjalmarson & Zawojewski, 2013). Many characteristics of MEA lend themselves to the design of an AA task which can mirror an open-ended workplace engineering problem. Therefore, my AA task, whose construct is mathematical modelling, is based on the MEA design.

MEAs are "a class of problems that simulate authentic real-world client-driven situations that small teams of 3 to 5 students work to solve" (Hamilton, Lesh, Lester, & Brilleslyper, 2008). Its six principles (Diefes-Dux, Hjalmarson & Zawojewski, 2013) ensure that each problem is in an authentic setting (reality principle) for the development of a client-driven mathematical model (model construction principle) that can be generalized in meeting the client's immediate and future needs (shareability and reusablity principle). Additionally, carefully selected sample data must be provided so that student teams can test and evaluate their ideas (self-evaluation principle). The problem also requires that the solution be communicated back to the client, with the end-users in mind (model documentation principle). The overall aim is to provide a significant learning experience with concepts or processes that students can draw upon when faced with new problem-solving situations (effective prototype principle).

Task

Main Task: Phase 1. In teams of four, students are given a map of an island with two points indicated on opposite sides of a swamp, and a memo (see below) from the project manager of an engineering firm laying down the project requirements. Teams must determine the most cost-effective pipeline route in connecting points A and B. The swamp area can be approximated to a simplified rectangular model. Costs associated with material and terrain type are given. They must come up with three mathematical functions for three routes: around the swamp (normal terrain), across the swamp (wetland) and a combination of both. For the third route, they should use differential calculus, and then compare the cost of each route to choose one with the minimum cost. The memo makes clear that the model must be generalizable and work for "other end-points that might be assigned to you in the later phase", i.e. further sample data. The teams must submit a report on their model and give a short oral presentation followed by a Q&A session.

Internal Memo

To: Engineering Team
From: Tan Eng Gin, Project Manager, Pipez Engineerng Pte Ltd.
Re: Pipeline Route on Pulau Ubin

Our firm has been hired by Energy Market Authority (EMA) to lay pipelines on Pulau Ubin, where there are wetland areas. Your team is tasked with installing the pipeline from Point A to Point B (please refer to attached Pulau Ubin map). Costs involved depend on material cost (cost of pipe is $7 per metre) and terrain type. Normal terrain installation costs $6 per metre, but installation in wetland requires an additional Track Hoe at a cost of $100 per hour. In a 10-hour day, the Track Hoe can dig approximately 100 metres of trench.

Your team is responsible for creating and evaluating a general procedure to determine the most cost-effective pipeline route in connecting various pairs of points on opposite sides of the swamp. By approximating the swamp area to a simplified rectangular model, please come up with 3 mathematical functions for 3 routes, each with its corresponding costs: around the swamp (normal terrain only), across the swamp (wetland only), and a combination of both.

As we are exploring the possibility of generalizing your model for future use, your model must be able to work for other similarly shaped wetland areas. So, as your team develops your model, you will need to analyse the accuracy and limitations of your model. That is, your team must quantify the cost of each route with the two given end-points of the pipeline, as well as other end-points which might be assigned to you in the later phase of the project.

In a report addressed to me, please reply with the following information:

- Your team's mathematical procedure for determining the minimum cost. Be sure to clearly state the reason for each step, heuristic (i.e. rule), or consideration in your procedure. You may use diagrams, flow charts (recommended), tables etc. in your report.
- The results of applying your general procedure to all the data provided.
- Use of any mathematical software in your modelling process should be indicated clearly.

Also, your team will be required to verbally present your model to me. Length of presentation should not exceed 10 minutes, followed by 5 minutes of Q&A.

Thank you,
Tan Eng Gin

Taking into consideration that workplace engineering problems typically require collaboration, the task is assigned as a group project. For first-year students, a problem that is too ill-structured may throw them off completely, but drawing on the finding that "ill-structured engineering problems include aggregates of well-structured problems", this project model is framed as three different mathematical functions, each of which is a well-structured problem. Given that "engineers use multiple forms of problem representation", teams may use diagrams, flow charts (recommended), tables and any mathematical software in their report, to encourage them to explore different forms of representation or even learn a new tool (mathematical software). Problem representation facilitates communication via reports, manuals etc. Therefore, I decided to include oral presentation as a further requirement, despite reservations regarding construct-irrelevance. This is because, besides giving them practice in public speaking, the presentation session is a good avenue for students to learn from other teams, and allows assessors to test students' understanding individually.

Main Task: Phase 2. At the end of the first week, students are to submit a preliminary report to their respective tutors. This phase allows teachers to give written formative feedback to each team. Together with the written feedback, teachers will inform the teams that due to environmental concerns and logistical issues (simulating unanticipated problems often encountered by engineers), the client is now considering four other possible pairs of points to connect the pipes. Teams are to test their models with the new sample data, evaluate and enhance their models if necessary (self-evaluation principle of MEA), and present all the results. The client will then weigh the different concerns to decide on the best route. The teams will be given a further two weeks to submit the final report.

The rubrics (Example 8.3.1), adapted from Diefes-dux et al. (2012), has an unusual layout. What is commendable is the inclusion of a general definition of each principle, for easy reference.

EXAMPLE 8.3.1 MEA rubrics with four dimensions

	Criteria	Description	Mark
Mathematical Model	Math functions for three different routes	All 3 functions correctly derived. Accurate use of Geometry or Trigonometry, with clear variables and constants, with domain stated for each variable.	7–8
		All 3 functions correctly derived. Accurate use of Geometry or Trigonometry, with clear variables and constants.	5–6
		All 3 functions derived. Mostly correct use of Geometry or Trigonometry for model, with minor errors in manipulation.	3–4
		<3 functions derived. Or incorrect use of geometry etc.	1–2
	Differential calculus	1st order Differentiation, Solution for the unknown variable obtained accurately.	5–6
		1st order Differentiation performed accurately. Unknown variable not solved correctly.	3–4
		1st order Differentiation performed accurately, but no attempt to solve for unknown variable.	1–2
	Data usage	All data sets provided used to generate the results.	4–5
		Some data sets used to generate the results.	3
		Only one data set used to generate the results.	1
Reusability		*A reusable procedure can be used by the direct user in new but similar situations: (1) identifies who the direct user is and what he needs in terms of the deliverable, criteria for success, and constraints, (2) provides an overarching description of the procedure, and (3) clarifies assumptions and limitations concerning the use of procedure.*	
	Reusability	Procedure clearly re-usable for similarly shaped areas (rectangles) of different sizes.	4–5
		Procedure might be re-usable, but 2 or 3 pieces of information are missing or need clarification.	3
		Procedure not re-usable because >3 pieces of information are missing or need clarification.	2
Modifiability		*A modifiable procedure can be modified easily by the direct user for use in different situations: (1) contains acceptable rationales for critical steps in the procedure and (2) clearly states assumptions associated with individual procedural steps.*	
	Modifiability	Procedure clearly modifiable for other geometrical shapes such as triangles and quadrilaterals.	4–5
		Procedure lacking acceptable rationales for 2 or 3 critical steps, and/or a few assumptions are missing or need clarification. Hence only fairly modifiable.	3
		Procedure lacks acceptable rationales for >3 critical steps in the procedure, and/or assumptions are missing or need clarification.	2

Shareability means that the direct user can apply the procedure and replicate results.

Shareability		
Results	All results from applying procedure to data presented appropriately.	4–5
	Not all results from applying procedure to data presented, or presented inappropriately, or results not consistent with procedure.	3
	Only one set of results presented.	1–2
Audience readability	Procedure easy for client to understand and replicate. All steps in the procedure clearly and completely articulated.	4–5
	Procedure relatively easy for client to understand and replicate. The following improvements needed: (1) two or more steps must be written more clearly and/or (2) additional description, example calculations, or intermediate results are needed to clarify the steps.	3
	Procedure difficult for client to follow.	2
Extraneous information	There is no extraneous information in the response.	1
	There is extraneous information in the response.	0
Oral Presentation	Main procedure and application of data presented clearly and concisely articulated. All students have "air-time", and questions well-answered, even when posed to selected members, showing the understanding and knowledge of all team members.	8–10
	Main procedure and application of data mostly clearly presented, but some parts unclear. All students have "air-time", but questions answered less adequately, especially when posed to selected members, showing uneven understanding and knowledge among team members.	5–7
	Main procedure and application of data not presented clearly. All students have "air-time", but questions not answered adequately, showing team's insufficient understanding and knowledge.	3–4
	There is a lot of missing information or misinformation in presentation. Not all students have "air-time", and most questions are not answered adequately, showing unpreparedness.	1–2

Total Mark 50

Example 8.4

Focus: Mathematics and statistics
Crafted by the Mathematics department of Wellington Girls' College (WGC), shared by Teo Chin Wen
Target group: 14–15-year-olds
Topic: Measurement
Achievement Standard 91030: Apply measurement in solving problems.

Context

The topic on measurement is typically very formulaic based and requires a lot of regurgitation of formulae – with or without understanding. A typical assessment comprising questions on measurement calculations does not necessarily capture the depth of understanding and the application to real life problems. As such, the mathematics department of WGC created this assessment task that requires students to go beyond formulaic calculations to solve a real-life problem. Through the task, students are put in the role of the manufacturer and have to consider many other aspects of packaging a product, not just focused on the calculations.

For this assessment task, students are to work in groups of threes or fours to investigate three packaging designs for packaging six Lindt chocolates which are spherical in shape. Students are provided with actual Lindt chocolates to work with. Groups will have four weeks to plan, measure, calculate and devise different packaging options. As a group, students will decide best how to present their work. This could be in the form of PowerPoint slides, storyboard, poster, website or other suitable formats. Students are to make the prototypes for each of their packaging designs using cardboard. A log will be kept of all progress that is made in each lesson. This will be in the form of a shared google document within the group and shared with the teacher. The teacher will monitor each group's progress and record evidence about how each student in the group is meeting the criteria for Achieved, Merit and Excellence. Groups will present their solutions to the class. Grades will be determined based on the evidence recorded during the completion of the task. Evidence for grades will come from students' logs, teacher's observations and the group presentation. The rubrics is shown in Example 8.4.1.

Instructions to students

LINDT Australia would like a new design to package six chocolates. Each chocolate is in the shape of a sphere. They would like you to investigate different ways of packaging the chocolates. They require six chocolates to be placed together in each package and would like the design to be appealing to consumers. Consideration should be given to the practical side of packaging, bulk transportation and the costs involved.

You need to provide at least three different shaped packages for consideration.

Specifications

- You need to provide at least three different shaped packages for consideration. At least one of the designs must include a curved surface.

EXAMPLE 8.4.1 Rubrics

Achievement criteria

Achievement	*Achievement with merit*	*Achievement with excellence*
• Apply measurement in solving problems.	• Apply measurement, using relational thinking, in solving problems.	• Apply measurement, using extended abstract thinking, in solving problems.

- Each design must be a neat fit for the six LINDT chocolates supplied.
- A special LINDT pattern is to be sprayed onto all outside surfaces of the package, 3 mls of pattern spray can cover 20 cm² of packaging.
- A special scented LINDT Ribbon (1 cm wide) is to be glued once around the outside of the box.
- The special scented LINDT Ribbon is also to be glued once around the outside of each of the six chocolates.

Make a recommendation to the company about which of your three designs you think would be best based on your calculations above and any other practical considerations. You must justify your decision.

While LINDT does not want to know the actual costs of packaging they would like to know the quantities of ribbon, cardboard and spray that will be required for each package of six chocolates.

As can be seen, the assessment standards are based primarily on Structure of Observed Learning Outcome (SOLO) taxonomy, a model that describes the different levels of students' understanding ranging from surface to abstract understanding.

Students are awarded an Achieved grade if they are able to apply measurement concepts in solving the problem, demonstrated through the following:

- Finding the volume, surface area, perimeter and/or area of the various shapes involved;
- Conversion of units and using the appropriate units for each of the measurements;
- Working out the size of the box to fit 200 packages of chocolates;
- Calculating the costs involved.

For a Merit grade, students have to be able to apply measurement concepts using *relational thinking* in solving the problem, demonstrated through the following:

- Working out the calculations to any two of the packaging correctly;
- Recommending the best packaging with justifications;
- and also relating findings to the context, and communicating thinking using appropriate mathematical statements.

For an Excellence, students have to be able to apply measurement concepts, using *extended abstract thinking* in solving the problem. This can be demonstrated through:

- Working out the calculations for any two of the packaging correctly;
- Communicating comprehensively and justifying the best packaging to use;

- Showing insight through discussions on other factors, such as bulk packaging and transporting in cuboidal boxes, wastage of spaces, transportation charges related to shape of boxes, best shape for shelf display in store to maximise shelf display space, etc.;
- *And* also using correct mathematical statements, and communicating mathematical insight.

Summary

Sometimes, AAs are compared unfavourably to the traditional paper-and-pen tests which are considered more "rigorous". In contrast, AAs are said to lack validity in that they may not reflect the underlying constructs, e.g. analytical reasoning ability (Terwilliger, 1997). The four examples in this chapter show that AA can be designed to reflect not only the real world but also the rigorous thinking and substantive knowledge in the disciplines. In other words, the AAs are simultaneously authentic to the discipline as well as the learner and the world outside of school (see Chapter 1).

References

Blalock, J. T. (2011). *The Impact of Singapore Math on Student Knowledge and Enjoyment in Mathematics*. Ruston, LA: Louisiana Tech University.

Diefes-dux, H. A., Zawojewski, J. S., Hjalmarson, M. A., & Cardella, M. E. (2012). A framework for analyzing feedback in a formative assessment system for mathematical modeling problems. *Journal of Engineering Education, 101* (2), 375–406.

Ginsburg, A., Leinwand, S., Anstrom, T., & Pollock, E. (2005). What the United States Can Learn from Singapore's World-Class Mathematics System (and What Singapore Can Learn from the United States): An Exploratory Study. American Institutes for Research.

Hamilton, E., Lesh, R. Lester, F., & Brilleslyper, M. (2008). Model-eliciting activities (MEAs) as a bridge between engineering education research and mathematics education research. *Advances in Engineering Education, 1*(2), 1–25.

Ministry of Education. (2016). *The New Zealand Curriculum Online*. Retrieved 13 September 2017, from http://nzcurriculum.tki.org.nz/The-New-Zealand-Curriculum#collapsible11.

MOE. (2012a). Mathematics syllabus: Primary one to five. Retrieved 7 June 2017, from https://www.moe.gov.sg/docs/default-source/document/education/syllabuses/sciences/files/primary_mathematics_syllabus_pri1_to_pri5.pdf.

MOE. (2012b). Mathematics syllabus: Secondary one to four. Retrieved 7 June 2017, from https://www.moe.gov.sg/docs/default-source/document/education/syllabuses/sciences/files/primary_mathematics_syllabus_pri1_to_pri5.pdf.

Sin, Y. (13 June 2017). Customising "Singapore maths" for use in schools abroad. http://www.straitstimes.com/singapore/education/customising-spore-maths-for-use-in-schools-abroad.

Tang, A. (23 October 2014). Singapore maths is travelling the world. *The Straits Times.* Retrieved 7 June 2017, from http://www.straitstimes.com/singapore/education/singapore-maths-is-travelling-the-world.

Terwilliger, J. (1997). Semantics, psychometrics, and assessment reform: A close look at "authentic" assessments. *Educational Researcher, 26*(8), pp. 24–27.

Yeap, B. H., Ferrucci, B. J., & Carter, J. A. (2006). Comparative study of arithmetic problems in Singaporean and American mathematics textbooks. In *Mathematics Education in Different Cultural Traditions-A Comparative Study of East Asia and the West* (pp. 213–225). New York: Springer.

9

AUTHENTIC ASSESSMENTS IN SCIENCES

Introduction

As in previous chapters, this chapter will present authentic assessment (AA) designed for a range of age groups (see Table 9.1). However, the AAs chosen focus on (1) scientific inquiry or (2) scientific literacy so that readers can compare and contrast how teachers approached the same topic. It is hoped that readers will see that while these AAs are good models, they are not the only possibilities. What teachers need are clarity of assessment objectives and good design principles; both of which can be seen in the examples provided.

Context

Science education in Singapore schools rests on the belief in the spirit of scientific inquiry (MOE, 2013, p. 1). Just like inquiry in the humanities where students work to investigate a real life issue (see Chapter 6), inquiry in the sciences also involve students engaging in activities to study the what (content) and the how (process) of understanding the natural and physical world around them. Throughout the student-directed, inquiry-based process, students take responsibility to pose and respond to questions, design investigations, before evaluating and communicating their findings.

It is hoped that such active learning will spark the learners' curiosity to explore the world around them. The three domains of scientific inquiry: in daily life, society and the environment, echoes the referent contexts for authenticity mentioned in Chapter 1. Here is clearly where the discipline intersects with the world of the child and real world outside school. As such, it is not surprising that AA lends itself very naturally to science assessment.

The national curriculum also argues that in this day and age, science education should go beyond teaching basic scientific concepts. Instead scientific literacy for the 21st century should encompass skills for reasoning and analysis, decision and solving problems; open-mindedness to learn new things and the ethics to engage in science-related issues as a reflective citizen.

It is thus instructive to see how the teachers have interpreted these principles to guide them in designing AAs for their learners. As such, each write-up of the AA is preceded by the contributor's exposition of these principles and the argument for AA.

TABLE 9.1 Summary of the AA presented in this chapter

Example	Level	Topic	Skills assessed
9.1	Primary	Heat and cycles of water	Scientific inquiry
9.2	Secondary	Properties of sound waves	Scientific inquiry
9.3	Secondary 2	Acids	Scientific literacy
9.4	Junior College	Qualitative analysis	Scientific literacy

Example 9.1

Subject: General science
Focus: Heat and cycles of water
Contributed by Tan Hui Zhen
Target group: 12-year-olds (Primary 6)

Relevant standards

- identifying possible research hypotheses from a given problem;
- isolating variables and determining whether they are independent, dependent or constant variables;
- designing suitable procedures to test the hypotheses;
- carrying out experiments and making and recording observations or measurements;
- interpreting experimental data;
- drawing upon experimental data and using scientific concepts to develop explanations and draw conclusions; and
- identifying flaws in the experimental design and suggesting improvements to be made in the re-design of experiments.

Context

One of the goals of science education spelt out by the Ministry of Education (MOE) is promote scientific literacy. As outlined in the MOE syllabus documents (MOE, 2013), scientific literacy is the capacity "to use scientific knowledge to identify questions and to draw evidence-based conclusions in order to understand and make decisions about the natural world" (MOE, 2013, p. 4). The implication is that, apart from learning scientific content, students need to engage students in scientific inquiry tasks in order to learn to reason scientifically. It is on this premise that I endeavour to design an AA task to assess students' scientific reasoning.

This AA is intended to be used with upper primary students who have learnt or are learning the topics of "heat" and "cycles in water". They are also expected to be taught the skills and processes detailed in the Primary Science Syllabus (MOE, 2012, p. 9–10) in other inquiry-based activities prior to attempting this task. As this task requires a higher amount of student self-direction (MOE, 2012, p. 14), it is suitable as a culminating performance to assess scientific reasoning.

Task

Read the following scenario and the instruction for the task that follows:

Kim and her friend, Jay, were at the school canteen. It was a warm day and they went to the drink stall to buy a glass of iced lemon tea. As usual, the stall vendor filled the glass with ice cubes all the way to the rim before pouring in the lemon tea, which was at room temperature, into the glass. Kim was very thirsty and did not take long to finish her drink. Jay noticed that there were many ice cubes left in the glass. The conversation below followed:

Jay: You know, Kim, why did stall vendor put so much ice into your glass?

Kim: Well, the more ice he puts in the glass, the colder the drink gets.

Jay: Are you sure about that?

Kim: Of course! It makes sense. More ice makes a cold drink, well … colder.

Jay: I think that more ice may help the tea cool down faster. But would it really make the water colder? Look, there are so many ice cubes left in your glass.

Kim: I like my drinks cold. The lemon tea was cold enough, so I gulped it all down. I can't help it that all the ice didn't melt. Besides, if all the ice were to melt, the lemon tea might have gotten colder and colder and maybe too cold to drink.

Jay: I don't know … How low can the temperature of the iced tea go? Could the tea become colder than the ice that is in it?

Kim: Well, I think so. Or maybe not. I don't really know.

Jay: We should find out! There are a few interesting questions we should investigate.

Instructions to students:

Based on the story above, generate two possible hypotheses and design an experiment to test each hypothesis. We will be doing this task over a few science periods. From the results of both experiments and your knowledge of the concepts from the topic of heat and cycles of water, you will help Kim and Jay explain the problem they face.

You are provided with the following apparatus and materials. You do not need to use all of them in your experimental design. You may request for other apparatus when necessary.

- 1 litre of tap water.
- 50 ice cubes of similar sizes.
- 100 ml measuring cylinder.
- Laboratory thermometers.

EXAMPLE 9.1.1 Rubrics for scientific inquiry

Criteria	Unistructural	Multistructural	Relational	Extended – abstract
Hypothesis generation	Identifies some of the variables related to at least one of the problems presented in the story but is unable to distinguish between the independent, dependent and constant variables. The research questions/hypotheses do not articulate the relationship between the independent and dependent variables.	Identifies the independent and dependent variable in at least one of the problems. Does not identify all the related constant variables. The research questions/hypotheses do not articulate clearly the relationship between the independent and dependent variables.	Identifies all the variables related to at least one of the problems presented in the story and can distinguish between the independent, dependent and constant variables. Expresses clearly the relationship between the independent and dependent variables in at least one of the hypotheses.	Identifies all the variables related to both of the problems presented in the story and distinguishes between the independent, dependent and constant variables. Expresses clearly the relationship between the independent and dependent variables in both hypotheses.
Experimental design	Experimental design contains some procedure to be taken, but lacks details and is difficult to follow.	Designs an experiment to investigate at least one of the research questions/hypotheses but has missing details (e.g., did not state how constant variables will be controlled in the procedures, or how independent variable is varied, how dependent variable is measured).	Experimental designs are comprehensive, easy to follow and appropriate to address at least one of the research questions/hypotheses, taking into account the following: • Describing independent and dependent variables in measurable terms; • Describing how the independent variable will be varied;	Experimental designs are comprehensive, easy to follow and appropriate to address both research questions/hypotheses, taking into account the following: • Describing independent and dependent variables in measurable terms; • Describing how the independent variable will be varied;

Communication of scientific data	Writes down some relevant information (e.g., findings) on the experiment but not in an organised manner.	Records relevant information using correct scientific terms and units.	• Describing how variables (other than independent variable) that will affect the dependent variables are kept constant; • Describing how dependent variable is measured using suitable apparatus. Presents findings in an organized manner using tables (with correct scientific terms and units). Uses graphical representations for data.	• Describing how variables (other than independent variable) that will affect the dependent variables are kept constant; • Describing how dependent variable is measured using suitable apparatus. Presents findings in an organized manner using tables (with correct scientific terms and units). Transforms data into effective graphical representations, which may include use of groups of colours for visual association, size to represent quantity etc.
Evaluation of experimental design	Some attempt to identify the flaws in the experimental design. Does not describe how the design can be further improved.	Some attempt to identify the flaws in the experimental design. Describes how the design can be further improved in a blow-by-blow manner without understanding how the improvements may have implications to one another.	Identifies the flaws in the experimental design and describes how the design can be further improved, so that one improvement can have a positive implication on another.	Identifies the flaws in the experimental design and points out how the data collection is affected. Describes how the design can be further improved, and how these improvements may have positive implications on similar experimental designs.

(continued)

EXAMPLE 9.1 (Continued)

Criteria	Unistructural	Multistructural	Relational	Extended – abstract
Drawing inferences and conclusions	States some facts related to the topic of heat but does not make any connection to the experimental data. States the trend of data collected as the conclusion of the experiment.	Describes the concepts related to heat transfer but does not use them to explain the experimental data. States the trend of data collected as the conclusion of the experiment.	Applies scientific concepts to explain the results of individual experiment and draws an appropriate conclusion for each experiment.	Applies scientific concepts to explain the results of the experiments and draws appropriate conclusions from both experiments to reach a complete understanding of the given problem.

- Glass beakers.
- Styrofoam cups.
- Stop watches.
- Electronic balance.

To help you in your task, your teacher will be giving you feedback on *one* of your experimental designs. Using the feedback, you will refine your design *before* you test it out in the laboratory.

For your second experiment, you will be on your own. You get to test out your design in the laboratory. It is okay if the design fails! As with all experimental designs, there will be flaws. You need to figure out what the flaw(s) are, how they affect your experiment and reflect how the design can be further improved. You will get a chance to test out your improvised design after that. See the rubrics in Example 9.1.1.

Example 9.2

Subject: Physics
Focus: Properties of sound waves
Contributed by Tan Boon Haur
Target group: 16-year-olds (Secondary 4)

Students' prior knowledge

Students have completed the chapter on general wave properties and know about the relationship between frequency, speed and amplitude. This lesson unit follows up from the introductory lesson on sound waves where students learned about the mechanical model of a sound wave and its transmission.

Relevant standards
Process skills

- Design and carry out an experiment to study the characteristics of a phenomena.
- Analyse experimental data to develop a scientific explanation.
- Justify the findings.

Concept and knowledge

- Identify and apply concept of waves motion to describe the properties of sound.
- Recognise and relate pitch of sound wave to frequency.
- Recognise and relate loudness of sound wave to amplitude.
- Recognise and relate waveform to the quality of sound.

Context

The call to make science learning relevant and meaningful to students is not unique to Singapore. The United Nations Educational, Scientific and Cultural Organization reiterated recently on the importance of basic science and mathematics education for the improvement of the human condition and world development (UNESCO, 2010). But unfortunately, students lose interest in science because they consider school science to be disconnected from their own lives.

In the Science Curriculum Framework crafted by Singapore's Ministry of Education Curriculum Planning and Development Division (MOE CPDD), the importance of a connection between science learning and the life of the student is underlined thus:

The [science] curriculum design seeks to enable students to view the pursuit of science as meaningful and useful. Inquiry is thus grounded in knowledge, issues and questions that relate to the roles played by science in daily life, society and the environment (MOE CPDD, 2013, p. 1).

Engaging students with science-related issues they might encounter in real life, now or in the future, requires understanding of authentic pedagogies and assessment approaches.

The background and the design of the following task are guided by these considerations of how real scientists "do science". The process skills and learning objectives emphasise the value of the lesson unit beyond classroom. Beyond acquiring factual understanding of sound waves, students learn to develop the disposition, processes and skills to problematise a situation that they may encounter in daily life to plan and conduct an informed investigation. The task scenario reinforces this aspect of authenticity by situating the subject of the inquiry in a familiar daily life situation.

Task

The students play the role of novice music students. In their music lessons, they are exposed to different kinds of musical instruments and music theory. However, the music instructor made frequent references to the quality of the sound produced by different instruments. As novice music students, while they can hear the difference, they may not comprehend the physics behind these differences. Hence the students are tasked to examine the nature of the sound produced by various musical instruments. See lesson in Example 9.2.1 and rubric shown in Example 9.2.2.

Reflection question

Note the different domains of scientific inquiry in this task and the previous. What advantages would each domain offer to the target learners?

EXAMPLE 9.2.1 Lesson

Lesson/Duration	Task design and activity

Lesson/Duration Task design and activity

Lesson 1 (2 h)
- Teacher clarifies lesson objectives, task requirements and assessment criteria.
- Teacher provides students with an online project management template to facilitate students' management of the inquiry work.
- Students discuss preliminary plan and work in groups of two to design their experiment, consulting their peers or the teacher where necessary. The deliverables at this stage include: (1) Statement of the inquiry question, (2) Plan for the conduct of the inquiry, including how data would be collected and they might be used.
- Teacher gives online feedback to students within one week.
- Teacher works with students to assemble the necessary instruments and sound recording tools.

Lesson 2 (2 h)
- (Two weeks after lesson 1) Students carry out experiments in groups of two and documents necessary work online. The deliverables at this stage include: (1) Procedure of data collection, (2) Representation of data collected.
- Teacher monitors each group online as well as in person to facilitate their inquiry.

Lesson 3 (2 h)
- Students analyse data and develop findings, consulting their peers or the teacher where necessary. The deliverables at this stage include: (1) Analysis of the data, informed by external information sources, (2) Develop and explain findings.
- Teacher will guide students to use prior knowledge of properties of waves to develop their explanations.
- Teacher monitors each group online★ as well as in person to facilitate their inquiry.

Lesson 4 (2 h)
- Students showcase their findings online. Each group will then evaluate 3 other groups using the rubric. The deliverables at this stage include:

  i. Respond to the peer-critique.
  ii. Make modifications, if necessary, to experimental design or analysis based on feedback.

- Teacher assesses the students' work and gives feedback within one week.

Lesson 5 (1 h)
- (1 week after lesson 4) Teacher discusses the learning with students.

★*Comment: Good meaningful use of ICT to facilitate and record peer feedback.*

EXAMPLE 9.2.2 Rubrics for scientific inquiry.

Criterion	Levels of understanding			
	Beginning	*Emerging*	*Developing*	*Competent*
Questions	Simple 5W1H query of what is observed, e.g., Why does a violin sound different from a guitar?	Queries the observed phenomena in relation to one or two isolated concepts, e.g., In what ways does the difference between the sounds of a violin and a guitar have to do with its frequency?	Queries the observed phenomena in relation to inter-related concepts, e.g., In what ways does the difference between the sounds of a violin and a guitar have to do with the wave equation?	Queries the observed phenomena in relation to a big idea, e.g., In what ways does the difference between the sounds of a violin and a guitar have to do with the conservation of energy?
Evidence	Uses a specified method of data collection independent of the context of the inquiry strategy.	Uses a specified method of data collection, with one or two modifications due to the context of the inquiry strategy.	Identifies and uses a known method of data collection.	Identifies and uses a known method of data collection, with modifications due to the context of the inquiry strategy.
Explanations and connections	Explanation is based solely on analysis of data.	Explanations show synthesis and analysis of data with one or two isolated concepts.	Explanations show synthesis and analysis of data with inter-related concepts.	Explanations show synthesis and analysis of data with a big idea.
Communication	States the explanation.	Logical arguments are constructed from one or two isolated concepts to justify the explanations.	Logical arguments are constructed from inter-related concepts to justify the explanations.	Logical arguments are constructed from the perspective of a big idea to justify the explanations.

Reflection question

Compare this rubric (Example 9.2.2) with Example 9.1.1 rubrics. Which do you prefer and why?

Example 9.3

Subject: Chemistry
Focus: Acids
Contributed by Charlene Seah
Target group: 13–14-year-olds (Secondary 1–2)

Relevant standards

- Pose questions.
- Determine evidence to collect.
- Formulate explanations.
- Connect explanations to scientific knowledge.
- Communicate and justify explanations.

Context

The term "literacy" is typically used to refer to the ability to read and write. Upon extension to other fields such as "scientific literacy", the term "literacy" is not intended to be descriptive but connotes an evaluation of knowledge mastery (Laugksch, 2000). Varying interpretations of the term "literacy" then give rise to different conceptions of the kind of knowledge that is deemed important in science. Three broad interpretations of "scientific literacy" may refer to someone who (1) is learned in the science; (2) competent in science, translated as possessing an intermediate level of ability to an adequate level of degree or quality; or (3) the most basic level of knowledge and skills needed for emancipation in society as citizens or consumers.

Amid such diverse views, Jon Miller's (1983) multi-dimensional conception emerged as a seminal consolidation of what "scientific literacy" entails. Miller conceived his definition upon a conceptual and empirical review of how the meaning of "scientific literacy" had evolved through the centuries. On the basis of his review and an extant society that is permeated by science and technology, Miller argues that "scientific literacy" is important for citizens to make informed decisions regarding science-related policies in a democratic society. As such, Miller's definition comprises three dimensions: (1) understanding the nature of science; (2) understanding key scientific terms and concepts; and (3) awareness and understanding of the impact of science and technology.

Major science education curricular reforms have also been influenced by the definition of "scientific literacy" that arises from the *Science for All Americans*, a product of Project 2061 undertaken by the American Association for the Advancement of Science (AAAS, 1993). In addition to scientific literacy for basic citizenry as Miller (1983) advocates, AAAS believes that the scientific knowledge of the general population is also important for the socio-economic development of the nation. Such a conception of scientific literacy implies a requirement of competence in science, beyond the minimum level. AAA's definition of "scientific literacy" then comprises

(1) a broad scope of content not limited to traditional science disciplines but also extending into related disciplines such as mathematics, technology and the social sciences; (2) understanding of the scientific endeavour, instantiated by the understanding of the scientific inquiry, the nature of such an enterprise, the relationship between science and technology and the relationship between science and society; and (3) the ways of thinking, the values and attitudes that are inherent in science.

AAA's (1989) conception of scientific literacy is closely mirrored by the OECD's (2013) definition for Programme for International Student Assessment (PISA) 2015. By viewing students as "consumers of science" rather than the "producers of science", PISA focuses on assessing process rather than the product. PISA's (2013) definition of scientific literacy consists of scientific concepts and ideas (content knowledge); plans and procedures employed in scientific inquiry (procedural knowledge) and ways in which scientific ideas are supported and legitimised (epistemic knowledge) (OECD, 2013). PISA (2013) elaborated that a scientific literate person would be able to "fulfil an enlightened role in making choices which affect their environment and to understand in broad terms the social implications of debates between experts". Such a situation of conflicting information is one that is commonly encountered in real-life, even by a lower-secondary student.

It may be discerned that more current definitions of scientific literacy include both (2) and (3) of Laugksh's categories, that is, encompassing both "basic competency" and "for citizenry and as a consumer". Therefore, in addition to Miller's constructs of epistemic knowledge, content knowledge, an awareness of the relationship between science and society, procedural knowledge as well as a scientific disposition manifested in thoughts and values are also encompassed within current definitions of scientific literacy. Although the multi-dimensional nature of scientific literacy has been widely recognized, dimensions of scientific literacy are still predominantly assessed as discrete entities (Laugksch, 2000). Apart from surveys and test items which PISA adopts, there appears to be few instruments available to measure scientific literacy, especially in an integrated manner (Laugksch, 2000).

Reflection question

Compare the context here with that in Example 9.4, both in terms of age group and how novice/advanced they are in science learning.

The AA task that follows is designed for Lower Secondary E/N(A) (LSS E/N(A)) students studying in the mainstream secondary schools in Singapore. Students at this level are still getting to know what science is and there is greater curricular space for exploration than preparing for imminent national exams. Therefore, Newmann and Archbald's (1992) definition of authenticity is favoured for my AA task because I wanted to foreground the use of assessment for authentic learning, placing greater emphasis on the achievement of scientific literacy to inform further teaching and learning, rather than for measuring attainment for placement. Although Newmann and Archbald (1992) did not specifically address the role of context in assessment task, my assessment task has taken that into account, Gulikers et al. (2004) and Wiggins' (1998) proposal to make available resources such as information and time to students which are typically accessible in real life. The task may be given to them as early as required so that students can be acquainted with the task before it is used in class, if they so wish to. That said, there are limits to the resemblance of the task to real life and this is due to the boundary and less open-ended nature of a classroom task which is to be expected and is unavoidable (Cumming, 1999). Indeed, as my target is the LSS students, it is important that my task should avoid the full complexity of real life so as not to render the learner helpless in his response to the task.

Task

(a) Students will be introduced to two conflicting sources regarding the acid-ity of the rainwater in Singapore. (http://newshub.nus.edu.sg/news/0909/PDF/ACIDRAIN-st-14Sep-pB1.pdf)

One view presented:

Acid rain may be wiping Singapore's native species to extinction.

The 20 species of animals plentiful in the Singapore's Bukit Timah Nature Reserve in the 1980s, including frogs, crabs and fish are slowly being wiped out.

This may be due to the acidity of a stream in the 80 hectare nature reserve, which offers great biodiversity in plant and animal life.

The stream, which covers 5 hectares of land, is more acidic after torrential rain. The water in the stream on the nature reserve has a pH value of 4.4 to 4.7, which is said to be more acidic now that it was 20 years ago.[1]

   • National University of Singapore (NUS) study led by Associate Professor David Higgitt

Other view presented:

"The acidity of rain water here, at pH 5, is no different from that of urban cities around the world. Rain water is no more acidic now than in the 1990s."

(b) Students will collaborate with students from other schools across the country to measure acidity of rainwater from Singapore. This enables them to synthe-size their own point of view concerning the conflicting information.

(c) They will discuss, as an online community, their approaches to determining the acidity of water in Singapore and how it may or may not affect Biodiversity in Singapore. The discussion may include issues such as what data to collect, how much data, analysis of the data and implications of the data in relation to the articles. The teacher will encourage learners to substantiate their online responses with rationale and evidence. Learners in the community will also be encouraged to critique, clarify and build on one another's responses.

(d) Assistance and resources will be made available to students to an extent that is rea-sonable within the means of the teacher and the school. In addition, the teacher will need to guide students on how to use the online platforms, including facilitat-ing students to co-establish common understanding of the rules of engagement.

(e) Students' learning will be captured through journals for individual reflection and online-databases and forums. They will also consider how their decisions may be linked to broader social issues, such as conservation of biodiversity or air pollution which causes acid rain. They will also reflect upon how they may exercise agency, based on their knowledge, in addressing some of these issues. The rubric is shown in Example 9.3.1.

EXAMPLE 9.3.1 Rubrics

	Exceeding standard	Meeting standard	Approaching standard	Beginning standard	Not meeting standard
Nature of science	Thoughtful understanding of the nature of Science, showing strong links between the integrated dimensions of the nature of Science and situations in daily life.	Clear understanding of the nature of Science, with coherent consideration of how its multiple dimensions are integrated to reflect the norms and methods of science.	Superficial understanding of the norms and methods of Science with attempts to relate a few dimensions of the nature of Science without effective integration.	Incomplete understanding of the norms and methods of Science with consideration of one or a few dimensions of the nature of Science in isolation of one another.	Poor understanding of the norms and methods of Science with inappropriate or no dimension(s) listed.
Scientific concept	Deep understanding of the science topic with correct reference to and effective integration of all related key concepts and applies this understanding to a new context.	Coherent understanding of the science topic articulated by correct reference made to and effective integration of all key concepts.	Vague understanding of the science topic with correct reference made to key concepts but lack integration.	Vague understanding of the science topic with correct reference made to only one or a few unrelated key concepts.	No understanding of the science topic with attempt or inappropriate reference to any key concepts.
Process of inquiry	Strong grasp of the process of scientific inquiry with critical understanding of the strengths and limitations of the steps taken in the process.	Good grasp of the process of scientific inquiry with an awareness of how the steps interrelate and contribute to the aim of the inquiry but without criticality.	Rudimentary grasp of the process of scientific inquiry with adherence to procedures with correct understanding of the rationale behind each step but unable to integrate the different steps.	Emerging grasp of the process of scientific inquiry with adherence to stated procedures but without understanding of rationale.	Lacking in attempts at the inquiry process or does not follow the procedures.

Example 9.4

Subject: Chemistry
Contributed by Darshini d/o Radha Krishnan
Focus: Qualitative analysis
Target group: 17-year-olds (Pre-university 1)

Relevant Standards

- understanding scientific concepts;
- correct application of scientific concepts;
- reason scientifically;
- use science to take position on scientific issues.

Context

This AA has been designed for Year-5 students of the Integrated Programme who have enrolled in chemistry as a subject to be pursued in their pre-university course. These students have undergone integrated science lessons in their first four years and have had the opportunity to engage in science research in Year 3 where they pursued a group research project.

The construct pursued through this assessment is scientific literacy. Scientific literacy is a big idea which is approached slightly differently by different people. For the purpose of this paper, I refer to the OECD PISA framework that defines scientific literacy as "the ability to engage with science-related issues, and the ideas of science, as a reflective citizen" (OECD, 2017, p. 1). The three underlying competencies displayed by a scientifically literate individual would then be the ability to "explain phenomena scientifically", "evaluate and design scientific inquiry" and "interpret data and evidence scientifically" (p. 2). The assessment hence targets the acquiring of seven scientific inquiry skills that allow for the attainment of the three competencies suggested above. Descriptive skills, conceptualisation skills, problem-solving skills, communication skills, collaborative skills, self-assessment skills and scientific attitudes and values are the skills that will be targets for development through this task.

The context of the assessment is set such that the student assumes the role of a water analyst tasked to propose to the Singapore government the suitability of one of its water catchment areas for the breeding of Koi, a freshwater fish. The subject matter that undergirds this assessment is qualitative analysis. The two-month long project is multi-layered, complex and consists of multiple tasks, characteristic of authentic tasks (Janesick, 2006). Students in this assessment contribute to their own learning through active engagement (Hargreaves, Earl & Schmidt, 2002).

The project is separated into three phases: The research, experimentation and presentation phases. Each phase targets particular scientific inquiry skills to be developed, as well as being designed such that the task allows for the highest potential of acquiring the intended skill. This assessment aims to develop higher-order thinking processes and competencies rather than lower-order processes such as rote recall. This is a characteristic benefit of AA (Cumming & Maxwell, 1999; Gulikers, Bastiaens & Kirschner, 2004; Janesick, 2006).

Instructions to students

Singapore is known as the "Ornamental Fish Capital of the World", being the top exporter of ornamental fish worldwide. The term "Ornamental Fish" is used to describe coloured fish that are bred and kept in captivity for the purpose of decoration. One of the most sought after ornamental fish in Asia is the Koi that symbolises good luck and fortune. To expand this ornamental fish business in Singapore which has a land scarcity, the government has decided to convert one of its water catchment areas into a Koi fish farm.

As a water analyst, you have been called in to analyse the suitability of the water in one of the water catchment areas for the breeding of the Koi fish.

There will be three phases involved in this project as follows:

Phase 1 – Research (individual work + group discussion)

You are required to research the conditions required for the successful breeding of freshwater fish. Following which, you will need to gather information on how the reservoir water could be tested for these conditions. Finally, you should come up with a plan for the testing of the water with suitable chemical/physical tests.

Phase 2 – Experimentation (individual work)

You are required to carry out your plan from phase 1 and to record your findings in a research logbook.

Phase 3 – Presentation (individual work)

You are required to present your findings from phases 1 and 2 in a written report. There will also be a 20 minute oral presentation to communicate your findings with the authorities.

Rubrics for assessment

Four different rubrics have been developed for this assessment; the first to assess the experimentation plan, the second to assess the logbook, the third to assess the written report and last to assess the oral presentation (see Example 9.4.1 for the rubrics for the first of the three rubrics on the following pages). In creating these rubrics, particular attention has been paid to ensure that it is construct-centred rather than task-centred and hence there is a substantial amount of generalizability (Messick, 1994). However, care has also been taken to ensure the rubrics are not excessively general rendering them useless (Popham, 1997). The rubrics contain between three to five evaluative criteria and are also short and make explicit the standards pursued in simple terms to allow students to understand them as well as well as to ensure that they appeal to teachers for usage (Popham, 1997). A written feedback section is included for the teacher to provide students with formative feedback targeted at allowing them to learn and improve. A section for reflection is also included for students to articulate and pen down their thoughts at the end of each phase, allowing the teacher to gain an inside view of their learning. The rubrics are presented to the students together with the task in order to make transparent the targets to be achieved so as to ensure that students are able to work towards achieving the goals of the assessment (Hargreaves, Earl & Schmidt, 2002; Wiggins, 1993) as well as to reduce their anxiety towards the assessment (Andrade & Du, 2005).

Again, compare the choice of these criteria used in Example 9.4.1 rubrics with those used in Example 9.3 rubrics. How are they the same or different and why?

Evaluation of the authentic task

Beyond ensuring validity of assessment results, the AA designer can also judge its merit against programme evaluation models such as the one by Stufflebeam (2001) which uses four criteria: feasibility, utility, accuracy and propriety, as the designer of Example 9.4 illustrates below.

Feasibility

Having had prior knowledge and experience in research, students should be able to handle the task with relative ease. The school is also in the process of building its research incubator and students will have access to iPad for their research within class as well. The collaborative and continuous feedback will also serve as a good scaffold for them. This coupled with the generous time of two months results in high feasibility of the task.

However, sufficient funds need to be allocated for the purchase of water testing kits and equipment that are not available in the laboratory. Safety is also a concern as the task involves on site tests as well as water collection. A protocol to ensure safe practice has to be implemented which involves the supervision of the teacher.

The assessment is also extremely time-consuming for the teacher and students alike and hence there might be resistance from these stakeholders in implementation. Hence, they have to be convinced of the vast skills that students are able to acquire through this task.

Utility

This task boasts high utility as it targets the big concept of science literacy rather than specific topics. The framework of this research task can be used in the pursuit of knowledge in other science topics as well. Furthermore, as is evident, the skills pursued in this task are not subject specific and hence the benefits of acquiring them are not limited to excelling in science alone, but improve the skill set of

EXAMPLE 9.4.1 Rubrics

Research phase

Criteria	Exceeding expectation 5 marks	Meeting expectation 3–4 marks	Approaching expectation 1–2 marks
Literature review	Strong evidence of having used reliable sources of information with a substantial number of sources used.	Evidence of having used reliable sources of information with a minimum of 5 resources used.	Evidence of having used insufficient and mostly unreliable resources.
Research findings • identification of conditions • identification of tests.	A substantial number of conditions have been accurately identified with appropriate tests for measurement.	At least five conditions have been accurately identified with mostly appropriate tests for measurement.	Five conditions identified are mostly accurate with mostly appropriate tests for measurement.
Experimentation plan	Procedure is detailed, appropriate and thorough. Steps of procedure are listed and sequential. All materials are listed.	Procedure is appropriate. Steps of procedure are mostly listed. Most materials are listed.	Procedure is inadequate. A few steps of the procedure are listed. No materials are listed.
Safety consideration	Safety issues have been addressed thoroughly.	Safety issues addressed are not complete.	Safety issues were not addressed.

Experimentation Phase

Criteria	Exceeding expectation 5 marks	Meeting expectation 3–4 marks	Approaching expectation 1–2 marks
Organisation of log book	All experiments are logged with all required sections present.	All experiments are logged but not all sections are present.	Not all experiments are logged.
Data Collection	Data was collected and recorded in a manner that accurately reflects the results of the experiment.	Data was collected and recorded in a manner showing incomplete representation of results.	Data was collected and recorded in a manner showing inaccurate representation of results.
Analysis	Thorough analysis resulting in conclusions that are accurate and supported by the data collected.	Analysis results in conclusions that are mostly accurate and supported by the data collected.	Inadequate analysis resulting in conclusions that are inaccurate and sometimes not supported by data collected.
Manipulative skills (based on checklist marking)	80–100% of the items on the checklist were achieved with particular attention paid to safety.	60–80% of items on the checklist were achieved with particular attention paid to safety.	Less than 60% of items on the checklist were achieved with insufficient attention paid to safety.

Presentation phase – research report

Criteria	*Exceeding expectation 5 marks*	*Meeting expectation 3–4 marks*	*Approaching expectation 1–2 marks*
Introduction	The introduction states the main topic and gives a good description of how the report is organised.	The introduction states the main topic and gives a description of how the report is organised.	The introduction states the main topic but does not adequately describe how the report is organised.
Organization	Report is organised such that there is a logical sequence of ideas with well-developed paragraphs.	Sequence of ideas is mostly logical with well-developed paragraphs.	Paragraphs are not adequately developed.
Conclusion	The conclusion restates the findings of the research strongly.	The conclusion restates the findings of the research.	The conclusion does not adequately restate the findings.
Language	Report is written well with the ability to communicate ideas and free of grammatical errors.	Report is written with the ability to communicate ideas and mostly free of grammatical errors.	Report mostly does not communicate ideas well and not free of grammatical errors.
Presentation APA Style	Format of report is according to the APA style with no errors.	Format of report is according to the APA style with little error.	APA style is not adequately followed in writing the report.

individuals due to its high transferability to other areas, a big benefit of this task. Equipped with the skills for inquiry, this task serves as a platform with the potential of propelling students to be self-directed learners as they gain the confidence to construct knowledge through research.

Accuracy

Each task in this assessment has been crafted in a way to ensure the skills pursued are indeed developed and assessed. The context where students assume the role of a water analyst is developed appropriately by allowing students to see the complexity that scientists face as well as the type of social interactions of science practice (Edelson, 1997). Hence there is a high level of alignment of the task to the intended outcome of science literacy. The contextualisation of the learning and assessment has also ensured validity (Cumming & Maxwell, 1999). In short, developmental care has been taken to ensure the relevance and accuracy of the assessment (Popham, 2010).

Propriety

The behavioural outcomes that are expected of students in this task are fitting, reasonable and within the capabilities of the students. These outcomes are clear indicators of science literacy and hence are appropriate for the judgement of students' performance.

Summary

The examples in this chapter show that with careful planning, AA is suitable for learners of different ages (12-year-olds in Example 9.1 to 16-year-olds in Example 9.4). As research shows (see Chapter 2), AA can benefit learners of various age groups and even those who typically score low on traditional, standardized assessment.

So, the question is why is AA not adopted more prevalently. It could be due to a variety of reasons (see summary in Chapter 2) but another reason not raised so far could be that AA is perceived as more taxing on teachers' time and attention. Hence, one can appreciate that teachers would need to balance feasibility, utility, accuracy and propriety (Stufflebeam, 2001) in the design of AA.

Note

1 Adapted from "Native species in Singapore may be wiped out by acid rain", by Amresh Gunasingham, 14 Sept 2009, Straits Times.

References

American Association for the Advancement of Science (AAAS). (1993). *Benchmarks for Science Literacy*. New York, NY: Oxford University Press. Also available at http://www.project2061.org/publications/bsl/online/index.php.

Andrade, H., & Du, Y. (2005). Student perspectives on rubric-referenced assessment. *Practical Assessment, Research & Evaluation, 10*(3), 1–11.

Bourdieu, P. (1986). Forms of capital. In I. Szeman & T. Kaposy (Eds.), Cultural Theory: An Anthology (pp. 81–93). Malden, MA: John Wiley & Sons.

Cumming, J. J., & Maxwell, G. S. (1999). Contextualising authentic assessment. *Assessment in Education: Principles, Policy and Practice, 6*(2), 177–194.

Edelson, D. C. (1997). Realizing authentic science learning through the adaptation of science practice. In B. J. Fraser & K. G. Tobin (Eds.), *International Handbook of Science Education* (pp. 317–31). Dordrecht, Netherlands: Kluwer.

Gulikers, J., Bastiaens, T., & Kirschner, P. (2004). A five-dimensional framework for authentic assessment. *Educational Technology, Research and Development, 52*(3), 67–87.

Hargreaves, A., Earl, L., & Schmidt, M. (2002). Perspectives on alternative assessment reform. *American Educational Research Journal, 39*(1), 69–95.

Janesick, V. J. (2006). *Authentic Assessment Primer.* New York: Peter Lang.

Laugksch, R. C. (2000). Scientific literacy: A conceptual overview. *Science Education, 84*(1), 71–94.

Messick, S. (1994). The interplay of evidence and consequences in the validation of performance assessment. *Educational Researcher, 23*(2), 13–23.

Miller, J. D. (1983). *Scientific literacy: A conceptual and empirical review. Daedalus, 112*(2), 29–48.

Ministry of Education Curriculum Planning and Development Division (MOE CPDD). (2013). *Science Syllabus Lower Secondary Express/Normal (Academic).* Retrieved 5 November 2011 from http://subjects.opal.moe.edu.sg/sciences/secondary/lower-secondary-science-e-n-a/syllabus.

MOE. (2016). Biology Syllabus: Pre-University. Retrieved 12 June 2017, from https://www.moe.gov.sg/docs/default-source/document/education/syllabuses/sciences/files/pre-university-h2-biology---2016.pdf.

MOE. (2013). Science syllabus: Primary. Retrieved on 7 June 2017, from https://www.moe.gov.sg/docs/default-source/document/education/syllabuses/sciences/files/science-primary-2014.pdf.

Newmann, F. M. & Archbald, D. A. (1992) The nature of authentic academic achievement. In H. Berlak, F. M. Newmann, E. Adams, D. A. Archbald, T. Burgess, J. Raven, & T. A. Romberg (Eds.), *Toward a New Science of Educational Testing and Assessment.* New York: State University of New York Press.

OECD. (2017). Pisa for Development Brief 10. Retrieved 16 June 2017, from https://www.oecd.org/pisa/pisa-for-development/10-How-PISA-D-measures-science-literacy.pdf.

OECD. (2013). PISA 2015 Draft Science Framework. Retrieved 16 June 2017, from https://www.oecd.org/pisa/pisaproducts/Draft%20PISA%202015%20Science%20Framework%20.pdf.

Popham, W. (1997). What's wrong – and what's right – with rubrics. *Educational Leadership, 55*(2), 1–7.

Popham, W. J. (2010). *Everything School Leaders Need to Know about Assessment.* California: SAGE.

Stufflebeam, D. (2001). Evaluation models. *New Directions for Evaluation, 89,* 7–98.

Tay, H. Y. (2014). Authentic assessment. In W. S. Leong, Y. S. Cheng, & K., Tan (Eds.), *Assessment and Learning in Schools.* Pearson: Singapore.

Tay, H. Y. (2015). Setting formative assessments in real-world contexts to facilitate self-regulated learning. *Educational Research for Policy and Practice, 14*(2), 169–187. DOI:10.1007/s10671-015-9172-5.

United Nations Educational, Scientific and Cultural Organization (UNESCO). (2010). *Current Challenges in Basic Science Education.* Retrieved 5 November 2011, from http:// unesdoc.unesco.org/images/0019/001914/191425e.

Wiggins, G. (1993). Authenticity, context, and validity. *The Phi Delta Kappan, 75*(3), 200–208, 210–214. Retrieved 9 April 2016 from cwtc.marinschools.org/Meetings/2011-10-07/ Assessment.pdf.

Wiggins, G. P. (1998). *Educative Assessment: Designing Assessments to Inform and Improve Student Performance.* San Francisco: Jossey-Bass Publishers.

10

AUTHENTIC ASSESSMENTS IN CHARACTER AND CITIZENSHIP

Introduction

There are currently some instruments that have been designed for measuring non-cognitive qualities such as aspects of character. For example, there are a number of instruments available for resilience. However, as concluded by Windle, Bennet and Noyes (2011) who reviewed a number of them, the conceptual and theoretical adequacy of a number of the scales is questionable. In any case, what respondents sometimes report may not cohere with what they actually do (Patrick & Middleton, 2002; Schunk, 2008; Turner, 2006). Also, in asking respondents to average across situations, surveys overlook important contextual factors that summon or constrain these qualities.

Some researchers have devised ways to overcome the inadequacies of self-report questionnaires. For example, to measure self-regulation, Zimmerman (2008) uses an event measure called microanalysis which uses a structured interview approach to capture the subtle changes in the learner's self-regulatory processes and motivational beliefs. At key points before, during and after learning, the learner is asked open- or closed-ended questions that produce both qualitative and quantitative data respectively. Others leverage technology. For example, to measure self-regulation, Perry and Winne (2006) designed a computer software, gStudy, to unobtrusively track how learners search for online information or draft their answers to get a better understanding of their use of self-regulated learning in real time. Innovative as this sounds, gStudy is not without detractors who question the validity of the results (Nolen, 2006).

Perhaps, as with 21st-century competencies (see Chapter 5), non-cognitive qualities are best assessed by teachers using real-life contexts that give ample opportunities for learners to manifest these qualities meaningfully. This chapter shows such

TABLE 10.1 Summary of the AA presented in this chapter

Example	Levels	Focus	Context
10.1	Primary	Responsibility and appreciation.	Orientation buddy programme.
10.2	Lower Secondary	Charity and volunteerism.	Madrasah (a school for Islamic education).
10.3	Secondary	Resilience.	My character quest.

examples. Although the tasks were designed for a particular group (see Table 10.1), they can be easily adapted for other age groups and contexts.

Context

Character and citizenship education (CCE) is literally at the heart of Singapore's education system. It features prominently in the centre of the national framework for "21st century competencies" (21CC) and student outcomes (MOE, 2017). It is argued that values shape the beliefs, attitudes and actions of a person. Expanding outwards from the character are desired social and emotional competencies[1]; and the emerging 21st century competencies.[2]

The CCE programme in Singapore aims to develop students of good character who are responsible to family and community through developing certain core values identified as respect, responsibility, resilience, integrity, care and harmony. The approach is based on a belief in active learning. As such, students play an important role in the assessment, often involving authentic tasks. They set their own goals, make decisions and monitor their own progress. The assessment criteria communicated to the students guide them in judging their own and their peers' work. Timely and comprehensive feedback by teachers is also encouraged.

Example 10.1

Focus: Responsibility and appreciation
Contributed by Ivy Ho
Target group: 11-year-olds (Primary 5)

Relevant standards

- Shows self-awareness and applies self-management skills to achieve personal wellbeing and effectiveness.
- Acts with integrity and makes responsible decisions that uphold moral principles.
- Acquires social awareness and applies interpersonal skills to build and maintain positive relationships based on mutual respect.
- Cares for others and contributes actively to the progress of our community.

Context

According to the Ministry of Education (MOE's) guideline, "CCE inculcates values and builds competencies to develop students into good individuals and useful citizens". So, what does being a "good" individual mean? Ryan and Bohlin (1999) stated that good character is about "knowing the good, loving the good and doing the good". "Knowing the good" refers to having the knowledge of knowing what is good and applies wisdom to make a right choice; "loving the good" means developing moral feelings and empathy, and having a contempt of what is wrong; "doing the good" involves the will to act and do what is right. In a similar vein, Lickona (1991) conceptualises good character as having the moral knowledge, moral feeling and moral action. In short, it is pertinent to consider these three aspects in the design of a quality CCE assessment to ensure construct validity and reduce construct irrelevance (Messick, 1994).

The context of learning and assessment in CCE often involves the use of real-world dilemmas, which prompt critical thinking, reflections, moral reasoning, and other higher-order skills to develop and justify their perspective and judgement (Wiggins, 1993). Besides the cognitive aspect, CCE also emphasizes the personal and social development of the students where the real audience involved in the authentic assessment (AA) serves as a good platform for the students to engage in social interactions.

Another strong argument for AA is that it offers opportunities to include other methods of assessing affective targets in the classroom: teacher observation, student self-report and peer ratings (McMillan, 2001). The open-ended assessment nature of CCE allows students to clarify, synthesize, reflect and develop their understanding in CCE. In contrast, decontextualized close-ended assessment involving regurgitation of the "morally" right response does not validly indicate students' character development.

In the task described in the following section, the Primary 1 (P1) orientation buddy system is used as the context of AA task. At the beginning of school term, each Primary 5 (P5) student is assigned to a P1 student to guide and assimilate him to the school environment. Leveraging the real context to authenticate both the P1 and P5 students' learning experience seems opportune as the natural platform sets the stage to cultivate responsibility and accountability for P5 students. In addition, it serves to help P1 students to develop a better understanding of appreciation. The target character traits and corresponding behaviour are explicated in Table 10.2 and a rubric is shown in Example 10.1.1.

Task

The objective of the task is to guide a primary one junior to adapt to the new school environment and increase his readiness for school. The orientation programme for the primary one junior will be carried out for the entire Term 1.

As a senior in school, you have the responsibility to role model school values and rules and show care and concern to other members in school. Through the task, you will have the opportunity to understand your role as a member of the school community better and practice the values and skills taught in class.

You may also refer to the guiding principles of a senior for more details on your role and responsibilities. Should you have any doubts, you can always clarify with your teacher.

Reflection

You are required to reflect on your experience (e.g., difficulties, challenges, concerns, learning, anecdotes) and record it on the journal on a weekly basis. This will help you to chart your progress with the P1 junior and record your learning as well.

At the end of Term 1, you will need to submit a reflection paper to conclude your learning from the guiding experience.

The reflection paper is framed by the three aspects of learning, namely (1) knowing the good, (2) loving the good and (3) doing the good. A detailed scoring rubric based on the above criteria is appended for your reference. Each criterion carries the same weighting. The sharing by the previous batch of primary six students will help you to have a better idea of the standards of the rubrics.

Guiding questions

Here are some questions to guide you in writing the reflection paper.

1. What happened during the course of interaction with the junior? Did you know the issues/difficulties faced by your junior? How did you find out? How did you apply your knowledge to help him? Do you think you played an important role to the junior? Why?
2. How did you feel before embarking on this journey? How do you feel now? Why do you feel that way? How would you describe your relationship with your buddy?
3. What did you do to help your buddy to increase his readiness for school? Why did you choose to do the above? Was it useful or helpful to him? If not, did you think of other ways to help him? How often did you render help to your junior?

The list of questions is not exhaustive and you may choose to highlight other learning points in your reflection as well.

TABLE 10.2 Unpacking of criteria and corresponding behaviour

Criteria	Behaviour

Knowing the good	• Able to identify the fears/issues of P1 buddy accurately:
	  ○ unable to buy food,
	  ○ feeling lost in such a new big environment,
	  ○ unfamiliarity of the school system such as school rules, hierarchy of staff, long school hours,
	  ○ does not know how to seek help.
	• Internalises the value of responsibility through:
	  ○ guiding the P1 buddy with care and patience,
	  ○ being approachable to allay fears and provide a sense of security,
	  ○ role-modelling the values and abide by the school rules,
	  ○ being an ambassador of school to transmit the abstract beliefs and culture,
	  ○ justifying the importance of the role as a senior.

Loving the good	• Enjoys building a strong, long-term relationship with the P1. • Derives great satisfaction and joy in guiding the young and affirms one's role and responsibilities as a senior. • Exhibits positive energy and feelings in establishing good relationships with others.
Doing the good	• Considers multiple perspectives and choices before deciding what to do to help the P1 buddy. • Displays responsible decision making in their role as a senior. • Takes initiative to connect and interact with the P1 buddy. • Builds rapport with the P1 buddy through genuine concern displayed. • Reflects on action and seeks to understand the P1 buddy through multiple ways.

Quality Feedback	• Content of the card
	  ○ P1 lists many thoughtful acts by the P5 and expresses gratitude sincerely,
	  ○ Artwork or drawing that captures the different caring acts by the P5 senior.

EXAMPLE 10.1.1 Rubric

Criteria	Keep trying! (1–2 marks)	Almost there! (3–4 marks)	Good job! (5–6 marks)	Excellent job! (7–8 marks)
Knowing the good (25%)	• Follows the specifications of the guidelines to fulfil one's responsibilities. • Vague description of one's role as a senior.	• Combines the specifications of the guidelines and the results of the diagnostic survey to identify the needs of P1. • Appropriate description of one's role as a senior.	• Compares and justifies the needs of the P1 through observation and results of diagnostic survey. • Relates to the experience of one's role as a senior and offers clear explanation.	• Accurately analyses the needs of the P1 through perspective taking, observation and results of diagnostic survey. • Makes connections and meaning from knowledge of responsibility and formulates ways to guide P1 to assimilate to school environment. • Critically reflects on one's responsibility as a senior and rationalizes the importance of one's role.
Loving the good (25%)	• Identifies some personal feelings about the experience.	• Shows attempt to build rapport with the P1. • Describes personal feelings about the experience.	• Builds rapport with the P1 centred round care. • Accounts of positive feelings about the experience.	• Establishes strong rapport and a caring relationship with the P1. • Insightful account of personal feelings throughout the experience and generates positive feelings about one's role as a senior, e.g., reflects affirmation of one's role and responsibilities.
Doing the good (25%)	• Limited attempt to help the P1.	• Adheres to the guideline and demonstrates some ways to help the P1.	• Applies the knowledge learnt and demonstrates a variety of ways to help the P1.	• Exercises judgment and demonstrates a variety of thoughtful ways to care for the P1. • Takes initiative to reflect on actions consistently and thinks of ways to do better.
Quality of feedback from P1 (25%)	• Poor feedback with areas of improvement.	• Neutral feedback with little comments.	• Good feedback substantiated with comments.	• Excellent feedback with quality comments to support the care provided.

Reflection question

Because character traits can often be nebulous, it is critical to carefully unpack character traits in terms of observable knowledge, skills and attributes (refer to Chapter 3 on Messick's construct-centred approach.) Examine how the target values are unpacked here, as well in the following two examples.

Example 10.2

Focus: Charity and volunteerism
Subject: Dirasat Deeniyyah (Islamic religious knowledge)
Target group: 13-year-olds (Secondary 1, Madrasah Al-Arabiah Al-Islamiah)

Contributed by Warintek binte Ismail

Relevant standards

- Care for others and contribute actively to the progress of our community.
- Reflect on and respond to community as an informed and responsible citizen.

Context

This AA is intended for a population of 120 students from Secondary One classes. The profile of the students varies from local Singaporeans to students of different nationalities. Among the local students, there are students who came from other Madrasah and National Schools.

The AA is a service learning task that requires students to apply their learning in an authentic context. The reasons for this approach are:

1. Retention of content and avenue for deep learning. Service learning contributes to students developing interest in the subject matter; Dirasat Deeniyyah and augmented their understanding of the academic content; Charity and Volunteerism (Astin, Vogelgesang, Ikeda & Yee, 2000).
2. Service learning aids students with the application of textbook content to a real-world experience (Prentice & Robinson, 2010).
3. Making the student's thinking, learning and depth of understanding visible to the students and the teacher throughout the term of work. Given that assessment is provided to students early in a term and given that the teacher is closely monitoring a student's progress, the formative approach where the student makes their thinking and learning visible to the teacher is a powerful form of teaching (Ritchhart, Church & Morrison, 2011).
4. Service learning amplifies the students' sense of civic responsibility (Astin, Vogelgesang, Ikeda & Yee, 2000). Character development is part of the process and is a critical component in a Muslim's life.

Overview

Rahmatan Lil Alamin' (RLA) or "Mercy to All Mankind" month was launched in September 2015. All mosques in Singapore will carry out various activities ranging from tree-planting to beach cleaning, fundraising and food distribution, to spread the message of doing good to all, regardless of race, religion or background.

The service learning in the form of performance task has three components: (a) analysis of information and planning; (b) service execution; and (c) individual reflection with every part generating evidence of learning for its focus. There are guiding questions for the problem analysis and individual deep understanding in components (a) and (c). Overall, it is an example of the kind of comprehensive assessment that is broad, complex and requires higher-order thinking and ample time for learners to achieve the intended learning goals (Brookhart, 2014). teachers' facilitate and monitor every stage of the assessment tasks. Please see Table 10.3 for an explanation of contruct, knowledge and learning objectives; and Example 10.2.1 for the rubrics.

TABLE 10.3 Construct, knowledge and learning objectives

	Concept of charity	*Concept of volunteerism*
Construct	Students will understand that:	Students will understand that:
	• Charity is giving without expectation. • Charity is part of humanity. • Charity changes life.	• Volunteerism is challenging yet rewarding. • Volunteerism requires passion and perseverance.
Knowledge	Students will know:	
	• The concept of charity/volunteerism. • The benefits of charity/volunteerism. • The significance of charity/volunteerism. • The challenges in practicing charity/volunteerism. • The misconceptions of charity/volunteerism.	
Learning objectives	Students will be able to:	
	• Explain the concept of charity/volunteerism in Islam. • Discuss the significance of charity/volunteerism. • Identify the challenges in practicing charity / volunteerism. • Discuss the misconceptions of charity/volunteerism. • Appreciate the benefits of charity/volunteerism. • Address the needs of the audience or issue of the selected area. • Be motivated to participate in charity/volunteer works.	

Task

In the spirit of RLA, students will be grouped to conduct a service learning project as part of their assessment. Students can choose one from the following broad themes to perform the service learning project:

• Caring for others in the community or
• caring for the environment.

The selection of the theme should be based on students' interests. The subject of the project work should have a high impact on the target audience.

Students are expected to perform the project by completing three components. Component A: Analysis of information and planning (30%), Component B: Service execution (70%) and Component C: Individual reflection.

There are many issues, in or out of school, that the students may wish to address. However, the decision to perform a service-learning project should be based on reliable information and realistic expectations. Students need to be clear about what issues they care about and where they think they can make the greatest impact. For instance, a group of students may not be able to solve the haze problem, but may bring greater awareness of the precautions to be taken at different Pollutant Standards Index (PSI) readings.

Procedure

Students will be given the AA task and the rubrics at the beginning of the unit. They are required to brainstorm ideas on things that interest them and will be given a few days to decide on the theme. Students are then to work on the following components:

1. Component A (30%): Analysis of information and planning
   In their own groups, students need to select a theme and complete three tasks: (i) Conduct a current state analysis to better understand the issue/problem that they will be working on; (ii) brainstorm according to the guiding questions provided to plan and execute the project work; (iii) fill in the timeline sheet that contains the list of tasks to be conducted. Students are to submit it to the teachers. Following that, teachers will assess and provide feedback for students to further improve the plan prior to task execution.

2. Component B (70%): Service execution
   Students may begin their project work. They are to record in detail the completed/incomplete tasks in addressing the selected issues as well as to provide the reasons for incompletion, if any.

3. Component C: Individual reflection
   After the completion of the project work, students are expected to pen down their reflection by answering the guiding questions:
   - Write a brief description of the problems or issues you had identified.
   - Outline your action plan and state your team's goal for the project.
   - Indicate what you have learned and possible challenges in executing the plan.
   - Did you meet your goal? What is the evidence of meeting or not meeting the goal?
   - Briefly describe one of the biggest challenges you faced; how you managed the challenge and then what you learned from the challenge.
   - What is charity/volunteerism (depending on the selected theme)? Support your response with evidence from your work.
   - Is there a relationship between "charity" and "volunteerism"? Explain and support with evidence from your personal and collective work.
   - Explanation whether you have emulated the Prophet s.a.w by being a mercy to others.
   - What is 1 thing you would do differently on the next service project?

   *Support your reflection with 'dalil' (evidences from the Qur'anic verses or Prophetic Tradition) whenever possible.

EXAMPLE 10.2.1 Rubrics

Content Rubrics	Pre & Uni-structural	Multi-structural	Relational	Extended Abstract
Charity/ volunteerism	• Student demonstrates a basic understanding of charity/ volunteerism.	• Student demonstrates some understanding of charity/volunteerism.	• Student demonstrates a deep understanding of charity/volunteerism. Student is able to explain and support the benefits and challenges of charity/ volunteerism.	• Student demonstrates a deep and sophisticated understanding of charity/ volunteerism. Student makes strong links between the local context and larger context of the world and is able to identify important questions related to the benefits and challenges of charity/ volunteerism.

Process rubrics	Pre & Unistructural	Multistructural	Relational	Extended abstract
Problem analysis and planning	• Student identifies and defines problems, issues and challenges with the help of teachers. • Student needs help and unsure of the details to implement the project.	• Student identifies and defines few problems, issues and challenges. • Student is able to identify few ideas to implement the project.	• Student identifies and defines some problems, issues and challenges and understands how they are connected. • Student is able to provide some ideas and original thoughts in planning and implementing the project and how one complements the other.	• Student identifies and defines genuine and major problems, issues and challenges thoroughly and understood how they are connected to other contexts in the real-world and able to suggest possible solutions. • Student is able to provide various ideas and original thoughts in planning and implementing the project and relates the ideas to other concepts and approach of service learning.

Task delegation	Student delegates the tasks poorly. Not all team members are tasked to do work.	Student delegates the tasks fairly well. Some team members are tasked more than the others.	Student delegates the tasks well. Almost every team member is tasked with the same amount of work and relevant to their ability and capacity.	Student delegates the tasks very well in consideration of other possible obstacles or hindrances. Almost every team member is tasked with the same amount of work and relevant to their ability and capacity.
Timeline and time management	Student is unable to set realistic timeline and struggles to complete the tasks.	Student attempts to set a timeline and completes a limited number of tasks.	Student sets achievable timeline that shows connection to proper planning. Student manages to deliver most tasks on time.	Student sets achievable timeline that shows proper planning, deep consideration and relates it to tasks' settings. Student manages to deliver tasks before deadline by anticipating possible delays.
Execution of service project and goal attainment	Student's service project does not address the needs of the audience or issues identified; and do not meet goals set for the project.	Student's service project addresses some of the needs of the audience or issues identified. Some goals for the project are achieved.	Student's service project is successful and tasks are integrated to coherently address the needs of the audience or issues identified. Most project goals are achieved.	Student's service project is successful by skilfully addressing the needs of the audience or issues identified. Student responds to and manages impromptu tasks. Goals are completely achieved.

(continued)

EXAMPLE 10.2.1 (Continued)

Collaborative skills rubrics	Pre & Unistructural	Multistructural	Relational	Extended abstract
Teamwork	• Student does not participate in the work and displays determination and perseverance sparsely.	• Student provides little support to the team and displays determination and perseverance occasionally.	• Student actively engages in the project, works towards achieving goals, responds to emerging needs and displays determination and perseverance most of the time and is able to relate the importance of these skills to the success of the project.	• Student is actively engaged in the project, works towards achieving goals effectively, shows initiative, fulfils commitments, responds to emerging needs, acts proactively, displays strong determination and perseverance thoroughly and applies other skills which contribute to the success of the project.
Social values	• Student barely exhibits empathy and compassion.	• Student exhibits some empathy and compassion.	• Student exhibits substantiated amount of empathy and compassion. Student is able to relate the importance of these values in completing the project.	• Student exhibits empathy and compassion significantly. Student is able to relate the importance of these values and exhibit other additional values required in completing the project.

Example 10.3

Focus: Resilience
Contributed by Sim Kooi Suen
Target group: 13–16years-old (Secondary 1–4)
Topic: "My Character Quest" (MCQ)

Context

The CCE syllabus emphasizes putting the student at the centre of the learning of CCE and encourages the active participation of the student with the teachers involved through collective collaboration using a constructivist approach. It further elaborates that assessment approaches can use "a variety of tools and strategies in authentic assessment tasks" (MOE – Primary, 2014 p. 38). Peer and self-assessment are encouraged to foster a deeper sense of ownership during goal setting, monitoring and in decision-making with the student.

These broad guidelines have led to schools customising their own approaches in assessing the character development of their students. From experience, schools have no structured rubrics or guides apart from referencing the broad guidelines set in the CCE syllabus guide. Teachers form impressions of their students through observations derived from their daily interaction during lessons, at co-curricular activities (CCAs) or any other platforms including camps and outings. The students are often told about the teachers' assessment only at teacher-student conference, when the students are asked how they intend to improve on their character and conduct. In short, for character development, the students seldom, if ever, have a chance to talk about their own personal journey in character development or have anyone from school personally journey and mentor them in character development. This task has been designed to address this gap. The key character trait chosen for illustrative purpose is resilience, but the process can be applied to other traits.

Task

The student embarks on a journal (see Example 10.3.1) to reflect on his resilience, a trait that the school has unpacked in terms of behavioural attributes.

EXAMPLE 10.3.1 Character trait: RESILIENCE

	A: What are the challenges I am facing now in these contexts.	B: Here are the steps I plan to overcome the challenges.	C: How will the factors like time, seeking help, affect my plan to improve?	D: How much of the challenges listed in 'A' have been overcome?
Class:				
CCA:				
Home:				
Others				

'Back to the future' reflection:

Spend some time to carefully think about what was done to improve the situation and what more can be done if the situation did not improve. Do not worry about language issues, e.g., spelling, grammar etc, just write and share. If you wish, you may want to draw or talk about this with the teacher assigned to you.

Reflection question

Notice that this AA takes an approach different from the previous two that are based on particular events. The assessment of the child's character here is through observations by adult mentors and child's self-assessment. What are the advantages and disadvantages of this approach?

At the same time, each child is assigned four significant adults who will observe, assess, as well as consult with the child on his character development. These significant adults comprise two of his classroom teachers, his CCA/committee teacher and one adult that represents his family/home. The role of each party is as follows:

1. The student: The development of the student is at the core of the programme so the student's view is paramount.
2. Teacher mentors: Teacher mentors (TMs) are teachers who interact with the student significantly and consequently their observations of the student are more valid, reliable and their recommendations more effective.
3. Parents or significant adult: Feedback from consultation with parents and significant adult from the child's home will provide a holistic and balanced assessment for the child to derive his or her own assessment of his or her attainment.
4. Others: Should the need arise for other adults to be involved, this shall be done in consultation with the child's parents or guardians. This is in the event if any external intervention or assessment is needed.

The mode of assessment and evaluation is done largely via the students' self-assessment and various consultations with the teacher mentors and other significant adults throughout the year. Attainment of the character traits are assessed based on the MCQ Rubrics and should be agreed upon by all parties concerned with input by all parties concerned. See Example 10.3.2 for the rubrics.

Summary

The discussion in Chapter 3 cautioned against merely layering on real-world conditions or contexts to make a task authentic. This is especially so when the real-life elements distract the learner from the domain of interest to the assessor. Instead, AA designers should use a construct-centred approach which focuses on defining and unpacking the construct of interest into observable behaviour, before designing tasks to elicit these behaviours (Messick, 1999; Tay, 2014).

One can see in this chapter how this construct-centred approach helps teachers design AA for psychological constructs like responsibility and appreciation (Example 10.1), charity (Example 10.2) and resilience (Example 10.3). Also note how the rubrics accompanying the tasks comprise standards that are qualitative in

EXAMPLE 10.3.2 Rubrics

Unistructural	Multistructural	Relational	Extended abstract
Developing Stage (Dy)	Pre-managing stage (PM)	Managing stage (M1–M3)	Exceeding stage (ES1–ES2)
Able to identify the components (A)–(D) in various areas in their lives	Able to identify and link components (A)–(D) and how they are linked	Able to gain insight into how the components (A)–(D) are linked and informs them on course of action in various contexts (Class, CCA, home)	Able to relate through reflection how their learning can be applied to the next stage(s) of their lives;
		M1 is awarded to a student who can only apply to one context and is still developing in the other two;	ES1 for students who thinks only about immediate future;
		M3 is awarded to a student who is able to see the course of action across 3 contexts.	ES3 for students who think far beyond the immediate to the next stage in life.

Comment: Refer to Example 10.3.1 for (A)-(D)

nature, using the SOLO framework (see Chapter 4). The clarity afforded by the descriptors in the standards provides the important formative feedback needed by learners to grow in character and citizenship.

Notes

1 Self-awareness, self-management, responsible decision-making, social awareness, relationship management.
2 As discussed in Chapter 5: Civic literacy, global awareness and cross-cultural skills; critical and inventive thinking; communication, collaboration and information skills.

References

Astin, A. W., Vogelgesang, L. J., Ikeda, E. K., & Yee, J. A. (2000). How service learning affects students. *Higher Education, 14*(10 April 2009), i–104. doi:10.1142/S1363919610002660.

Brookhart, S. M. (2014). *How to Design Questions and Tasks to Assess Student Thinking.* Virginia: ASCD.

Gulikers, J., Bastiaens, T. M., & Kirschner, T. J. (2004). A five-dimensional framework for authentic assessment. *Educational Technology Research and Development, 52*(3), 67–86.

Lickona, T. (1991). *Educating/or Character.* New York: Bantam.

McMillan, J. H. (2001). *Classroom Assessment: Principles and Practice for Effective Instruction.* Massachusetts: Allyn & Bacon.

MOE. (2012). Character and citizenship syllabus (primary). Retrieved 10 June 2017, from https://www.moe.gov.sg/docs/default-source/document/education/syllabuses/

character-citizenship-education/files/character-and-citizenship-education-(primary)-syllabus-(english).pdf.

MOE. (2017). 21st Century Competencies. Retrieved 26 May 2017, from https://www.moe.gov.sg/education/education-system/21st-century-competencies.

Messick, S. (1994). The interplay of evidence and consequences in the validation of performance assessment. *Educational Researcher, 23*(2), 13–23.

Nolen, S. B. (2006). Validity in assessing self-regulated learning: A comment on Perry and Winne. *Educational Psychology Review, 18*(3), 229–232.

Patrick, H. & Middleton, M. J. (2002). Turning the kaleidoscope: What we see when self-regulated learning is viewed with a qualitative lens. *Educational Psychologist, 37*(1), pp. 27–39.

Perry, N. E., & Winne, P. H. (2006). Learning from learning kits: gStudy traces of students' self-regulated engagements with computerized content. *Educational Psychology Review, 18*(3), 211–228.

Prentice, M., & Robinson, G. (2010). Improving student learning outcomes with service learning. *American Association of Community Colleges*, 1–16.

Ryan, K. and Bohlin, K. E. (1999). *Building Character in Schools: Practical Ways to Bring Moral Instruction to Life.* San Francisco, CA: Jossey-Bass.

Ritchhart, R., Church, M., & Morrison, K. (2011). *Making Thinking Visible: How to Promote Engagement, Understanding, and Independence for All Learners.* San Francisco: Jossey-Bass.

Schunk, D. H. (2008). Metacognition, self-regulation, and self-regulated learning: Research recommendations. *Educational Psychological Review, 20*(4), 463–467.

Stoll, S. K., & Beller, J. M. (1998). Can character be measured? *Journal of Physical Edcuations, Recreation & Dance, 69*(1), 19–24.

Tay, H. Y. (2014). Authentic assessment. In W. S. Leong, Y. S. Cheng, & K. Tan (Eds.), *Assessment and Learning in Schools.* Pearson: Singapore.

Turner, J. C. (2006). Measuring self-regulation: A focus on activity. *Educational Psychology Review, 18*(3), 293–296.

Wiggins, G. (1993). *Assessing Student Performance.* San Francisco: CA: Jossey-Bass.

Windle, G., Bennett, K. M., & Noyes, J. (2011). A methodological review of resilience measurement scales. *Health and Quality of Life Outcomes, 9*(8), http://doi.org/10.1186/1477-7525-9-8. Retrieved May 26, 2017, from https://www.ncbi.nlm.nih.gov/pmc/articles/PMC3042897/.

Zimmerman, B. J. (2008). Investigating self-regulation and motivation: Historical background, methodological developments, and future prospects. *American Educational Research Journal, 45*(1), 166–183.

11

PERSONALISING ASSESSMENT IN SPORT SCIENCE

Ben Jenkinson

Introduction

This chapter is a case study of how authentic assessment is used at Camberwell Girls Grammar School (GS), Melbourne, Australia, specifically in sport science. The design of the unit is based on Understanding by Design and is focussed on delivering personalised learning through authenticity in learning and assessment.

Background

According to the Melbourne Declaration on Educational Goals for Young Australians (2008), for young people to be successful learners, their teachers need to provide personalised learning that aims to fulfil the diverse capabilities and interests of each student. The principles underpinning personalised learning are quality teaching and learning; consultation; collaborative practice and planning. Knowing the student's background, strengths, interests and goals is crucial for educators implementing a successful personalised learning agenda.

Context

In recent years, the teaching and learning agenda at Camberwell Girls GS has focused heavily on achieving deeper personalisation in learning for each individual student. Underpinning this personalised learning approach in the Senior School has been the development of an Understanding by Design™ (UbD) curriculum framework that emphasises the learning of enduring understandings within and across subject discipline areas.

A key feature of this UbD framework is where assessment tasks are designed to elicit clear and authentic evidence of understanding, through performance tasks that require students to transfer their learning to a new context (Wiggins & McTighe, 2005). Whilst the school is still on its learning journey with UbD, the Year 10 exercise sport science subject provides an exemplar of this blended UbD framework and personalised assessment pedagogy in practice.

Case study: Year 10 Exercise Sport Science

Year 10 Exercise Sport Science at Camberwell Girls GS is a semester-length, elective pathway subject. Linked primarily to the Victorian Curriculum domains of science and health and physical education, this course addresses a wide selection of Year 10 standards and capabilities. A list of the relevant Victorian Curriculum Achievement Standards is provided in the appendix.

Usually studied by 15- to 16-year-old students with clear interests and experiences in competitive sport, the subject also attracts girls with non-sporting interests such as those participating in high-level dance competitions, as well as some who may consider themselves simply to be recreational fitness enthusiasts. The resultant outcome being that in each class grouping, a wide variety of different passions, experiences and levels of skill, might prevail, but they are united as individuals within the class group by the subject's core focus and enduring understanding:

> that athletes and coaches can use sport science concepts to improve their personal performances.

By design, the curricular pursuit of this enduring understanding is framed as a simple, essential question (Wiggins & McTighe, 2013) to drive student inquiry:

> "How can I use sport science to improve my own sporting performances?"

Students of the Exercise Sport Science course are guided by their teacher through a series of learning modules which comprise different aspects of sport science theory that have relevance and inspiration for each and every different physical pursuit that aligns with a student's interest.

As an exemplar of quality assessment and personalised learning practice, the Year 10 Exercise Sport Science course leverages the students' individual interests and strengths (see Figure 11.1). It affords them the opportunity to use their preferred learning styles to critically evaluate a spectrum of sport science theories that they believe have relevance to their own personal agenda of improving performance in their chosen physical pursuit (e.g., track athletics, basketball, contemporary dance, freestyle swimming, general fitness, etc.).

The assessment challenge

Given the heavy personalisation agenda and the practical nature of the course, the student learning pathways in Exercise Sport Science are very diverse. In a

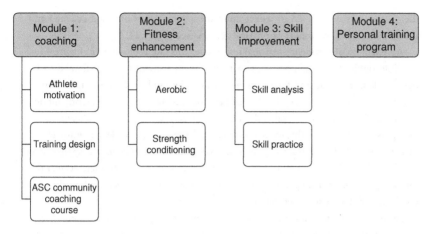

FIGURE 11.1 Year 10 Exercise Sport Science Curriculum – module overview.

conventional sense, this variety could provide difficulty for the teacher in achieving consistent standards for assessment across the student cohort. For example, in a class of 20 girls, with each pursuing a different sporting activity and each possibly investigating a different aspect of sport science, how can the teacher ensure all students are learning? How can the teacher assess their level of achievement and growth in learning? How can their progress be compared and ranked within the cohort?

A solution born from the UbD philosophy

The solution implemented by this course was to take an UbD approach to assessment of each module, whereby each girl is exposed to similar theoretical concepts in sport science, but their assessment of understanding is based on the evidence they demonstrate individually, across multiple small performance tasks. That is, each girl is expected to identify and transfer, to their best ability, relevant aspects of theory to suit their needs for improvement in their personal sporting context. The sophistication of understanding demonstrated in these student responses determine their learning achievement in the assessment tasks and help formatively, to provide direction for future learning pathways in the subject.

Collectively, the sum of these many smaller, formative assessment tasks would contribute to an overall level of academic achievement in the subject, but the greater emphasis at all times, is on the individual's growth in learning and their personal capabilities in applying it to new and relevant contexts.

Example Assessment Task 1: Reflection on my coach's use of motivation

From the very first module of learning (Module 1 Coaching), students were exposed to motivation theory as a mechanism that sport coaches use to improve the performance of their athletes. To assess their preliminary understanding of motivation theory, students were asked to reflect upon their experiences of being coached and motivated in their own sport or physical activity (see Figure 11.2).

An example of a student's personal response to this task is provided in Figure 11.3.

Philosophically, it was important that this first assessment task was framed to be open-ended, reflective and formative, as it was to be used to drive the next step in learning through student inquiry. As planned, the students were subsequently guided by the teacher's formative, oral and written feedback (Glasson, 2009; Wiliam, 2011) into personal inquiry pathways that encouraged them to delve deeper into related theories associated with the topic (e.g., arousal, anxiety, etc.). Given the open-ended nature of this task, the variety of responses in the student reflections dictated that the follow up inquiry learning caused each girl to enhance her understanding through researching different sub-theories.

By design, this task was not to be assessed by letter grades, nor any other form of subjective mark that would compare or rank students. For the teacher, each individual's response to the task would yield evidence of their understanding of motivation theory and their ability to connect and apply it to their own real life experiences through an empathetic and self-aware lens.

"One time, my coach …" (approx 250–300 words)

Complete a short reflection on a specific time that your coach used a particularly successful strategy to motivate you to perform your best.

Please include specific details about the context prior to your coach's motivational intervention and also, the resultant positive outcome and why you think it worked for you.

To deepen your reflective analysis, it would be good to outline why a different coaching motivational strategy may not have worked as effectively to motivate you.

FIGURE 11.2 Reflective learning task – stimulus.

A specific time when my 'coach' used a particular successful strategy to motivate us to perform our best was towards the end of last year. I was at my very last dance class before our concert and we were all feeling a bit nervous. Our teacher, who had always been really encouraging throughout the year, gave us a short motivation speech about just doing our best at the concert. He was very calming and helpful and made me feel better about performing the next week. I think this calming, motivational speech worked because I was nervous before hand and was towards the 'stress' side of the arousal theory graph, but his techniques brought me back to the optimal level. Part of what he said in his speech was just to have fun and reminded us that this isn't a competition so we didn't need to worry about being the best. Therefore, the motivation was derived from intrinsic sources rather than extrinsic sources. The outcome of this, was that we did really well in the concert and I was not nervous before going on stage because I remembered his speech. I personally get very worked up about things, so this technique worked for me. If he had been more forceful or rough with his motivational speech, it would have made me freak out about the concert more and would have put on pressure. A harsh approach would not have been affective.

FIGURE 11.3 Reflective learning task – example student response.

According to McTighe and Wiggins (2004), application, empathy and self-awareness are among the six key "facets of understanding" to be exhibited in assessment of student learning.

Example Assessment Task 2: Skill acquisition video analysis

A different example of effective personalisation in assessment occurred within the third module of the course: Skill Analysis. In this performance task, students were provided with an opportunity to tailor a skill acquisition task to enable them to improve a physical motor skill that is essential to their sporting performance (see Figure 11.4).

Your task is to analyse (using video) your execution of a specific skill, then train to improve it.

There are 4 areas for your final product to address:

1. Identifying incorrect skill technique
2. Theory evidence (research) on correct technique for optimal performance
3. Skill training to improve/rectify technique deficiency
4. Final performance demonstrating improvement in technique

You may present/submit this task in one of the following ways:

- 1–2 minute video file – with technique annotations and theory voice over (preferred).
- Lab report format – with annotated still images and theory text
- Oral presentation – accompanied by graphics and video evidence.

FIGURE 11.4　Skill acquisition task – stimulus.

Camberwell Girls Grammar School — 10 Exercise Sport Science – M3 Skill Improvement **Skill Analysis Task**			
Student: _____ Sport / Activity: _____ Skill: _____ Date: _____			
Criteria:	Low Understanding	Medium Understanding	High Understanding
Identification and analysis of skill error Visual evidence was provided of a deficient skill technique requiring improvement. Relevant theoretical information was provided to help explain why it was deemed to be impacting negatively on performance.	1	2	3
Theory evidence of good/optimal technique Referenced research theory was interpreted and used to outline the preferred/optimal/good technique for successful execution of the chosen skill.	1	2	3
Skill training methodology for improved technique A clear and practical training methodology was documented and followed to help improve the desired skill technique.	1	2	3
Evidence of improved performance Visual evidence was provided for comparison to illustrate improved performance. Annotations of skill analysis enhanced the comparison.	1	2	3
Participation in practical training sessions to improve their chosen skill. The student was self-motivated and self-directed when training to improve their skill. They also provided collaborative coaching assistance in support of other students as required.	1	2	3
Feedback comments: *see online feedback comments in SEQTA learn			
Total Marks:　/15			

FIGURE 11.5　Skill acquisition task – assessment rubric.

A simple assessment rubric (Figure 11.5) was developed for this performance task, with clear emphasis on the student demonstrating their interpretation and application of sport science theory to a context different to any of those used in the teaching delivery or subject notes.

Identification and analysis of skill error

The skill error affected is to do with the linear and angular motion in a netball shot. Through video analysis it is evident my body; during preparation for the shot, is too straight (0 degrees from vertical) to be able to achieve an accurate shot (image 1). This then affected the optimal angle of release, and the angle was too obtuse (115 degrees) when it should be much more acute (image 2). From the same still image, arm extension from the elbow was observed showing to be far too obtuse (145 degrees) (image 3).

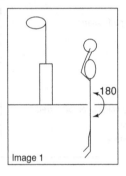

Image 1

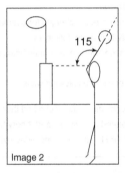

Image 2

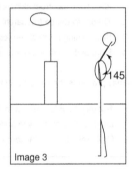

Image 3

Theory of good technique

I sourced evidence of a good netball shooting technique from: Julie R Steele (1993) *Biomechanical factors affecting performances in netball.*

The theory specifies for an optimal shot, you must be leaning around 15 degrees back wards when preparing to shoot. When squaring up with your arms, the optimal angle between elbow flexion is between 90–104 degrees. The last part of theory for a good netball shot is the angle of release, which should be approximately 60 degrees, and the ball should spin 1–1.5 revolutions.

Evidence of improved Performance:

There is now an angle to my vertical position 167 degrees (image 6). In turn has allowed me to bend without altering the flexion of my elbow and keep between the optimal degrees (image 5). The angle of release has also improved tremendously by almost getting it to the 60 degrees.

FIGURE 11.6 Skill acquisition task – student response (snippets).

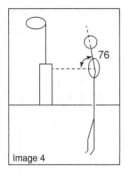 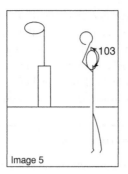 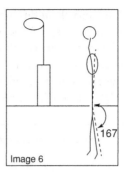

Image 4 | Image 5 | Image 6

FIGURE 11.6 (Continued).

As identified in the student response above (Figure 11.6), the learner's scientific understanding of the biomechanical principles of angle and height of release has clearly grown to become more sophisticated and informed throughout the task. To clarify, this student first encountered these biomechanical principles with her peers through a teacher-led practical and theoretical example of the athletics field event, the javelin throw. Her subsequent learning work was to investigate the theory to a deeper level, as relevant to her, and then transfer it to her own sport to demonstrate evidence of her understanding.

Content versus understanding

In summarising the pedagogical approach to assessment of curriculum in this Exercise Sport Science course, it can be said that the educational pursuit of developing student understanding through practical application and transfer, trumps the approach of simply teaching to impart theoretical content and knowledge. Essentially, the full volume of the sport science theoretical knowledge and content that could be learned in this course has become of lesser importance than the student's individual ability to apply relevant aspects of it to a new context for her own personal benefit.

It is important to acknowledge that content and knowledge are important in the learning process (Gardner, 2000), so to diminish the significance of subject-specific content and knowledge when pursuing student learning is not easily reconciled by many subject teachers in secondary schools in Australia. Consequently, this approach to assessment may not suit all assessments, subjects and student demographics.

Fundamentally, this Exercise Sport Science course strives for and achieves personalised assessment because it places greater importance and emphasis on the learners demonstrating their understanding in an authentic, practical way that is relevant to them as individuals, capitalizing on their personal strengths, interests and backgrounds. This is opposed to more traditional methods of assessment such as tests, projects and examinations that might prioritise low-level knowledge recall of content knowledge with little evidence of genuine understanding through application (transfer) to new contexts.

Unfortunately in this subject-area, past iterations of similar skill acquisition tasks shown in Figures 11.5 and 11.6, often utilised the test format that would first provide the theory concept, then ask students to link it to a sporting skill example (e.g., tennis serve, soccer penalty kick, basketball lay-up, etc.).

These learning tasks often had a detrimental effect on student engagement with the subject. Examples of such assessment questions are provided in Figure 11.7.

---

7. Give four examples of sequential force summation.

(i) _____ (ii) _____

(iii) _____ (iv) _____ /4

8. In the performance of the standing broad jump:

    (a) Which body parts provide the force for the jump?

_____ /2

    (b) Which type of force summation is used?

_____ /1

---

10. Give 2 examples of sporting situations where friction is increased to improve performance.

(i) _____
_____

(ii) _____
_____ /2

FIGURE 11.7 Examples of traditional assessments in similar skill acquisition tasks.

Unfortunately, this type of questioning rarely demanded any higher-order thinking or evidence of true depth of understanding as per the foundational aims of teaching for understanding (Blythe, 1998; Gardner, 2000) or the UbD approach (Wiggins & McTighe, 2005). In this teacher's experience, this type of assessment task does not meet the objectives of personalisation, nor was it successful in inspiring young people into deeper inquiry in the topic area.

For the teacher of this Exercise Sport Science course, personalising the assessment is a natural and productive way to foster engagement in each student learner, including the independent ability to use his or her sport science knowledge and understanding in practical and relevant ways for his or her benefit. In the case of Exercise Sport Science at Camberwell Girls GS, it is assured that after completing this course of learning, each girl has developed the independent ability to research and apply whichever aspect of sport science theory she may deem relevant to improve her sporting performances, now and into the future. Importantly, these students also reached this empowering, enduring understanding by themselves, through their own academic endeavour; their teacher did not simply give it to them on a handout of class notes, nor test them on it.

Appendix

Victorian Curriculum Achievement Standards – Science

- VCSIS135 – Planning and conducting – Levels 9 and 10
  Independently plan, select and use appropriate investigation types, including fieldwork and laboratory experimentation, to collect reliable data, assess risk and address ethical issues associated with these investigation types.
- VCSIS136 – Planning and conducting – Levels 9 and 10
  Select and use appropriate equipment and technologies to systematically collect and record accurate and reliable data, and use repeat trials to improve accuracy, precision and reliability.
- VCSIS138 – Analysing and evaluating – Levels 9 and 10
  Analyse patterns and trends in data, including describing relationships between variables, identifying inconsistencies in data and sources of uncertainty, and drawing conclusions that are consistent with evidence.
- VCSIS140 – Communicating – Levels 9 and 10
  Communicate scientific ideas and information for a particular purpose, including constructing evidence-based arguments and using appropriate scientific language, conventions and representations.
- VCSSU115 – Science as a human endeavour – Levels 9 and 10
  Advances in scientific understanding often rely on developments in technology and technological advances are often linked to scientific discoveries.
- VCSSU133 – Physical sciences – Levels 9 and 10
  The description and explanation of the motion of objects involves the interaction of forces and the exchange of energy and can be described and predicted using the laws of physics.

Victorian Curriculum Achievement Standards – Health and Physical Education

- VCHPEM152 – Moving the body – Levels 9 and 10
  Perform and refine specialised movement skills in challenging movement situations.
- VCHPEM153 – Moving the body – Levels 9 and 10
  Evaluate own and others' movement compositions, and provide and apply feedback in order to enhance performance situations.
- VCHPEM154 – Moving the body – Levels 9 and 10
  Develop, implement and evaluate movement concepts and strategies for successful outcomes.
- VCHPEM155 – Understanding movement – Levels 9 and 10
  Design, implement and evaluate personalised plans for improving or maintaining their own and others' physical activity and fitness levels.
- VCHPEM156 – Understanding movement – Levels 9 and 10

Analyse the impact of effort, space, time, objects and people when composing and performing movement sequences.

- VCHPEM159 – Learning through movement – Levels 9 and 10
  Transfer understanding from previous movement experiences to create solutions to movement challenges.
- VCHPEM160 – Learning through movement – Levels 9 and 10
  Reflect on how fair play and ethical behaviour can influence the outcomes of movement activities.

Victorian Curriculum – General Capabilities

- VCCCTQ044 – Questions and Possibilities – Levels 9 and 10
  Suspend judgments to allow new possibilities to emerge and investigate how this can broaden ideas and solutions.
- VCCCTQ045 – Questions and Possibilities – Levels 9 and 10
  Challenge previously held assumptions and create new links, proposals and artefacts by investigating ideas that provoke shifts in perspectives and cross boundaries to generate ideas and solutions.
- VCPSCSO050 – Collaboration – Levels 9 and 10
  Evaluate own and others contribution to group tasks, critiquing roles including leadership and provide useful feedback to peers, evaluate task achievement and make recommendations for improvements in relation to team goals.
- VCCCTM051 – Meta-Cognition – Levels 9 and 10
  Critically examine their own and others thinking processes and discuss factors that influence thinking, including cognitive biases.
- VCCCTM053 – Meta-Cognition – Levels 9 and 10
  Investigate the kind of criteria that can be used to rationally evaluate the quality of ideas and proposals, including the qualities of viability and workability.

References

Blythe, T. (1998). *The Teaching For Understanding Guide.* San Francisco: Jossey-Bass.

Gardner, H. (2000). *The Disciplined Mind.* New York: Penguin Group.

Glasson, T. (2009). *Improving Student Achievement: A Practical Guide To Assessment For Learning.* Carlton, Australia: Curriculum Corporation.

Ministerial Council on Education, Employment, Training and Youth Affairs (2008). *The Melbourne Declaration on Educational Goals for Young Australians.* Federal Government of Australia.

Wiggins, G. & McTighe, J. (2004). *Understanding By Design – Professional Development Workbook.* Alexandria, VA: ASCD.

Wiggins, G. & McTighe, J. (2005). *Understanding by design.* (2nd ed.). Alexandria, VA: ASCD.

Wiggins, G. & McTighe, J. (2013). *Essential Questions: Opening Doors to Student Understanding.* Alexandria, VA: ASCD.

Wiliam, D. (2011). *Embedding Formative Assessment.* Moorabbin, VA: Hawker Brownlow Education.

12

DEVELOPING EMPATHY THROUGH AUTHENTIC ASSESSMENT

Eric Chong King Man

Introduction

This chapter examines a case study aimed at planning and implementing authentic assessment by using both an empathy model and experiential learning principles in classroom learning and field-based experiential learning. The learning unit is in the context of Personal, Social and Humanities Education (PSHE) in a Hong Kong secondary school. The case study intends to shed light on how authentic assessment can be incorporated into a PSHE learning unit of junior secondary Life & Society subject that combines both classroom learning and experiential learning, and suggest how effective assessment tasks can contribute to the development of students' empathy in terms of understanding other people and seeing things from their perspective. The intervention is conducted in two junior secondary one classes in a Hong Kong secondary school, with about 24 students in each class. The age group in both classes is between 12 and 13 years old. English is the medium of instruction for this learning unit, and students belong to the medium and high academic capability range. However, during experiential learning activities, when students interact with the local population, the spoken dialect of Cantonese is used in verbal communications.

Background

As a special administrative region of China after the resumption of sovereignty in 1997, Hong Kong is basically a Chinese community that believes in rational decision-making (Cheng, 2000). People believe there are fundamental rights and wrongs in education policies and that "the rational dimension refers to the objective and impartial basis of decision-making", which is "often related to the collection, analysis and utilization of data and information" (Cheng, 2000, p. 74). Regarding the educational context in Hong Kong, the school organisation promotes a context-dependent orientation in which people are valued as part of the organisation (Wong, 2000). Well-known examples are the School Management Initiative implemented by the government in 1991, and the subsequent implementation of the Incorporated Management Committee in 2010. Lee (2000a) argues that such an orientation of development represents a clear departure from the traditional bureaucratic and administrative orientations of Hong Kong, as it enables decentralisation at the school level and school-based management. In addition, in this context-dependent orientation, parents, teachers and alumni representatives participate in each school's management committee, thereby paying more attention to the people involved in decision making (Lee, 2000a). Regarding assessment, Hong Kong schools are expected to guarantee and accredit learning standards to students; therefore, assessment generally dominates school learning, and examinations often determine what is taught and how it is learned (Biggs & Watkins, 1995), since the effect of the examination on teaching did matter since the 1980s (Coniam, 2015). It was a major concern of the Hong Kong Examinations and Assessment Authority (HKEAA). While the use of examination-like assessments as a practice is usually not supported by proponents of assessment for learning (Gipps, 2002), the practices persist, especially where stakes or consequences for examination performance are large such as this present case in Hong Kong.

The 1993 Target Oriented Curriculum represents a significant landmark in the curriculum reform in Hong Kong schools. Griffin, Falvey and Owen (1993, p. 18) describe the reform as "one of the most ambitious changes attempted by an education system" that "represented a very fundamental attempt to reform the key elements of the curriculum, especially the forms of assessment and the styles of teaching used, and the learning styles promoted" (Adamson & Morris, 2000, p. 14). In short, Hong Kong teachers are asked to develop school-based curricula (Brown, 2000). This educational initiative encourages teachers to become involved in the development of curricula directly relevant to the particularities of their schools and students (Brown, 2000). However, the lack of time, money and reference materials; the lack of appropriate skills or training; the schools' or Education Department's lack of provisions to reduce teachers' workload; and the emphasis on hierarchy, control, uniformity and accountability of the bureaucratic operation of school-based curriculum projects in Hong Kong (Chun, 1989; Morris, 1990) all merely contribute to teachers' exhaustion.

Assessment in Hong Kong is often associated with the summative evaluation of students' performance after a teaching episode, usually quantitatively conceived. Assessment has been tied up with identification, classification, placement and ongoing monitoring of students (Lachat & Spruce, 1998). In progressive assessment, the student's final grade is determined by performance throughout the course, but in terminal assessment, the grade is usually determined by performance in a final examination at the end of the course (Biggs & Watkins, 1995, p. 16). Biggs & Watkins (1995) also suggest that there are two major approaches to assessment: Assessing for selection and assessing for the effects of education. While the former is based on the assumption that students have fixed abilities, assessing educational outcome is based on the assumption that students change through learning. Meanwhile, feedback must occur during the learning process if it is to be formative for the learners being taught or prepared for the final summative assessment (Scriven, 1991). Therefore, teachers frequently use assessments during instruction that mimic high-stakes examinations, partly as test-taking preparation and partly as a means of providing feedback about performance on test-like assessments (Brown, et al., 2009).

In recent years, Hong Kong has been seeking to increase the use of "assessment for learning" rather than rely on "assessment of learning" (Brown, et al., 2009), mainly through the efforts of the Education Bureau (EDB) of Hong Kong SAR government. The HKEAA also administers examination and produces assessment syllabus for promulgation on various school subjects and learning areas for Hong Kong teachers (HKEAA, 2017). Through developing a focus on "assessment for learning", Hong Kong teachers have been encouraged to view assessment not only as examinations and tests, but also as part of a learning process that can provide feedback to students to help them improve their learning (Curriculum Development Council, 2001). The Curriculum Development Council (2001) also suggested that (a) teachers provide feedback to students of their strengths and weaknesses, and (b) schools include key attitudes, self-management, and moral and civic qualities in report cards as part of student achievement and for further improvement (Brown, et al., 2009). Hong Kong teachers also see holding students accountable in their learning as consistently associated with learning improvement (Brown, et al., 2009).

Amidst this context of assessment reform, this learning unit on understanding poverty was created by teachers and project team for the subject Life & Society, by combining both classroom-based inquiry learning and experiential learning activities. In particular, it aims at developing their students' perspective taking and empathy. This chapter examines how assessment tasks can enhance students' learning experience by enabling them to be more empathetic towards other people. A variety of methods are used to assess learning outcomes in different ways instead of simply using traditional assessment forms, such as quiz or examinations.

Context

The school in this case study is a co-educational school in Hong Kong, which serves students coming mainly from neighbouring communities and districts. Like many secondary schools in Hong Kong, the school is sponsored by a Protestant church that supports its incorporated ethos management committee and offers religious study as a subject. Since its foundation in 1950, the school has been well established. Like other local aided schools in Hong Kong, it mainly serves local Hong Kong Chinese students. Regarding the medium of instruction in this school, both English and Chinese are used depending on the language skills of the students, and students are thus arranged into separate classes. The focus of this learning unit of junior secondary Life & Society is poverty. It uses both formative and summative

TABLE 12.1 The aims, goals and learning activities of this experiential learning to understand poverty issues

Aim	Nurture young people's empathy towards the poor
Learning goals	Students should be able to: examine the issue of poverty; see from others' perspective; develop their empathy towards others in need; and cultivate a willingness to take action to alleviate poverty in their lives
Experiential learning activities	Experiencing the lives of those living in rooftop housing (temporary flats on the rooftop), interviews, spending time to experience the lives of elderly people who collect vegetables on the streets.

assessment methods to inform teachers about the learning progress of students at different stages. Table 12.1 presents a summary of this learning unit.

The focus on the unit, empathy, is conceived as constituted by "shared emotional response" and "perspective taking" ability (Krznaric, 2008): it is a strong drive for one to take action and tackle injustice, for the sake of others and the betterment of the world. Empathy education encourages development of the two interrelated aspects of empathy: comprehending and sharing emotional responses of another person (affective empathy); and understanding the perspective of others through the imaginative act of stepping into their shoes (cognitive empathy). According to Krznaric (2008, p. 10): "perspective-taking empathy concerns the ability to step into the shoes of another person and comprehend the way they look at themselves and the world. It allows us to make an imaginative leap into another person's being. Although one can never fully understand another person's worldview, we can develop the skill of understanding others' viewpoint, and on this basis, we will be able to predict how they will think or act in particular circumstances". Perspective-taking in empathy education enables students to:

(a) link oneself to the local community and the world, understanding the perspectives and feelings of others;
(b) form positive relationships with other people, value diversity of people and avoid prejudice, as well as, to understand ourselves better; and
(c) be motivated to take action to tackle the impact of social injustice.

Objectives and design of authentic assessment

This action research (McNiff, 2013; Hart & Bond, 1995) case study (Stake, 1995 2006) aims at developing an experiential learning curriculum to understand poverty issues in a Hong Kong secondary school, with a learning goal to develop student's empathy. Generally, learning in Hong Kong focuses on teaching declarative knowledge to the students (Biggs & Watkins, 1995), out of practical constraints of cost and benefits of large class size. Direct instruction mode is also commonly found across Hong Kong's classrooms, with flavours of "transmission" or "content-driven". In contrast, this authentic assessment involves experiential learning activities using Kolb's Experiential Learning Cycle, in which applying, experience, reflection and generalization are emphasized in a series of experiential learning and reflection activities. The key proposition is that experience can be the source of learning and development (Kolb, 1984) based on Kolb's principle that a person would learn through discovery and experience. Specifically, in this unit, the experiential learning activities adopted by the teachers could be described as aligning to different stages of Concrete Experience – Reflection – Hypothesising – Testing, where student learning through action and reflection takes place.

In addition, this experiential learning intervention is informed by the thinking–feeling spiral model developed by Skolnick, Dulberg and Maestre (2004). This model aims at developing student empathy through inviting them to experience the shared emotions, to understand the feelings of others and to take on the others' perspective. The thinking–feeling spiral includes the following four teaching steps: (1) making concrete and personal connections; (2) inquiring and imagining; (3) investigating content resources; (4) acting as if. The teachers planned this learning unit based on these steps in enabling learning, action, feeling and reflection taking place together.

The lesson units use both formative and summative assessments. Specifically, the former is used to inform teachers of their students' progress and to monitor student learning with ongoing feedback that teachers can use to improve their teaching. As part of a learning process, providing feedback to students helps them improve their learning (Curriculum Development Council, 2001). Examples of formative assessments in this case study include asking students to:

- draw a concept map in class and present their understanding of poverty;
- use their previous knowledge to brainstorm their understanding about definition of poverty; and
- submit one or two sentences identifying the impact of poverty.

Before the experiential learning activities, students were asked to think about what poverty meant to them. Some students answered that poverty meant facing hunger or a lack of food, while others replied that poverty meant having poor health and even facing death. Then, the teachers asked them to draw a concept map to connect all of these understandings.

Other means were also used to assess students' previous knowledge of poverty. Students were asked to a draw a picture to show their understanding of the relation between the rich and the poor. The pictures showed how students usually associated the difference as having high and low status in society and sometimes even facing discrimination. Next, students were asked to give a short skit dramatising their perception of the relation between the rich and the poor. Both activities

TABLE 12.2 Effects of poverty on family

The effects of poverty			
Family	Good or bad?	Aspect?	Explanation
A			
B			
C			
D			

enabled the teachers to understand how their students perceived the connections between various groups in society, e.g., the middle class and working class; and rich and poor people. These activities can be an important source of data on address and self-expression (Esland, 1973). On the causes of poverty, students learnt from the materials given by the teachers that poverty can be related to economic changes and personal reasons such as health or accident. Teachers encouraged the students to further explore the causes of poverty during the experiential learning activities afterwards by observing, interviewing and thinking.

One exercise also required the students to examine the effects of poverty. Students were asked to reply in Table 12.2.

Students proposed the following examples of "aspects" and "explanations" in Table 12.2.

1. "Children's education: children pick up cardboards, broken iron and soft drink cans in the streets to earn a living after school and during holidays. They may not have enough time to study and do homework."
2. "Parent-child relationship: parents may feel sorry for being poor and little children may complain and feel sad. Poverty may cause family conflicts."
3. "Living conditions: poor people live in the inner city where flats are small, dirty and crowded. Flats are old and unstable and thus at risk of collapsing. Children are forced to do their homework sitting on their bed. It can be bad for their growth and health."
4. "Transport: poor people have to walk or cycle to save money. Children may be tired when walking for long hours."
5. "Recreation: recreation is minimal for poor people to save money. Poor people spend most of their time at home during holidays."

To deepen students' sense of poverty on individual aspects, teachers created the following flowchart, shown in Table 12.3, and asked the students to imagine the possible effects.

TABLE 12.3 Brainstorming the effects of poverty on individual aspects

Immediate effects →	Intermediate effects →	Long-term effects

Some examples of students' entries on the effects of poverty on an individual include the following.

- Immediate effects

    1.   Health: hungry, lack of energy.
    2.   Living conditions: poor and unsafe.
    3.   Education: lack of good study conditions, may be unable to use the Internet to do homework, may not hand in homework on time.
    4.   Recreation.

- Intermediate effects

    1.   Sick: lack of money to see a doctor and get medicine from the store.
    2.   Education: may not want to go to school because they cannot manage their study.

- Long-term effects

    1.   Death, thin, skinny.
    2.   Lack of nutrition.
    3.   Poor memory due to poor health.

After studying some data about poor families in Hong Kong, the students were then asked to research on the causes of poverty. They gave the following various causes.

- Hong Kong has shifted from an industrial city to an international trading and financial centre since the 1980s. As a result, many factories moved to mainland China, and thus low-skilled workers lost their jobs. Moreover, they can only find low-income jobs, e.g., security guards or cleaning workers. They also face difficulties in changing jobs because of their low level of education.
- Older people can only find jobs with low income. Additionally, many retired without retirement benefits. If they suffer from a long-term illness, they spend a lot of money on doctor's appointments.
- As new immigrants are not well educated, they can only find low-income jobs. Women generally take care of family members; therefore, they can only work part time and earn low income.

The preceding examples were used to compare students' previous understanding of the effects of poverty with what they found in the media regarding the causes and effects of poverty. The classroom observation highlights that students can identify differences between their previous understanding and what is reported by mainstream media. In particular, they found that some media portray the poor as unfortunate and pitiable but without adequate analysis of the causes and pitfalls of poverty. This is where experiential learning can help students enhance their understanding of poverty, and more importantly, cultivate an empathetic attitude towards the poor.

Formative assessments after each visit to a poor district as part of their experiential learning included students' written reflections based on these three main questions:

- What did you learn during the visit?
- What did you discover and what do you want to know more about?
- Your reflection/comments after the visit.

Students wrote comments such as the following.

> "I learned more about the causes of poverty, and I just wonder what the government can do to help poor people. I would like to see what I can do to help them; perhaps I should start with a search on the Internet."

> "What I remember most today is an old man saying that what is lacking in this society is not space, but productivity that can create jobs. I think poor people should be given training to improve their productivity."

In one specific activity, designed to study the streets of a poor district, students were asked to use their five senses (taste, sight, touch, smell and hearing) to describe their experiences. The students were then asked to fill in Table 12.4.

The activity using the five senses guides students to collect data that includes their contact with people, what they see in stores and buildings and what they hear and smell while walking in the streets. All of these experiences enable students to improve their perspective-taking ability in a community that may be quite different from their own, and to develop a sense of empathy towards people coming from different backgrounds. From the type of language they hear during the visit, students can discover the relationship between social class and language, insofar as a working-class community has its own language use preferences (Lee, 2000b). Students hear how the community uses the public language (or restricted language; Bernstein, 1973), which is "characterized by a high proportion of short commands, simple statements and questions where the symbolism is descriptive, tangible, concrete, visual and of a lower order of generality; and the emphasis on the emotive rather than the logical implications" (Lee, 2000b, p. 157). With such experiences using the five senses, students may also be able to understand how a particular

TABLE 12.4 Experiences during their visit to a poor district

Street:		Street:	
Sight			
Touch			
Smell			
Hearing			
Overall impression		Overall impression	

community can be referred to as a speech community (Hudson, 1980, p. 25), while at the same time understanding the social organisation of society and the social experiences of its members.

Finally, the goal of summative assessment is to evaluate the learning progress of students at the end of the learning unit. First, students were asked to discuss their views on the following question: "What can you do for local poverty?" Some examples of the students' views are included as follows.

- Become a social worker.
- Volunteer.
- Visit the poor.
- Write a card.
- Recycle old clothes using recycle bins.
- Raise money.
- Build a canteen that is affordable.
- Respect poor families.
- Sell flats to the poor.

Next, a final group report and an examination served the summative purpose. The final group presentation aimed at reporting what the students learned about poverty and their answers to the following questions set by their teachers.

- What are the causes of poverty?
- Where did you go during the experiential learning activities?
- What are the effects of poverty on individuals and their families?
- What is your reflection after visiting different types of poverty sites?
- What can the government do to reduce poverty?
- What can you do to help improve the situation?
- What can different stakeholders, such as the community and NGOs, do to help solve the poverty issue?
- Do you have any questions?

Indeed, students reported that the experiential learning activities had a profound effect on them and deeply affected their understanding of the topic. Here are some examples of their presentations that demonstrate how the preceding questions required them to use their thinking abilities, and help to develop their empathy in terms of understanding other people and seeing things from their perspective.

"Regarding the causes of poverty, first, most poor people were poorly educated and thus had a low level of skills. Nowadays, most jobs require highly educated and high-skilled workers. Therefore, they cannot find a high-paying job or even have an income. Another reason is social policy. Most poor families cannot get support over time."

"Why is there free lunchbox delivery? It is because some people do not have the chance to work (they have a low education level and many jobs require a high education level). Renting a flat is also expensive. They cannot afford it despite earning money. They simply cannot pay high rent."

"Poor people and their families may face problems with living conditions. Most of their homes do not have enough space. The smallest are only 50 square feet and they are not safe. Additionally, poverty may affect children's education and their examination results, which may later prevent them from finding a job easily."

"The government can use the law to lower house rents in some districts, so the poor can save more money. Additionally, the government could build more public housing; thus, the poor could live in a better environment."

"I feel pity for the elderly who come to collect free vegetables. I can get free food from my family. Today, I learned that I should not waste food."

"I think I can donate some money, equipment and books. The government can also help them, e.g., by building more public housing."

"We can share the lives of rough sleepers in the streets on the Internet, so people can know more about them and help them. We can also become volunteer workers, so we can help them."

"Nevertheless, some families need to live in these rooftop houses. I wonder why there are rough sleepers in the streets? Is there not enough public housing for them? Or maybe they cannot find a job?"

Although the final report and its presentation in the final class of Life & Society can demonstrate students' understanding of the lives of poor people, the examination assesses their knowledge and conceptual attainment by comparing them with a standard or a benchmark. Teachers found that students could elaborate on their thinking about issues of poverty in the examination, and they could answer the questions by applying what they have seen in the experiential learning activities. Also, they could generalize from experience into some tangible solutions in their written answers. Thus, teachers felt that the summative assessment affirmed the benefits of combining classroom-based inquiry and experiential learning activities.

In short, the results of students' summative assessments inform teachers and guide their curriculum planning for the next school year. The teachers thus gain concrete ideas on how to improve experiential learning, such as incorporating brainstorming activities for students to develop interview questions themselves and establish a better connection between classroom-based inquiry learning and experiential learning activities outside of school.

Reflection on the design and review of the project

The following section provides a review of what I learned about designing assessment methods. First, authentic assessment conducted to measure educational learning outcomes can be composed of different types of assessment, such as a combination of formative and summative assessments, which can serve different purposes. For instance, formative assessment helps students identify the learning areas they can improve and help teachers recognise where students are struggling and specifically address these issues. Formative assessment can also enable the teachers to make use of authentic learning materials, such as what they have seen and felt, in asking students to write down their feeling, thinking and analysis, and reflection. Regarding summative assessment, teachers can gain more information about what students have learned after completing the experiential learning processes. For example, the students' answers in the examination enable the teachers to know more about their cognitive understanding about the causes, impacts and solutions on poverty. This case study's finding agrees with the findings by Frisby (2001) that supplementing traditional standardized tests with more authentic measures of the abilities of students with cultural and linguistic differences promotes the application of knowledge and skills in situations that closely resemble real world activities.

Second, when using assessment methods, students should receive feedback on their performance during learning processes. This is assessing educational outcome based on the assumption that students change through learning (Biggs & Watkins, 1995). In other words, teachers agree that formative assessment, however short or simple, should be adopted to inform them about the learning progress of students, whether such kinds of assessment is verbal, written, visual or motor. Modification can further be made to teaching plans afterwards.

Third, the medium of instruction is also a concern during the planning stage of a learning unit. The use of English may prove difficult for local students when learning about the complex issue of poverty. Spinelli (2008) found that existing research indicates that there is a disproportionate number of students with cultural and linguistic differences are misidentified as learning disabled when their problems are due to cultural and/or linguistic differences. The HKEAA has been working on producing language proficiency standards specifications and an assessment syllabus for promulgation to Hong Kong teachers in using English language (Coniam, 2015). by the same token, using learning materials written in English in this case study can thus be a hindrance for students to effectively understand the issue at stake. However, the lesson learnt in this case study is that it can be mitigated by having instructions on the activity sheet, as well as teachers giving coaching and facilitating by questioning techniques and checking during the classroom-based inquiry learning activities and the experiential learning in different sites.

Furthermore, students' reflection, observed in their presentations, reports and in-depth understanding of the causes and effects of poverty and highlighted by the examination results, help teachers to decide whether they should keep this experiential learning programme for the next school year and what should be further improved. Teachers found that students could conduct their analysis and clearly express their views on poverty issues during examinations despite using English which is not their native language. To certain extent, this finding of examination affect future teaching could be an interesting area for further investigation, especially since the concept of "Washback" (see, e.g., Alderson, 2004; Cheng, 2005; Choi & Lee, 2010), which relates to the positive effect that changes to examinations have on teaching. It has been taken very seriously the notion that examinations could encourage worthwhile classroom practices (Coniam, 2015). Therefore, it would be interesting to examine and compare how this examination affects teaching "imperative" in the context of other Asian nations or other jurisdictions.

Finally, there were positive results in both presentations and examinations. The teachers pointed out an example from a group presentation when students reported that they learn about how poor people can have a positive life by facing challenges in a positive way.

With such positive evidence of student learning at the junior secondary level, the teachers gained information about what to teach at the senior secondary level. For example, the teachers think that next year the same cohort of students should experience service learning with services targeting the elderly to deepen their understanding of the local community. Also, this same cohort of students can apply their interview and communication skills that they have already learnt in the future service learning activities. In senior forms, this cohort of students should face greater challenges of community exploration, where they meet with much more complex and intricate issues of poverty and urban redevelopment. In short, the learning evidence obtained from these assessments enabled the teachers to be more confident about using an experiential learning approach in their teaching.

Conclusion

This chapter discusses a case study based in a Hong Kong school that combined classroom-based inquiry learning activities and experiential learning in order to develop student's empathy towards the poor. It reveals that both formative and summative assessments can be quite effective at enhancing student learning and informing the next stage of teaching. Of course, this is situated in the local context of an assessment reform agenda that has focused on "assessment *for* learning" rather than "assessment *of* learning". Finally, this chapter poses several questions of assessment within the parameters of classroom teaching and experiential learning in Hong Kong. For example, how can we make a better connection between classroom and out-of-classroom learning, and what can be adopted for authentic assessment outside of schools? Nevertheless, it has implications for understanding authentic assessment in general, and specifically how it can be used to promote and assess students' empathy.

Appendix A: Student artefacts

Student artefacts can be found in their work throughout the learning unit to understand poverty and what actions that they can take.

On the other hand, I think they will face some difficulties such as lack of money, homeless, poor health and low education level of their children.

I think I can donate some money, equipment and some books.

The government can help them, e.g., build more public housing for them.

TEXT. 1 What problems are the poor families facing in Hong Kong?

These show how students understand the concept of poverty during the learning. As seen, student learning is well informed and as they progress, their thinking about the concept becomes much richer.

In particular, one group of students wrote about the reflection on sleeping in the street and what actions that the government and themselves shall take to address such social problem.

Experience from sleeping in the street

The target of this activity is let us try to become a street sleeper and learn what they feel.

I have already visited the rooftop house. The houses were so small and it can just fit one to two people in each.

Nevertheless, some families need to live in these houses. I wonder why do the street sleepers appear? Is there not enough public housing for them? Or maybe they cannot find jobs

TEXT. 2 Student reflection on sleeping in the street and solutions

Below is another group of students who wrote about what they feel can be done to help to the homeless.

The government can provide more jobs to the street sleepers. This can let them earn money by themselves. The government can build more houses so that the rent can be lower (because there are many houses in the Hong Kong).

We can share about how the street sleepers' life in the internet so that the people can know more about them and help them. We can also be volunteer workers so that we can know more about them and help them.

TEXT. 3 Student reflection on what can the government and themselves do to help the street sleepers.

Finally, on what they can to help reduce poverty in Hong Kong, students told in their presentations that:

> "We can visit the poor people and chat with them. We can also be friends and care about them."

> "NGOs can provide more activities to help the poor people like giving them some meal boxes or vegetables."

> "The government can see how to make the rent of the houses lower so the poor people can spend less on rent. Also, the government can build more public housing, so the poor people can live in a better environment."

> "We can be a volunteer, donate money, and share the situations with others to let more people know about them, care about and help them."

References

Adamson, B. & Morris, P. (2000). Changing Hong Kong's schools. In B. Adamson, T. Kwan, & K. K. Chan (Eds.), *Changing the Curriculum – The Impact of Reform on Primary Schooling in Hong Kong* (pp. 7–20). Hong Kong: Hong Kong University Press.

Alderson, J. C. (2004). Foreword. In L. Cheng, Y. Watanabe & A. Curtis (eds.), *Washback in Language Testing: Research Contexts and Methods* (pp. ix–xii). Mahwah, NJ: Lawrence Erlbaum Associates.

Bernstein, B. (1973). Some sociological determinants of perception. In B. Bernstein (Ed.), *Class, Codes and Control*, Volume I Theoretical Studies towards a Sociology of Language (17–30). New York & London: Routledge Taylor & Francis Group.

Biggs, J. & Watkins, D. (1995). *Classroom Learning – Educational Psychology for the Asian Teacher.* Hong Kong: Hong Kong University Press.

Brown, H. O. (2000). Teachers and teaching. In G. A. Postiglione & W. O. Lee (Eds.), *Schooling in Hong Kong* (pp. 95–116). Hong Kong: Hong Kong University Press.

Brown, G. T. L., Kennedy, K. J., Fok, P. K., Chan, J. K. S., & Yu, W. M. (2009). Assessment for student improvement: understanding Hong Kong teachers' conceptions and practices of assessment, *Assessment in Education: Principles, Policy & Practice*, 16(3), 347–363, DOI:10.1080/09695940903319737.

Cheng, K. M. (2000). The policymaking process. In G. A. Postiglione & W. O. Lee (Eds.), *Schooling in Hong Kong* (pp. 65–78). Hong Kong: Hong Kong University Press.

Cheng, L. (2005). *Changing Language Teaching Through Language Testing: A Washback Study.* Cambridge: Cambridge University Press.

Choi, C. C. & Lee, C. (2010). Developments of English language assessment in public examinations in Hong Kong. In L. Cheng & A. Curtis (Eds.), *English Language Assessment and the Chinese Learner* (pp. 60–76). New York & London: Routledge.

Chun, L. Y. (1989). A review of the characteristics of school-based curriculum projects in Hong Kong schools. In *Proceedings of the International Conference on School-Based Innovation: Looking Forward to the 1990s*, The University of Hong Kong.

Coniam, D. (2015). Half a century of English language assessment in Hong Kong. *Journal of Applied Research in Education*, 19, 1–14.

Curriculum Development Council (2001). *Learning to Learn: The Way Forward in Curriculum.* Hong Kong: Curriculum Development Council.

Esland, G. (1973). *Language and social reality*. Bletchley: The Open University Press.

Frisby, C. L. (2001). Academic achievement. In L. A. Suzaki, J. G. Ponterotto, & P. J. Meller (Eds.), *Handbook of Multicultural Assessment* (2nd ed.) (pp. 541–568). San Francisco: Jossey-Bass.

Gipps, C. (2002). Round table on school-based assessment: Discussant presentation. Paper presented at the International Association for Educational Assessment (IAEA) Annual Conference, 1–6 September 2002 in Hong Kong.

Griffin, P., Falvey, P., & Owen, J. (1993). Targets and Target-Related Assessment (TTRA): Implications for Hong Kong of Experience Elsewhere. *Curriculum Forum*, 3(1): 14–8.

Hart, E. & Bond, M. (1995). *Action Research for Health and Social Care*. Buckingham: Open University Press.

Hong Kong Examinations and Assessment Authority (HKEAA) (2017). Assessment literacy training. Available on http://www.hkeaa.edu.hk/en/our_services/assess_literacy_training/.

Hudson, R. A. (1980). *Sociolinguistics*. Cambridge: Cambridge University Press.

Kolb, D. A. (1984). *Experiential Learning*, Englewood Cliffs, NJ: Prentice Hall.

Krznaric, R. (2008). You Are Therefore I Am: How Empathy Education Can Create Social Change. *Oxfam Great Britain Research Report*. Available on http://www.oxfam.org.uk/~/media/Files/Education/Global%20Citizenship/Oxfam%20GB%20-%20You%20Are%20Therefore%20I%20Am.ashx.

Lachat, M. & Spruce, M. (1998). Assessment reform, equity, and English language learners. Office of Educational Research and Improvement, Northeast and Island Regional Educational Laboratory at Brown University. Retrieved 30 September 2006, from http://www.alliance.brown.edu/pubs/asellbib.pdf.

Lee, W. O. (2000a). Schooling and the changing socio-political setting: an introduction. In G. A. Postiglione & W. O. Lee (Eds.), *Schooling in Hong Kong* (pp. 1–21). Hong Kong: Hong Kong University Press.

Lee, W. O. (2000b). Social class, language and achievement. In G. A. Postiglione & W. O. Lee (Eds.), *Schooling in Hong Kong* (pp. 155–174). Hong Kong: Hong Kong University Press.

Morris, P. (1990). Bureaucracy, professionalization, and school-centered innovation strategies. *International Review of Education*, 36(1): 21–41.

McNiff, J. (2013). *Action Research – Principles and Practice* (3rd ed). London & New York: Routledge.

Scriven, M. (1991). Beyond formative and summative evaluation. In M. W. McLaughlin, & D. C. Phillips (Eds.), *Evaluation and Education: At Quarter Century*, 90(2), 19–64. Chicago: NSSE.

Skolnick, J., Dulberg, N., & Maestre, T. (2004). *Through Other Eyes: Developing Empathy and Multicultural Perspective in the Social Studies*. Toronto: Pippin Publishing Corporation.

Spinelli, C. G. (2008). Addressing the issue of cultural and linguistic diversity and assessment: Informal evaluation measures for English language learners. *Reading and Writing Quarterly*, 24(1), 101–118.

Stake, R. (1995). *The Art of Case Study Research*. Thousand Oaks, CA: Sage Publications, Inc.

Stake, R. (2006). *Multiple Case Study Analysis*. New York: The Guilford Press.

Wong, K. C. (2000). Organizing and managing schools. In G. A. Postiglione & W. O. Lee (Eds.), *Schooling in Hong Kong* (pp. 81–94). Hong Kong: Hong Kong University Press.

CONCLUSION

The many practical examples in Part II serve to illuminate the theory undergirding authentic assessment (AA) as explicated in Part I. To recap, AA can be thought of as assessments that require performances that parallel those in the real world (Messick, 1994). However, unlike what is commonly thought, the real world can have three different and possibly overlapping referent contexts: the real world of the students' life, the working world outside school or the world of the discipline.

For example, in Chapter 6 (AA in humanities), the AAs are designed to tap into the learners' everyday life, such as writing a journal entry on a topical geographical issue (Example 6.2). However, in Chapter 7 (AA in languages), the learners are required to interact with a live audience from the real-world context outside their school. Example 7.3 describes students interviewing visitors at tourist attractions as way of assessing their spoken communication, while polytechnic students in Example 7.4 are required to present their research to industry representatives. But one notes that learners are also engaging in the world of the discipline as they engage in intellectual work that is "grounded in the substantive knowledge of the disciplines" (Newmann, 2000, p. 2). The fact that AA can be designed to satisfy all three referent contexts of authenticity can be seen more clearly in the examples in Chapters 8 (AA in mathematics) and 9 (AA in sciences) where learners are guided to investigate everyday problems in a similar manner to experts in the field to induct them into the ways of thinking practised in the discipline.

This reference to the context of the discipline guards against threats to validity that sometimes come with replicating superficial "real world" contexts, resulting in construct under-representation and construct irrelevance variance (see Chapter 3 How do you design quality AA). In fact, validity is foremost with Messick's construct-centred approach as seen in the various examples where the AA design starts with unpacking the construct of interest before designing the tasks. In Example 8.2, the construct of formulating a mathematical problem into three criteria: understanding the problem in the real world, making assumptions to simplify the problem and representing the problem in the real world. These then guided both the task design as well as the rubric. This approach is particularly useful when planning authentic assessment of complex psychological constructs such as those involving character and citizenship (see Chapter 10, AA in character and citizenship).

When the constructs are thoughtfully unpacked into key performance criteria, this facilitates the construction of rubrics to accompany the assessment (see Rubric Example 7.3 to assess spoken communication, 8.2 to assess formulating a mathematical problem, 9.2 to assess scientific inquiry, 10.1 to assess responsibility and appreciation). The other key element of quality rubrics is clarity of standards, which can be achieved through using a research-based framework such as Structure of Learning Outcomes (SOLO) taxonomy (see Chapter 4, How do you design quality rubrics to accompany the AA). The different SOLO levels make clear the differentiated levels of success which provide explicit feedback to learners on their present performance as well as how to modify their work to progress. As such, such rubrics can both measure performance as well as enhance learning.

Similarly, as argued in Chapter 2 (Why bother with "authenticity" in assessments?), AA can also serve dual purposes of evaluating as well as advancing learning. The last two chapters (Chapter 11, Personalising assessment in sport science and Chapter 12, Developing empathy through AA) show that AA is far from being the token activity to engage students at the end of the unit; in fact, AA helps facilitate learning that can be said to be more authentic because it is directly related to the life of the learner, and more representative of the world outside school and the discipline.

> The great waste in the school comes from the child's inability to utilize the experiences he gets outside of school in any complete and free way within the school itself; while, on the other hand, the child is unable to apply in daily life what he is learning at school. That is the isolation of the school – its isolation from life.

Though it seems to be describing the current state in schools, this statement was made more than 100 years ago by John Dewey (1899, p. 67). What the AA examples in this book have shown is one way to bridge the gap between schools and life to make learning more meaningful for our learners.

References

Black, P., & Wiliam, D. (1998). Inside the Black Box: Raising Standards through Classroom Assessment. London: School of Education, King's College.

Dewey, J. (1899). The School and Society. Chicago: University of Chicago Press.

Messick, S. (25–26 October 1994,). Alternative modes of assessment: Uniform standards of validity. Paper presented at the Evaluating Alternatives to Traditional Testing for Selection, Bowling Green, OH.

Newmann, F. M. (2000). Authentic intellectual work: What and why? [Electronic Version]. *Research/Practice,* 8. Retrieved 24 September 2017, from https://www.researchgate.net/publication/255607299_Authentic_Intellectual_Work_What_and_Why_1.

INDEX

References to tables are denoted by the use of **bold**. References to figures are denoted by the use of *italics*.

Taylor & Francis eBooks

www.taylorfrancis.com

A single destination for eBooks from Taylor & Francis
with increased functionality and an improved user
experience to meet the needs of our customers.

90,000+ eBooks of award-winning academic content in
Humanities, Social Science, Science, Technology, Engineering,
and Medical written by a global network of editors and authors.

TAYLOR & FRANCIS EBOOKS OFFERS:

A streamlined
experience for
our library
customers

A single point
of discovery
for all of our
eBook content

Improved
search and
discovery of
content at both
book and
chapter level

REQUEST A FREE TRIAL
support@taylorfrancis.com

 Routledge
Taylor & Francis Group

 CRC Press
Taylor & Francis Group